The
Big Book
of
Indispensable
Wisdom

The Classics

My Grammar and I...
Or Should That Be Me?

Easy as Pi

A READER'S DIGEST BOOK

The Classics
   Copyright © 2011 Michael O'Mara Books Limited

My Grammar and I...Or Should That Be Me?
   Copyright © 2011 Michael O'Mara Books Limited

Easy as Pi
   Text copyright © 2011 Jamie Buchan

   Illustrations on pages 352, 353, 355, 357, 360, 368, 369, 376, 377, 379, 385, 390, 391, 392, 394, 398, 400, 404, 406, 411, 412, 413, 414, 415, 416, 421, 425, 426, 428, 430, 433, 434, 437, 438, 440, 443, 444, 445, 448, 450, 451, 456, 457, 458, 459, 462, 470, 472, 474, 475, 477, 488, 490, 493, 494, 496, 498, 500, 511 © Andrew Pinder 2011

   Illustrations on pages 366, 384, 387, 452, 465, 469, 481, 482, 484, 505, 506, 507, 509 © 2011 Claire Buchan

   Illustrations on pages 351, 371, 383, 409, 455 © Shutterstock

ISBN: 978-1-60652-351-3

PROJECT STAFF
The Classics
   Consulting Editor: Barbara McIntosh Webb
   Canadian Project Editor: Pamela Johnson

My Grammar and I...Or Should That Be Me?
   Project Editors: Sarah Janssen, Abigail Wilentz
   Copy Editor: Siobhan Sullivan
   Canadian Project Editor: Pamela Johnson

Easy as Pi
   U.S. Project Editor: Siobhan Sullivan
   Copy Editor: Barbara McIntosh Webb
   Canadian Project Editor: Pamela Johnson

READER'S DIGEST TRADE PUBLISHING
   U.S. Project Editor: Kim Casey
   Copy Editor: Barbara Booth
   Project Designer: Jennifer Tokarski
   Project Production Coordinator: Wayne Morrison
   Senior Art Director: George McKeon
   Executive Editor, Trade Publishing: Dolores York
   Associate Publisher, Trade Publishing: Rosanne McManus
   President and Publisher, Trade Publishing: Harold Clarke

We are committed to both the quality of our products and the service we provide to our customers. We value your comments, so please feel free to contact us.

   The Reader's Digest Association, Inc.
   Adult Trade Publishing
   44 S. Broadway
   White Plains, NY 10601

For more Reader's Digest products and information, visit our website, www.rd.com (in the United States)

Printed in China

1 3 5 7 9 10 8 6 4 2

❧ Contents ❧

MY GRAMMAR AND I...OR SHOULD THAT BE ME?
How to Speak and Write It Right

Easy as Pi
The Countless Ways We Use Numbers Every Day

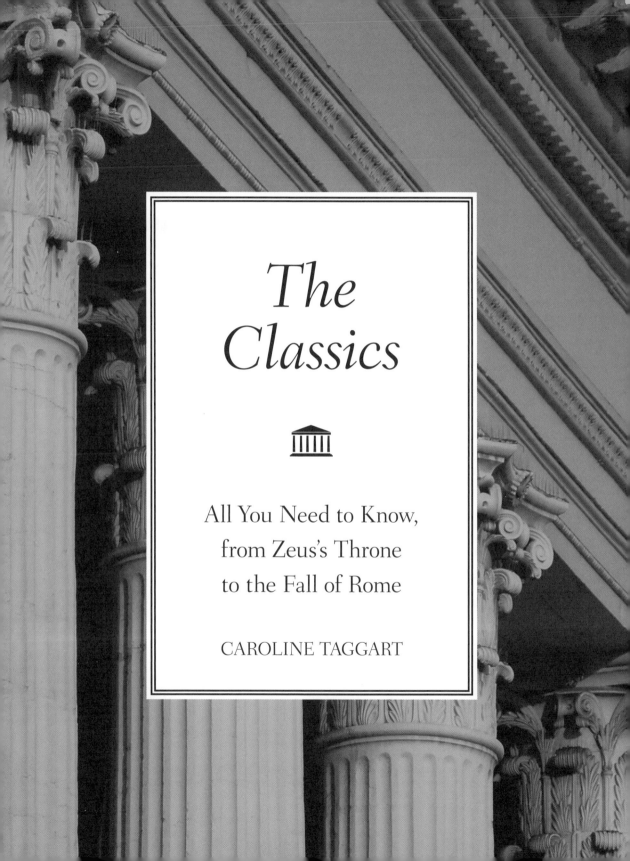

The Classics

All You Need to Know, from Zeus's Throne to the Fall of Rome

CAROLINE TAGGART

"Education is learning what you didn't even know you didn't know."

—Daniel Boorstin, American Historian

Before I Begin…

Two things: a decision and a question.

The decision, with a book like this, is what to include and what to leave out. For most people, "classical" means the Ancient Greeks and Romans, and I have stuck to them except when they came up against people such as the Persians or the Carthaginians who couldn't be ignored. The first great Greek writer was Homer, in around the ninth century B.C., while the last great Roman ones wrote in the second century A.D.; most of the famous philosophers, inventors, politicians and emperors lived in between. Obviously the mythology came before Homer—because that is what he was writing about—and the Roman Empire went on for a bit longer, so don't hold me to those dates, but they are my rough parameters.

The question is, "Who cares?" After all, it was all a very long time ago, it has no relevance to us, and it isn't as if the Greeks and the Romans were the world's first civilizations anyway. And it's all sooo boring… isn't it?

True, Buddha and Confucius both died before Socrates was born, so the Greeks can't claim to have invented philosophy. As anyone who saw the Tutankhamen exhibition knows, the Egyptians were doing some pretty sophisticated stuff with gold in the fourteenth century B.C., and building pyramids over a thousand years before that. The Babylonians created huge stepped structures known as ziggurats, and topped them off with temples, in around 2000 B.C.; the Assyrians had magnificent palaces by 800 B.C. The Sumerians had a written language as early as 3500 B.C., as did the Hittites 2,000 years later—but that was still 600 years or more before anything was written down in Greek. So the Greeks didn't invent art, architecture or culture, either. Why all the fuss?

I suppose the answer is that they invented *our* art, architecture, culture and philosophy. In the twenty-first-century Western world, there are classical influences all around us. A civic building that looks serious and important is likely to be in the classical style. Whether we know it or not, we put together a logical argument following principles laid down by Aristotle. We do geometry and trigonometry because the Ancient Greeks showed us how. (Perhaps not the strongest argument in their favor.) Our language is full of references to *Herculean tasks* and having *the Midas touch*. Judges still *ad lib*, comedians hold sessions *in camera*—or should that be *vice versa*? Even if we don't study the classics, there's simply no getting away from them.

Unlike most of the earlier Middle Eastern civilizations, the Greeks and Romans also left us a massive amount of writing. We know what their lives were like, we know about their wars and their politics, their crimes and misdemeanors, their wives and lovers. Quite a lot more than is any of our business about their lovers, actually. We know that they were just like us. Lines such as "We are just statistics, born to consume resources" might have been written yesterday, and "You may drive out nature with a pitchfork, yet she'll be constantly running back" might have come straight from the mouth of British broadcaster and gardener Alan Titchmarsh. Yet they are both Horace, writing (and gardening, evidently) in the first century B.C.

Which brings me to the not insignificant point that the classical writers are fun. Admittedly there aren't many laughs in the Greek tragedies, but anyone who tells you that the classics are dull hasn't read Herodotus, Ovid, Horace or Tacitus, or seen the plays of Euripides or Sophocles performed. And, if I may mention this without lowering the tone too much, Aristophanes, Catullus and Juvenal all produced a considerable amount of pure filth that still has the power to amuse or arouse.

Until very recently, the classical world was an integral part of our education system. Less than a century ago, George Bernard Shaw could call a play *Pygmalion* and expect his audience to understand why. Yet over the past twenty years, the number of students taking Latin has diminished and almost nobody learns Greek. It seems a shame, because there is so much in the classics that speaks to us today.

Still, *nil desperandum.* Perhaps some of the snippets in this book will encourage you to seek *bona fide* sources and overturn the *status quo.* As for me, this introduction was the last bit of the book to be written, so *nunc est bibendum*—in other words, I've finished, so I'm off to have a glass of wine.

1
The Wordy Stuff: Classical Languages

At a conservative estimate, about half of modern English derives from Latin, and a lot of that has Greek origins, with the result that just under a third of the words in an average English-speaker's vocabulary are ultimately drawn from Greek. So, though few people learn either language these days, and most of us would be hard pressed to tell an ablative from an aorist, we nevertheless babble away in these ancient tongues all the time.

But it has to be said that there is something slightly off-putting about your first glance at Greek…

The Greek alphabet

This is a very different beast from the Roman alphabet we use today, although the Romans developed theirs from a classical Greek original.

Greek letter	Symbol	English equivalent
Alpha	A, α	a
Beta	B, β	b
Gamma	Γ, γ	g
Delta	Δ, δ	d
Epsilon	E, ε	e (as in *met*)
Zeta	Z, ζ	z or ds (as in *gods*)
Eta	H, η	e (as in *meet*, sometimes as in *may*)
Theta	Θ, θ	th
Iota	I, ι	i
Kappa	K, κ	k
Lambda	Λ, λ	l
Mu	M, μ	m
Nu	N, ν	n
Xi	Ξ, ξ	x
Omicron	O, o	o (as in *hot*)
Pi	Π, π	p
Rho	P, ρ	r
Sigma	Σ, σ	s
Tau	T, τ	t
Upsilon	Y, υ	u
Phi	Φ, φ	ph
Chi	X, χ	ch (as in *loch*)
Psi	Ψ, ψ	ps
Omega	Ω, ω	o (as in *slow*)

Most people are content to sail through life without worrying about this, but if you do any amount of math or science, you will come across π, ρ, θ and many others; if you read the Bible, you will find "I am Alpha and Omega, the beginning and the ending"—which is just the Greek way of saying "I am A and Z, not to be confused with a street directory"; and if you are an outstanding scholar in the United States, you might be honored with the ΦΒΚ (Phi Beta Kappa) award. That said, what really matters to most of us are not the letters but the words.

A touch of logorrhea

That's a fancy word for "verbal diarrhea," and just to prove the point that it is not all Greek to any of us, here are some examples of everyday words with Greek roots.

Asterisk	*asteriskos* (little star)
Biology	*bios* (life) *logia* (study)*
Catastrophe	*kata* (down) *strophe* (turning)
Clone	*klon* (twig, i.e., from which a new plant is created)
Democracy	*demos* (people) *kratos* (rule)
Dyslexia	*dys* (impaired) *lexis* (word)
Economy	*oikos* (house) *nemein* (to manage)
Geography	*ge* (earth) *graphein* (to write)
Helicopter	*helikos* (spiral) *pteron* (wing)
Hippopotamus	*hippos* (horse) *potamos* (river)
Homeopathy	*homoios* (similar) *pathos* (suffering)
Horoscope	*ora* (time) *skopein* (to observe)
Monogamy	*monos* (one) *gamos* (union)
Pantomime	*pantos* (all) *mimos* (mimic)†
Rhinoceros	*rhinos* (nose) *ceros* (horn)
Telephone	*tele* (far) *phone* (voice)
Xenophobia	*xenos* (stranger) *phobos* (fear)
Zoo	*zoion* (animal)

---

* And all sorts of other *bio-* words such as *biography, biosphere, biodegradable,* and *-ologies* such as *geology, astrology, sociology, theology.* See? You learn one thing and you find you know lots more.

† There are lots of other *pan-* words, too: *panacea* (see page 142), *pancreas* (literally "all flesh"), *pantechnicon, panorama.* Sadly, *panda, pangolin* and *pantyhose* are completely irrelevant here.

The root of the matter

Being aware of a few basics can help enormously with vocabulary and spelling, as the *bio-* and *pan-* examples show. Switching to Latin, for instance, *mater* and *pater* mean "mother" and "father," so that's a clue to the meaning of anything beginning with *matri-* or *patri-*: *patricide, patrimony, matriarch, matrilineal.**

Lux and its genitive form *lucis* mean "light," which helps with *lucid* and *elucidate.*

Vertere means "to turn," hence *vertigo, subvert, advertisement* (literally something you turn toward).

Intra means "within" and *inter* means "between," which explains the difference between the *Internet*, which is a link between various networks, and an *intranet*, which is confined to an individual company. Anything beginning with *pre-* has a good chance of meaning "before"; *post-* is likely to mean "after."

In *herbivore* and *carnivore*, the *-vore* is concerned with eating. So if you come across a *fructivorous* monkey or *sanguivorous* bat, you can at least be confident that you are being told about their diet, even if you aren't quite sure what it is they eat.

---

* *Matrimony* also comes from *mater* and has a complicated derivation that involves a no-longer-used meaning of "an inheritance from one's mother." *Patrimony*, however, still means "an inheritance from one's father" and has nothing to do with marriage.

Et cetera, et cetera, et cetera

Not only does half our language derive from Latin, but there are also still many Latin expressions in common use. Below are a few you'll come across most days of the week in perfectly unpretentious company.

It is worth noting that Latin didn't go in for silent letters in the way that English does, so you should pronounce every syllable. The exception is the *vice* in *vice versa*, which is now often a single syllable but would originally have been pronounced something like "wee-keh." In the Latin alphabet, the letter *v* could be used as either a vowel (when it served the same purpose as *u*) or a consonant (pronounced as *w*, which didn't exist as a separate letter until much later). Similarly, Latin had no *j*, but used *i* as a consonant in words such as *iustitia*, "justice," which would originally have been pronounced as if it began with a *y*. The same applies to other words associated with the law, such as *jury* and *adjudicate*, and also to words associated with youth such as *juvenile* and *junior*. And yes, clever dogs, you do sometimes see it spelled *IVSTITIA*.

ad hoc: literally "toward this," used to mean "for this special purpose" or "just to be going on with," as in "Heath Robinson made a number of ad hoc contraptions."

ad infinitum: "until infinity," usually in the sense of "and so on and so on."

ad lib: *ad libitum*, literally "according to pleasure." In other words, making it up as you go along, performing a play or giving a speech without sticking to the script, or indeed without having a script at all. Call it improv if you like.*

ad nauseam: "until nausea," usually in the sense of "and so on and so on until the listener is so bored they throw up."

alibi: literally "in another place." Originally an adverb, as in "The maid's evidence proved that the butler was alibi," now generally used as a noun: "The maid's evidence provided the butler with an alibi."

ars gratia artis: "art for art's sake." See the note about Corinthian columns on page 123, or find the song on *10CC's Greatest Hits.*

bona fide: literally "with good faith," usually used to mean "genuine," as in "a bona fide example of a Latin expression." Sometimes also a noun, meaning much the same as "credentials" (which comes from a Latin word meaning "to be believed"): "He presented his bona fides to the senior manager."

coitus interruptus: Oh, come on, you know what that means. But it does prove the point that Latin has some fairly basic uses. (Or, a cynic might say, that Latin is perhaps a bit outmoded after all.)

---

* *Libido*—also (some say) connected with pleasure—comes from the same root. Women's *lib*, which may not have anything to do with pleasure, is from a different source: It's short for *liberation* and is connected with *liberty* and *libertine*. *Librarians* and *Libras* are, as I'm sure you'll agree, another thing entirely.

cui bono: literally "for whose good?" Used in the more pretentious type of whodunit to establish who benefits from a crime and is therefore likely to have committed it. See *modus operandi*, below.

de facto: "in fact," or more explicitly "actual, though not officially recognized," as in "After Bill's resignation, Ben became the *de facto* chairman of the board." If Ben were later formally confirmed in the position, he would become the chairman *de jure*, "by law."

e.g.: *exempli gratia*, "for example," "e.g. this is an example." Not to be confused with *i.e.*, below.

et al.: *et alii*, "and other people." Used a couple of times in this book (see pages 113 and 137) to mean "and the rest of those guys."

etc.: *et cetera*: literally "and other things," widely used to mean "and so on."*

i.e.: *id est*, "that is," "i.e., not the same thing as *e.g.* and to be used when clarifying a statement rather than giving an example of it."

modus operandi: "way of working." Abbreviated as "MO" in detective fiction, it means that someone who goes around strangling people with silk scarves is unlikely to be the murderer of a victim who has been struck over the head with a poker.

---

* I think I am proving my point here. If it weren't for these Latin phrases, we would have to say "and so on" all the time, and that would be pretty dull.

N.B.: *nota bene*, literally "note well." "N.B. This abbreviation is not to be confused with *P.S.*, below."

non sequitur: "it doesn't follow." Originally a term from formal logic (see page 161, especially the bit about *post hoc propter hoc*), this is now used more widely to describe any statement that isn't relevant to what has gone before. As in "It was a non sequitur for Bill to claim that, having vacationed in Greece, he knew all about Aristotelian logic."

per annum: "each year," usually used to refer to salaries and sometimes abbreviated, as in '$100,000 p.a." Also, **per diem**, "each day," as in a consultant being paid a per diem rate of $10,000, or used as a noun, as in receiving a $100 per diem.

per capita: literally "by the heads," as in "the equivalent per capita expenditure was $7 a week."

per se: "in itself," as in "I don't need to win the lottery per se, but a sudden inheritance of half a million would come in rather handy."

pro rata: "in proportion," often applied to part-time jobs: "Three days a week, salary $25,000 pro rata" (meaning: salary appreciably less than $25,000).

P.S.: *post scriptum*, "after writing." Formerly used if you wanted to add something to a letter after you had signed it; nowadays more usually replaced by a second email headed "And here it is with the attachment this time." *Postscript* has also gone into the language as a noun denoting any afterthought or supplement, and if you put a capital *S* in the middle you get the name of what Wikipedia calls a "dynamically typed concatenative programming language." But of course you knew that already.

Q.E.D.: *quod erat demonstrandum*, "which was the thing that was supposed to be demonstrated," written (in the good old days, at least) at the end of a calculation in geometry, showing that you had worked out what you were supposed to have worked out. Also used more or less facetiously to mean "I've proven my point."

quid pro quo: "something for something," giving something in exchange or recompense for something else. Along the lines of "You scratch my back and I'll scratch yours" and not necessarily as vindictive as "tit for tat."

requiescat in pace: Never heard of it? Well, it abbreviates to *R.I.P.* and literally means "May he or she rest in peace." Most frequently seen on cartoon gravestones (and a few real ones) and Halloween decorations.

And lest you think that all Latin expressions are obsessed with money or death:

status quo: "the existing state of affairs," as in "If neither Johnny Depp nor George Clooney is available, I will have to put up with the status quo."

vice versa: "the other way round," as in "I could marry Johnny Depp and have an affair with George Clooney, or vice versa."

Less common but still around:

alea iacta est: "the die is cast." Allegedly said by Julius Caesar when he crossed the Rubicon (see page 87), it means "There's no going back now." Widely used in the *Asterix* books by Roman soldiers whenever something goes wrong.

carpe diem: "seize the day," so make the most of the opportunity, have fun, you may be dead tomorrow. From an ode by Horace (see page 118), whose philosophy of life this pretty much sums up.

caveat emptor: "let the buyer beware," meaning lift up the carpets and check for dampness, because it'll be your problem later.

de mortuis nil nisi bonum: "of the dead, nothing unless it is good," in other words: Don't speak ill of the dead.

in camera: literally "in the room,"* usually used in a legal sense of "behind closed doors," not in open court.

in situ: "in the original place," as in "The archaeologists could date the fossil because it was discovered *in situ*."

in vino veritas: "in wine, truth." A nonsensical expression that suggests you tell the truth when you are drunk, when it should of course be "*in vino* gross exaggeration, distorted reality and maudlin self-pity."

---

* The modern word *chamber* derives from *camera*, as does, surprisingly enough, the modern word *camera*.

ipso facto: "by the fact itself," as in "An illegal immigrant, *ipso facto*, cannot be issued a passport."

res ipsa loquitur: "the thing speaks for itself," meaning "It's obvious, isn't it?" Briefly brought back from oblivion when British politician Boris Johnson used it as a justification for learning Latin.

sine qua non: "without which not," as in "Reliability is the *sine qua non* for success."

sub rosa: literally "under the rose," meaning "in secret," from the Roman habit of hanging a rose over a council table to indicate that all present were sworn to secrecy.

Singulars and plurals

Neither Latin nor Greek formed plurals by putting an *s* on the end of a word, which is one of the many reasons we have some irregular-looking words in English that not everyone recognizes as plurals.

Greek neuter words ending in *-on* had a plural form ending in *-a*, so *phenomenon* and *criterion* are singular, *phenomena* and *criteria* are plural.

Latin neuter words ending in *-um* also end in *-a* in the plural, leaving us with *medium/media, datum/data, bacterium/ bacteria.*

Latin feminine nouns ending in *-a* have *-ae* in the plural; not common in modern English, but *formula/formulae* is one example; masculine nouns ending in *-us* are pluralized as *-i*: *alumnus/alumni* and, come to think of it, if they are women, *alumna/alumnae*.

Some Latin nouns ending in *-is* changed to *-es* for the plural: *crisis/crises, thesis/theses*.

And then there are some oddities (which were perfectly regular in Latin): *opus/opera, genus/genera, index/indices, matrix/matrices, species/species*.

Speaking of genera and species

Another common use of Latin in English (as it were) is in the "technical" naming of plants and animals. An eighteenth-century Swede named Linnaeus developed what we now call **taxonomy**, which means that he classified all the known plants and animals into genera and species (and orders and all sorts of other things that are outside the scope of this book). Many of his names were descriptive, so that if you come across a plant whose name has *folia* or *folium* in it, you know that it is talking about the leaves (think *foliage*), and if it has *aurea* or *aureus*, it is golden. *Rosa canina* is the dog rose (think about it), and *Helleborus foetidus* is the stinking hellebore.

And finally...

Throughout history we have had to invent new words for new things or new concepts, and not everyone is as well informed about Latin and Greek as they used to be. Hence *television* (literally "far seeing") is a confusion of a Greek beginning and a Latin ending; and that once widely used word *psychedelic* is what the *Oxford Dictionary* describes as "irregularly formed": If it had been coined by a classical scholar, it would have been *psychodelic.*

2
The Made-Up Stuff: Religion and Mythology

The **Greek gods** were a complicated lot, partly because there were so many of them, partly because of their penchant for incest, and partly because there are a number of conflicting stories about their origins and activities. The bible—for lack of a better word—on the subject is Hesiod's *Theogony*, a poem composed in around 700 B.C., but Homer, Ovid and Uncle Tom Cobley have their own variations. So don't write in, OK?

Each god was responsible for his or her own area of expertise, so the Greeks would seek support from Aphrodite in matters of love, or make sure Poseidon was in a good mood before going on a sea voyage. Priests were on hand to conduct sacrifices on holy days, or check the omens to see whether a certain day would be auspicious for a particular journey or marriage, but there wasn't the modern concept of "going to church." For the most part, the humble mortal could go along to the relevant temple with his gift of wine or honey, or a piglet, and offer it to the god on his own account. Some gods required an animal to be sacrificed, while others could be mollified with a few plumes of smoke, leaving the sacrificial meat for the humans to eat.

The gods' family tree

In the beginning, reasonably enough, there was a state of nothingness known as **Chaos**, from which was born **Gaia** (Earth, also spelled Gaea, Ge and sundry other ways). She produced a son, **Uranus** (heaven), who also became the father of her children. If this shocks you, you might like to skip the rest of this section.

The children concerned were a whole horde of giants, including two **Titans** named Oceanus and Tethys, whom Homer calls the progenitors of the gods. Hesiod, however, suggests that Uranus was overthrown by another Titan son, **Cronus**, who in turn was overthrown by his own son, **Zeus**. There are lots of contradictory accounts involving castration and the swallowing of their own children, but we haven't got room for that here.

Some versions of the story have Zeus drawing lots with his brothers **Poseidon** and **Hades**, but however it happened Zeus became king of the gods and married **Hera**, who was also his sister. They lived on **Mount Olympus**, where they did wonders for property prices, luring all the major gods to the neighborhood. Tradition has it that there were twelve "Olympian" gods, though not always the same twelve. In due course, the Romans adopted them all and gave them new Latin names, shown in parentheses here:

Zeus (**Jupiter** or **Jove**), lord of the skies, was prone to throwing thunderbolts at anyone who displeased him, and to changing himself into a variety of forms in order to have sex with anything that moved. He turned into a swan to seduce Leda, fathering Helen of Troy and the twins Castor and Pollux (now better known as the constellation of Gemini); into a bull with Europa, who gave birth to Minos, king of Crete (see page 46); and into a shower of gold to impress Danaë, who was suitably dazzled and gave birth to Perseus (see page 52). He also had affairs with Semele, producing Dionysus (Bacchus), the god of wine; with Maia (see *Hermes*, page 39) and many more. Zeus's legitimate offspring with Hera included Hephaestus and Ares (see page 34), and Athena sprang fully armed from his head—or at least that's what Zeus told Hera when he came home after a particularly heavy night and spent the next day groping for Tylenol.

Poseidon (**Neptune**) came second in the lot-drawing contest and got to be god of the sea. Notoriously short-tempered, he wrought havoc if anyone offended him, using a trident that could shake the earth. Appeasing the temperamental gods was always a good move, and staying on the right side of Poseidon was vital for anyone thinking of setting foot on a boat. The bearded version of Neptune who still appears on ships crossing the equator is a much jollier character.

Pluto or **Hades** (**Dis**) drew the shortest straw and became god of the Underworld (the place itself is also called Hades). He fell in love with Persephone (Proserpina), daughter of Demeter (Ceres), the goddess of corn and agriculture,* and abducted her to live in the Underworld with him. Demeter neglected her agricultural duties while searching for her daughter and the earth became barren. Eventually Pluto agreed to let Persephone spend six months of the year above ground, as long as she spent the other six months in the Underworld with him. Demeter remained in mourning while her daughter was absent—thus creating autumn and winter—but returned to the daily grind during the other two seasons.

Although he was king of the Underworld, Pluto wasn't a devil. There are plenty of bad guys kicking around in classical mythology (and some pretty mean women too), but no equivalent of Satan or Lucifer. That said, people certainly suffered in Hades. There's Tantalus, for example, doomed to perpetual hunger and thirst because the water he stood in receded whenever he bent down to drink, and the fruit above his head remained—wait for it—*tantalizingly* out of his reach. But the Elysian Fields, the nearest classical mortals got to what we might call Heaven, were also in the Underworld. There's more about all this in the box on page 35.

Hera (**Juno**) was the goddess of marriage and a particular protector of married women. Zeus's chronic infidelity meant that jealousy and strife were commonplace in stories featuring

---

* …and namesake of corn-based breakfast *cereal*, from Cocoa Puffs to Corn Pops.

Hera. And when she became angry at someone, she stayed angry at them and could be pretty drastic: See, for example, the Labors of Hercules (page 44), although that is far from being the only time she let her temper get the better of her.

Hestia (**Vesta**) was the sister of Zeus and Hera, and goddess of the hearth. A rather homely figure, she was a virgin goddess, perhaps to make up for the total lack of chastity among some of her peers. Vesta is unusual among Roman goddesses in that her worship was not influenced by her Greek counterpart: In Roman times, she was the patron of the Vestal Virgins, priestesses whose virtue was inviolable—they were buried alive if they were caught with a man in their room—and whose duties included guarding the sacred fire that was never allowed to go out.

Ares (**Mars**) was the son of Zeus and Hera, and the god of war. Interestingly enough, more of a problem child than a dignified deity—he liked to stir up trouble but frequently behaved in a cowardly and unchivalrous way. When Hephaestus discovered him with Aphrodite (see page 38), he caught the two of them up in a net and exposed them to the ridicule of the other gods. The Roman figure was a little more respectable: The Campus Martius, scene of great chariot races, was dedicated to Mars, and the word *martial* (as in "martial law") derives from his name.

Athena (**Minerva**), the one who was born in that rather unconventional way (see *Zeus*, page 32), was the goddess of war and of wisdom, with a particular interest in Athens. Her

About the Underworld

The **Underworld**—sometimes called Hades, sometimes Avernus—appears in so many myths and legends that it deserves a box to itself. The best description of it comes in Book VI of the *Aeneid* (see *Virgil*, page 117), when Aeneas is escorted by an ancient prophetess called the Sibyl to visit his father, Anchises, and see evidence of the future glories of Rome. Virgil puts the entrance to the Underworld somewhere near Mount Vesuvius and says, in the (loosely translated) words of the Sibyl, "The descent to Avernus is not hard. It's getting back that's tricky."

To get into the Underworld you had to be rowed across the **River Styx** by the boatman **Charon**, who charged a fee, which explains why corpses were buried with a coin in their mouths. You also had to get past **Cerberus**, the three-headed dog, which the Sibyl did by throwing him a drugged cake she had prepared earlier. Other rivers of the Underworld included the **Acheron** and the **Cocytus**, which were just black and swirly and nasty, and the **Lethe**, the Underworld's solution to overcrowding. This could be a problem even in those days, so, after a thousand years, souls down below were allowed to take on another body and go back up to Earth as someone else; drinking the waters of the Lethe made them forget everything that had gone before.

At the entrance to the Underworld, the road divided, leading you either to Hell (**Tartarus**) or to Heaven (**Elysium** or the **Elysian Fields**). Tartarus was pretty grim. It had a burning river called the **Phlegethon**, and **Tisiphone**, one of the Furies (see page 41), spent her time whipping the inmates and threatening them with snakes. Elysium, on the other hand, let you play music and dance or whatever else had turned you on when you were alive.

The very few people who weren't dead managed, for various reasons, to get down to the Underworld and back. They included:

• **Hercules** (see page 44)

• **Theseus**, whose mate Pirithous lusted after Persephone. The two of them were caught by Pluto, but Hercules eventually liberated Theseus, leaving Pirithous to his fate.

• **Orpheus**, the great musician, whose wife **Eurydice** had died. Orpheus was grief-stricken and wheedled his way into the Underworld to beg for her return. His heart softened by Orpheus's music, Pluto agreed, on condition that Orpheus did not look back at Eurydice "until they had reached the upper air." Alas, Orpheus couldn't resist the temptation, and Eurydice was drawn back into the Underworld for good. Orpheus himself was killed shortly afterward and thus reunited with his wife. His lyre was placed in the heavens as the constellation Lyra, and a nightingale is said to sing more sweetly over his grave than anywhere else. Orpheus's story has inspired many great musical works, including what some consider the first opera, by Monteverdi.

symbol was the owl, which remains the symbol of the city to this day. She is also known as Pallas Athena.

Apollo (**Apollo**) was the son of Zeus and Leto, a minor goddess in her own right. When she became pregnant, Leto had to travel the world looking for somewhere to give birth, since everyone was terrified of incurring Hera's wrath if they let her in. Eventually she found refuge on the tiny island of Delos, which has remained sacred to Apollo ever afterward. He was the god of, among other things, music and of light: Every morning he harnessed his chariot and drove the sun across the sky (in this context he is also known as Phoebus Apollo, or just Phoebus).

Apollo inherited his father's libertine tendencies and spent a lot of his time pursuing nymphs: Daphne's father turned her into the tree that bears her name so that she could avoid his advances, which is why Apollo is often depicted wearing a laurel crown (the daphne being a member of the laurel family, for the non-gardeners among you). He also took a shine to Cassandra, daughter of Priam, King of Troy, and granted her the gift of prophecy; when they had a tiff, he added the curse that no one would believe anything she said. She, poor lass, later wandered around the ruins of Troy muttering, "I told you so. Don't take in that horse, I said. But would anybody listen? Oh, no." But of course nobody paid any attention.

The **Oracle at Delphi**, famous for its unhelpful, ambiguous predictions, but also for giving the ancient Greeks advice on political matters, was sacred to Apollo.

Artemis (**Diana**) was the twin sister of Apollo, and goddess of hunting and the moon. Another virgin. The story goes that the hunter Actaeon came upon her when she was bathing; she was so outraged that she turned him into a stag and he was torn apart by his own hounds. Two paintings by Titian depict this story, and it is interesting to note that, even in the second one when she has had time to get dressed, pick up her bow and arrows and lace up a complicated pair of sandals, the modest maiden still has a breast hanging out of her dress.

Aphrodite (**Venus**) was the goddess of love and beauty. There was nothing virginal about her, and some unpleasant diseases are named after her. Some say she was the daughter of Zeus and Dione,* others that she rose from the sea on a scallop shell, as in the painting by Botticelli. Aphrodite was married to her brother Hephaestus (see page 39) but had an affair with her brother Ares. She also fell in love with a particularly beautiful youth called Adonis (no relation), who was later killed while out hunting. There's a long poem by Shakespeare about this.

Aphrodite's son **Eros** (**Cupid**) is generally portrayed as a chubby baby who mischievously shoots arrows at people to make them fall in love, usually with someone who couldn't be less interested. Contrary to popular belief, the statue in London's Piccadilly Circus that celebrates the work of the Victorian philanthropist Lord Shaftesbury doesn't depict Eros at all; it's his brother,

---

* The sources are vague about who Dione was. She may have risen from the sea.

Anteros, who represents requited, rational love. But as they looked rather similar, it's a mistake anyone could have made.

And speaking of words derived from the names of gods, we can add *erotic* and *cupidinous* here—neither of them closely associated with Victorian philanthropy.

Hermes (**Mercury**) was the son of Zeus and Maia, daughter of Atlas (see page 49). Hermes was the messenger of the gods and got around with the help of a winged helmet and winged sandals; he also carried a rod entwined with two serpents known as the caduceus. Famous for his cunning, he was the god of wealth and presided over both merchants and thieves.

Hephaestus (**Vulcan**), son of Zeus and Hera (or, if you believe Hesiod, Hera alone), was the god of fire, and the blacksmith and armorer of the gods. His forge sat under Mount Etna in Sicily. An ugly baby, he was banished from Heaven either by Hera because she couldn't stand the sight of him or by Zeus for taking Hera's side in a quarrel between the two (as I have mentioned, there was never any shortage of those). Hephaestus may have been born lame or broken his legs as he fell from Olympus. Either way, he ended up crippled as well as ugly, but was given the beautiful Aphrodite as his wife as a reward for forging Zeus's thunderbolts. Unsurprisingly, it turned out not to be a marriage made in Heaven (see various references to her infidelities, above, never mind the fact that she was his sister).

These are the principal gods of Olympus, although there was occasional to-ing and fro-ing. Some say that Hestia went to live among mortals and gave up her place to Dionysus; others mention that Pluto actually lived in the Underworld, so there was a spare room, sometimes occupied by Demeter.

There are many other **demigods, heroes, nymphs** and what have you (as you might expect with all that fooling around going on); the most important of them turn up when the mood takes them in various parts of this book.

The female of the species

In addition to the main gods, there are several groups of women—goddesses, primeval beings, call them what you will—who crop up again and again in the myths and can be confusing. And there are times when it is important to know the difference between a goddess who will inspire you to write beautiful poetry and one who will turn you to stone if you so much as look at her.

The Nine Muses

More daughters of Zeus: Their mother was Mnemosyne, another Titan and the goddess of memory.* The Muses lived on **Mount Parnassus** and inspired musicians and artists. They were:

• **Calliope:** the muse of epic or heroic poetry
• **Clio:** the muse of history

---

* Hence *mnemonic* devices.

- **Erato:** the muse of lyric and love poetry*
- **Euterpe:** the muse of music
- **Melpomene:** the muse of tragedy
- **Polymnia:** the muse of sacred song
- **Terpsichore:** the muse of dance
- **Thalia:** the muse of comedy
- **Urania:** the muse of astronomy

The Three Fates or *Moirae* (*Parcae* in Latin)

Controlled the lifespan of mortals and immortals alike:

- **Clotho** spun the thread of life from her distaff
- **Lachesis** assigned and measured each lifespan's length
- **Atropos** cut it and therefore decided when and how mortals died

The Three Furies or *Erinyes*

The personifications of vengeance: **Alecto**, **Megaera** and **Tisiphone**. They were particularly hot on crimes against the ties of kinship, which is why they pursued Orestes so violently after he had killed his mother, Clytemnestra. (You may think they had a point, but he got off in the end—see page 109.) Aeschylus's *Oresteia* calls these ladies the Eumenides or "Gracious Ones," but this is probably just a feeble attempt to appease a group of angry crones surrounded by snakes.

---

* A word much beloved of crossword puzzlers. It is the only possible answer to the entry e_a_o, which appears surprisingly often.

The Gorgons

Another group of angry crones, the most famous of whom was **Medusa**. They had serpents in their hair and girdles, and anyone who met their gaze was turned to stone. Medusa was killed by Perseus, who chopped off her head while she was sleeping, having avoided looking directly at her by using her reflection in the shiny shield he had been given by Hermes. Which, when you think about it, is pretty darned clever, and would have taken quite a bit of practice in front of the bathroom mirror. Medusa was pregnant by Poseidon at the time and the winged horse Pegasus sprang from her blood.

The great thing about being a Gorgon was that you retained the ability to turn people to stone even after you had died and had your head cut off. How cool is that?

The Harpies

In Homer and Hesiod these were violent winds that carried people away to their deaths. By the time of Virgil, they had turned into birds with the faces of women, but the effect was the same.

During the Middle Ages, there were continued literary references to harpies. In his *Inferno*, Dante envisages the tortured wood infested with harpies, where the suicides have their punishment in the second ring.

The Sirens

At last, some halfway decent-looking women! The problem with the Sirens, though, was that they sang in a hypnotic way that lured seafaring men to their deaths on the rocks. Orpheus, passing near them, played beautifully on his lyre to drown them out; Odysseus protected his men by stuffing their ears with wax, which, according to one version of the story, caused the Sirens to drown themselves in a (rather drastic) fit of pique.

Scylla and Charybdis

Scylla was a (female, of course) sea monster who seized and devoured sailors who passed too close to her cave; Charybdis dragged them into a whirlpool nearby, so the two made for a particularly tough navigational challenge. Odysseus, who was a bit of a smartass, survived them, as did Jason and the Argonauts. Tradition has it that Scylla and Charybdis are in the Straits of Messina, between Sicily and Italy, where a natural whirlpool makes sailing tricky to this day. The expression "between Scylla and Charybdis" is still sometimes used to mean much the same as "between the Devil and the deep blue sea," that is, stuck with the choice of two unattractive options, or "between a rock and a hard place," given that Scylla's cave was cut out of a rock.

The Labors of Hercules

So after gods and monsters come superheroes, and other bits and pieces of mythology that have lingered on in our culture and vocabulary. People still talk about a Herculean task, which might mean as little as cleaning up after a dinner party. The original twelve Labors of Hercules were rather tougher.

Hercules is the Roman name for the Greek Heracles, and I'm using the Roman form here because it's more familiar to most of us, but either way he was a great hero, known for his strength, courage and hearty appetite (for all sorts of things). He was a son of Zeus by Alcmene, daughter of the King of Mycenae, and—in common with many of Zeus's other out-of-wedlock offspring—was persecuted by Hera; indeed, she sent a load of serpents to kill him in his cradle, but he strangled them effortlessly, which pretty much set the pattern for the rest of his life.

Thanks to Hera, Hercules was later overcome by a fit of madness and murdered his wife and children; when he asked the Oracle at Delphi how he could purify himself of this crime, he was told to go to Tiryns and serve King Eurystheus, who happened to be his worst enemy and could be guaranteed to give him a hard time. It was Eurystheus who imposed the Labors. As is so often the case, sources and details vary, but the usual list is:

To kill the Nemean Lion. This lion was such a fearful thing that a club wasn't good enough, so Hercules strangled it, skinned it and thereafter wore the skin as a mantle— scaring Eurystheus half to death when he went back to Tiryns to report success.

To kill the Lernaean Hydra. The Hydra was a monster with many heads, each of which regrew whenever cut off. Hercules enlisted the help of his friend Iolaus, who sealed the stumps with a "burning brand" as Hercules cut off each head. (Some sources report that there were nine heads, only one of them immortal, and Hercules ended up burying that one under a rock.)

To capture the Hind of Ceryneia. This was a deer with golden horns, sacred to Artemis, so Eurystheus included it specifically to get Hercules into trouble with the goddess. Hercules chased it for a year before running it down.

To capture the Erymanthian Boar. He tired it out by driving it through a snowdrift, and then caught it in a net. Erymanthos is a mountain, so relying on a snowdrift in Greece is not as silly as it sounds.

To clean out the Augean Stables. Sounds easy enough, but the problem here was that there were a lot of cattle, the stables hadn't been mucked out for thirty years, and Hercules had only one day to do the cleaning (which seems mean given that he was allowed to spend a whole year chasing a hind). He diverted a couple of rivers and flushed the stables out.

To get rid of the Stymphalian Birds. These were allegedly man-eating monsters, and Hercules scared them from their coverts using a brass rattle and either shot them or drove them away.

To capture the Cretan Bull, probably the one that had fathered the Minotaur (see page 56). The bull was rampaging all over Crete, so Minos was perfectly happy for Hercules to take it. He released it in Mycenae, where it carried on rampaging, finally settling near Marathon and eventually being killed by Theseus.

To tame the Horses of Diomedes, because they were fed with human flesh. Hercules killed Diomedes and fed his flesh to the horses, which seems to have turned them off the whole carnivore thing.

To capture the Girdle of Hippolyta, Queen of the Amazons, because Eurystheus's daughter wanted it. Hippolyta was going to be nice about it (hey, she was a queen, she probably had other girdles), but Hera persuaded the rest of the Amazons that Hippolyta was being abducted and the whole thing degenerated into the sort of battle you see on the opening day of the December 26th sales.

To capture the Oxen of Geryon. This involved going to the very western edge of the known world, where the Pillars of Hercules (on either side of the Strait of Gibraltar) mark the spot. Hercules accomplished the journey by forcing the sun god Helios to give up the golden bowl that carried him back to the east at the end of every day. Hercules then killed Geryon, captured the cattle and brought them home in the golden bowl. These cattle ate human flesh, too, but presumably Hercules had figured that one out by this time.

To capture the Apples of the Hesperides. These golden apples had been given to Hera on her wedding day, and the Hesperides were the girls who guarded them. The problem was that Hercules didn't know where they were. He got around this with a trick: either conning a sea deity called Nereus into telling him where the gardens were, or conning Atlas, who was father to the Hesperides, into getting the apples for him.

To capture Cerberus, the three-headed dog who guarded the Underworld (see page 35). Hercules descended to the Underworld with the help of Hermes and Athena (both of whom Hera hated, so we are in the realms of "my enemy's enemy is my friend" here), overpowered the dog with brute strength, took him to Eurystheus to show that he could do it, and then took him home again.

The Judgment of Paris

This was one of the most important decisions in all mythology. There's a lesson to be learned from this story: Invite people to parties; they'll be offended if you don't.

Eris, the goddess of Discord, was the only one of the gang not invited to the wedding of Peleus and Thetis (don't worry about who they are—they're just the ones around whom the action happens). Hanging around outside, she threw a golden apple among the guests, inscribed "For the fairest." Hera, Athena and Aphrodite all made a grab for it and then called on Zeus to arbitrate. Well, you know what it's like at weddings—everyone's a tad overwrought, one wrong word and *someone*'s going to end up in tears—so Zeus wisely passed the buck to Paris.

Remember that these are gods we are dealing with. They're used to getting their own way, and bribing the judge is all in a day's work. Hera offered Paris power and wealth if he chose her, Athena promised that he would win glory in war, and Aphrodite suggested he might like to marry the most beautiful woman in the world.

No prizes for guessing which he chose.

The most beautiful woman in the world was **Helen**, who was married to **Menelaus**, King of Sparta. Not allowing this detail to stand in his way, Paris invited himself to stay and, with the help of Aphrodite, persuaded Helen to elope with him to **Troy**. Where very soon they found there was a war on, with Hera and Athena firmly on the other side. Remember I mentioned that when Hera got mad she stayed mad? Well, this war lasted ten years and she didn't let up.

Turn to page 105 for Homer's version of the rest of the story. And if you are getting married in the near future, be careful with your guest list.

Miscellaneous myths

I've included some famous mythological figures in the chapter on literature (see page 105), but here are a few more that might otherwise have slipped through the net:

Atlas: A son of one of the Titans, and involved in their revolt against the gods of Olympus. As punishment he was condemned to hold up the pillars separating heaven and earth. This image frequently appeared as the frontispiece of books of maps in the sixteenth century, which is why they are "atlases" now, not "books of maps." Atlas was inhospitable to Perseus (see page 52), who used the head of Medusa to turn him into a mountain range in North Africa, which takes almost as much talent as cutting someone's head off while looking at their reflection in a shield, and makes me think that Perseus could have taught David Copperfield a thing or two.

Jason and the Argonauts: Stop me if you've heard this one, but there was this ram with a golden fleece. Oh, there just was, OK? The ram was sacrificed to Zeus, and its fleece hung up in a place called Colchis, over to the east of the Black Sea (absolutely the back end of beyond, in mythological terms).

For reasons too complicated to explain, it became Jason's task to get it back. He set off with fifty other heroes on a ship called the *Argo*, so the men aboard it were the Argonauts.

You could have written an *Odyssey* about the adventures they had on the way, only somehow a *Jasony* doesn't have the same ring to it. Once they got to Colchis, though, the king agreed to hand over the fleece as long as Jason performed a number of ludicrous tasks. These included yoking to a plow a pair of fire-breathing oxen with brass feet and sowing the teeth of a dragon, from which would spring armed men who would turn on the sower. The king's daughter, Medea, who conveniently happened a) to be a sorceress, and b) to have fallen in love with Jason, helped him to do all these things, and also to dope the dragon that guarded the fleece. So, mission accomplished, the Argonauts set off for home, with Medea tagging along because Jason had promised to marry her. Yeah, that old line. For Euripides's version of what happened next, see page 111, and to see how this became useful in philosophy, see page 156.

Midas: King of Phrygia, who was granted a wish by Silenus, a companion of Dionysus. Midas wished that everything he touched would turn to gold, not realizing that this would include his food, the water he tried to wash in and, in some versions, his daughter. When he explained very quietly and reasonably to Dionysus that he hadn't really meant it, the god sent him to wash in the River Pactolus, and Midas went back to normal. A later king of the area, Croesus, became proverbially rich because he could mint money (literally by the bucketload) from the gold dust in the river. It's sort of true, too: Croesus is the only person in this section who probably existed, and there are deposits of gold in the bed of the Pactolus to this day. Despite this cautionary tale, to have "the Midas touch," meaning to find it easy to make money, is generally considered a good thing.

The other story about Midas is that he was called upon to judge between the music of Pan and Apollo and found in favor of Pan. Apollo, understandably annoyed (he was, after all, god of music, whereas Pan was merely god of shepherds and tootled on the occasional pipe in his spare time), punished Midas by making a pair of ass's ears sprout from his head.

Pandora: The first woman, created by Hephaestus at Zeus's instruction and endowed by the gods with "all the gifts" (that's what her name means). The idea, according to one version of the story, was to punish both Prometheus for stealing fire from Heaven (see next page) and man for accepting the gift. Another version says that Pandora (that is, woman) was sent by Zeus as a blessing to man, so you can believe whichever you prefer, according to your gender, marital status and frame of mind. Either way, she had been given a mysterious box and told by Zeus never to open it. When she inevitably did open it, she released all the evils that have since afflicted the world, from rheumatism and colic to spitefulness and jealousy. Only hope was left behind. The moral of the story being that, whatever sorrows may afflict us, hope is always there to provide comfort. Sweet.

Perseus: Had a head start on some of the other heroes because he was the son of Zeus, which is a bit like being Superman without having to worry about kryptonite. His big task was to kill Medusa, one of the Gorgons (see page 42). That done, he was flying around using Hermes's winged shoes, when he came upon Andromeda chained to a rock and about to be devoured by a sea serpent. He was able to stab the serpent, rescue the girl and marry her. Then, after one of those laughable misunderstandings that are all too common in mythology, he killed his grandfather[*] and took himself off into exile in Asia, where his not-very-imaginatively-named son Perses became the first king of the not-very-imaginatively-named Persians.

---

[*] With chilling parallels to the story of Oedipus (see page 110), there had been a prophecy when Perseus was born that he would kill his grandfather, and the old man thought he could get around it by sending the baby away. A word of warning: When you are a character in mythology and you try to stop a prophecy from coming true, *it never works.*

Prometheus: One of the Titans, whose name means "forethought." With his brother Epimetheus ("afterthought") he was given the task of creating man, and giving him and the animals all the qualities that they would need in order to survive. Epimetheus was so generous, handing out wisdom to the owl, strength to the lion, a hard shell to the tortoise and so on, that when he came to man, who was supposed to be superior to the rest, he had nothing left to give. At his instigation and with the help of Athena, Prometheus went up to heaven, lit his torch from the heat of the sun and brought fire down to earth for the first time. This was the gift that made humans able to produce tools that would till the land, make weapons, keep themselves warm in winter, and a number of other things with which the animals couldn't compete. Zeus wasn't very pleased with this presumptuousness and had Prometheus chained to a rock where an eagle perpetually pecked at his liver, which grew again every night.

Pygmalion: Sculpted a statue of a woman so beautiful that he fell in love with her. In answer to his prayers, Aphrodite brought the statue to life, Pygmalion married the woman he had created and, according to Ovid, they lived happily ever after.

Before this happened, though, Pygmalion spent a lot of time admiring the brilliance of his own work, much like Professor Higgins in Shaw's play but with more actual groping. In Shaw's version, first performed in 1913, the only references to the legend are in the preface and postscript, not in the text itself—he presumably expected his audience to know what the title meant. By the 1950s, this would no longer have been a safe assumption, and so *My Fair Lady* was born.

Galatea, the name of the statue, was popularized by W. S. Gilbert (of Gilbert and Sullivan fame), who wrote a comedy on the subject; it doesn't appear in the early sources.

3
A Detour: Crete

This section goes much further back in time than most of the Greek history covered in the next chapter, but there are two reasons for that:

- You can't ignore Crete just because it doesn't fit in with the time frame.

- It provides a useful link between mythology and history. Yes, it has improbable stuff about Minotaurs and labyrinths and balls of thread, but the fact that you can still visit the ruins of the **Palace of Knossos** suggests that there are some elements of truth to the story. Rather like Croesus and the river full of gold dust (see page 51), it can't *all* have been made up by bards to wile away a long winter's evening.

It seems to be pretty certain that there was a settlement in Crete as early as 6000 B.C., and the **Minoan** civilization—named after a great king, or possibly a number of kings, called **Minos**—flourished until about 1500 B.C., most probably destroyed by a volcanic eruption and/or an earthquake. The palace once had glorious frescoes showing the bull-leaping to which the Cretans were prone, but most of what remains of these is now in the Archaeological Museum in the capital, **Heraklion**.

More than one expert describes the ruins of Knossos as labyrinthine, so it's not unreasonable to imagine that there was once a labyrinth here—and that's where myths become intertwined with history.

The story goes that Poseidon had given King Minos a bull, which Minos then refused to sacrifice to him. In punishment, Poseidon caused Minos's wife **Pasiphaë** to fall in love with the bull and give birth to the **Minotaur**, a creature that was part-man, part-bull.* Bulls were quite the thing in those days—the Minoans practised bull-leaping and bull sacrifice, and archaeologists have found remnants of bull masks and bull horns. But interestingly, Minos wasn't best pleased to be saddled with the bastard offspring of his wife and her taurine paramour.

In order to keep the Minotaur under control, Minos got the master craftsman **Daedalus** to construct a maze or labyrinth for the creature to live in. Every year the Minotaur was fed the seven youths and seven maidens that Minos demanded from Athens as an annual tribute. (They did that sort of thing in those days, and you can imagine that a Minotaur might

* See page 30 for advice on not annoying Poseidon.

have a hearty appetite.*) Anyway, **Theseus**, an Athenian hero, determined to put a stop to this shocking waste of Athenian youth, came to Knossos to destroy the Minotaur. Minos's daughter **Ariadne** fell in love with him and provided him with a ball of thread so that he could find his way out of the labyrinth.

Monster destroyed, ritual sacrifice abolished, hero and heroine united—end of story, you might have thought. Unfortunately, Theseus got tired of Ariadne and abandoned her on the island of Naxos, where she became the subject of an opera by Richard Strauss. She was subsequently taken up by the god **Dionysus,** the Greek equivalent of Bacchus, the god of wine. So presumably she lived happily ever after, unless bacchanalian orgies were not to her taste.

There are lots of other vaguely familiar legends tacked on to this story, so let's get them out of the way while we remember:

• When Minos died he became one of the judges of the Underworld, and assigned the dead to the afterlife task of his choice (see page 55 for more about the options he had there).

• Daedalus was later imprisoned in the labyrinth himself and, being the clever craftsman he was, made wings for himself

---

* Come to think of it, the Minotaur is another example of a creature you might have expected to be an herbivore preferring to eat human flesh—see the Labors of Hercules on page 39. Clearly the four stomachs of the ruminants still had some evolving to do.

and his son **Icarus**[*] so that they could escape. Icarus, getting above himself in more senses than one, flew so close to the sun that the wax on his wings melted and he fell into the sea and drowned.

• Theseus already had a son, **Hippolytus**, by the Amazon queen **Hippolyta** (the one who had the girdle that Hercules needed to steal; see page 46). Having abandoned Ariadne, Theseus then got involved with her sister **Phaedra**, who promptly fell in love with Hippolytus, a virtuous youth who rejected her advances. Lots of lies and denouncing and curses followed (at least they did in the play by Racine that you may have done for French 101), with the result that both Phaedra and Hippolytus were killed, and Theseus was left to ponder whether chastity might not be the answer from now on.

---

[*] From the wax and feathers that just happened to be lying around in the labyrinth, you understand.

4

The Old Stuff I: Ancient Greek History

It's difficult to know with a book such as this precisely how far back in time to go. The Persian Wars, for example, are an important part of the history of Athens, but the entry for Persian Wars in *The Oxford Companion to Classical Literature* begins "The Assyrian empire had collapsed with the fall of Nineveh in 606 B.C., and had been followed by the Median empire under Cyaxares and Astyages." To me that single sentence raises five questions beginning with the words *who*, *what* and *where*, so I think I had better just jump into the middle somewhere.

By about the ninth century B.C., the ancient Greeks spoke mutually comprehensible dialects and worshipped the same gods, but politically the area we now call Greece was divided into **city-** or **citizen-states** (*poleis*, singular *polis* as in *metropolis*). These were ruled by kings and later by aristocratic families (*aristo-* means "the best"), who served as both magistrates and priests.

Although in these early days there were other important city-states—Corinth was one—**Athens** soon emerged at the top of the heap. Legend associates the founding of the city with Theseus (see page 57), who may or may not have existed, but certainly most of the great Greek dramatists and philosophers came from or worked in Athens, as did a couple of famous orators and politicians. Oh, and the Athenians invented democracy.

Aha! That might be the place to start.

The birth of democracy

As time went on, the dominance of the aristocratic clans lessened and they tended to be replaced by individual monarch-style rulers whom the Greeks called **tyrants**. The word didn't have quite the negative overtones that it does in modern English, but it still wasn't a compliment. Power continued to be inherited by sons who weren't always up to the job; at the same time increased trading produced a handful of wealthy merchants whose lack of important relatives disqualified them from public office.

Disaster waiting to happen, you say?

Well, not really, because the Athenians were basically a rational people who preferred to solve their problems through the rule of law rather than revolution if they could. But there was a certain amount of unrest.

The first famous figure to emerge from this was **Draco**, who has given his name to very harsh measures in any context, as well as to a character in *Harry Potter* who provokes the audience to hiss whenever he appears. The original Draco amended the laws of Athens so that crimes were no longer punished by private vengeance (believe it or not, the norm up until then) but by a system of public justice, establishing tribunals a bit like a modern judicial court. This may not sound all that draconian, but Draco did make liberal use of the death penalty, if that isn't a contradiction in terms. What I mean is, you could be executed for almost anything. Within thirty years another important politician, **Solon**, had come along and repealed almost all of Draco's laws.

Solon has gone down in history as "the law-giver" and, although he wasn't the only one by any means, he is generally considered to have been the wisest. One of his great concerns was the freedom of the Athenian people. Up until his time (he became chief magistrate in 594 B.C.), one Athenian citizen could enslave another who owed him money; Solon made this illegal and instituted a system whereby any citizen could seek justice from any other, regardless of the status or wealth of the individuals concerned. For the first time, wealth rather than class became a qualification for public office.

It's an interesting insight into the Athenian mindset that both Draco and Solon were aristocrats, so they were cleaning up the system from the inside. They also marked a firm departure from the notion that law-givers were divinely inspired—the priestesses of the Oracle at Delphi had previously been known to accept the occasional bribe in order to give the answer that a tyrant wanted.

These two also paved the way for a guy named **Cleisthenes** to go one step further.

Now here's another interesting thing. At the time we're talking about (508 B.C., if you're taking notes), this man was a highly regarded elder statesman in Athens, so he had been around for a while and done other stuff; he then made a speech that changed the course of world politics forever—and I'd never heard of him until I started work on this book. Why isn't he as famous as Socrates or the Magna Carta? Did he die in vain?

Not really. What happened was that he stood up in a public meeting and said, "I know. Let's give power to the people."

It was, almost, as simple as that. There had been troubles in the preceding couple of years, Solon's constitution was not working as well as it had been, and the Athenians needed to be rid of aristocratic and tyrannical rule once and for all. What Cleisthenes introduced was a system based not on family groups but on what we might now call parishes; he called them **demes**, a word derived from *demos*, meaning "the populace." Every male citizen over the age of thirty could register with his local deme. To supplement the existing Senate, Solon had created a "lower house" or council, which sometimes opened discussion to a larger public assembly, the

Ecclesia; under Cleisthenes, membership of the council was opened to all, and more important, the Ecclesia—and therefore every male citizen over thirty—was given a say in every major public decision. And each man, regardless of his wealth or who his father was, had one vote and one vote only.

Of course all of this was of no use whatsoever if you were a woman, a foreigner or a slave, but for everyone else it was phenomenal.

Cleisthenes also invented a way to stop people from screwing up the system, called **ostracism**. The name derived from *ostrakon:* pieces of broken pottery on which voters would write the names of anyone they felt the state could do without for a while. Every year the Ecclesia would take a vote on whether they felt the need for an ostracism; if so, and providing at least 6,000 votes were cast, the man whose name came up most often was exiled for ten years. By the time he came back, it was assumed, the issue about which he'd been kicking up a fuss would be old news, and he would have learned his lesson and would just sit at the back of the room and keep quiet from now on.

The Athenian Empire

Athens by this time had acquired quite an empire, which, along with territories loyal to Athens, extended north from the city and along the entire eastern coastline of modern-day Greece, across to Byzantium and down into the southwestern corner of

Turkey, encompassing almost all the islands of the Aegean. Growth in both population and wealth meant that the Athenians needed to import food and could export other things (they had discovered a nearby source of silver, and had plenty of slaves to mine it, which helped the balance of payments greatly). In short, they had become an international force to be reckoned with. And when that happens, history does tend to bring along someone who wants to reckon with you.

Enter the **Persians**. Skipping over that stuff about Nineveh and Cyaxares I mentioned earlier, what matters here is that for about a hundred years (*ca.* 550–465 B.C.), three Persian kings—**Cyrus** (known as "the Great"), **Darius** and **Xerxes**— steadily extended their sphere of influence across the eastern Mediterranean. They took over Lydia (the place in Asia Minor, not the character from *Pride and Prejudice*) and various Ionian Greek cities,* and inched their way into mainland Greece. The Greeks did not normally present a united front, but at a time like this they pulled together, in theory at least, against a common enemy.

Note the words *in theory*. The **Battle of Marathon** is a good example of how it worked in practice.

Date: 490 B.C. Scene: the plain of Marathon, about 23 miles (37 km) northeast of Athens. An Athenian force of 10,000 realizes

---

* *Ionian* or *Ionic* in this context refers to the area on the west coast of Asia Minor known as Ionia, which was part of the Athenian Empire until the Persians came along. It's not to be confused with the modern Ionian Sea, which lies to the west of Greece and contains Corfu and Kefalonia. Asia Minor is, for all intents and purposes, Turkey.

it is not strong enough to resist the invading Persians, so it sends its fastest runner, **Pheidippides**, to ask the Spartans for the help they had promised. The historian Herodotus (see page 66), never one to miss out on a good story, says that Pheidippides covered the distance—about 155 miles (250 km) each way—in two days. The Spartans, for reasons of their own, refused to set out before the full moon, by which time the Persians had somehow got confused about whether or not to attack Athens and had let the Athenians win after all. Pheidippides then ran from Marathon to Athens to announce the victory and dropped dead of exhaustion the moment the words were out of his mouth. (This last part may not be true—Herodotus says there is no evidence for it—but it certainly ought to be.*)

This was under Darius, who died shortly afterward. The Persians did better when Darius's son Xerxes became king (see *Sparta*, page 69, for more about this). They even managed to sack Athens, but in 480 B.C. the Athenians bounced back under the leadership of a man named **Themistocles**. Thanks to him, Athens had built up a powerful navy, and he now came up with a cunning plan to lure the Persian fleet into a narrow channel separating the island of Salamis from the mainland. A resounding victory for the Athenians followed, and it was not long before the Persians were pushed out of Greece and the city-states could go back to fighting among themselves.

---

* The first "modern" marathons were run over distances varying from about 22 to 25 miles (35 to 40 km), roughly the distance from Athens to Marathon. Then, according to the website of the International Association of Athletics Federations, in 1908 the distance was officially set at 26 miles 385 yards (42.195 km).

About Greek historians

When you go back 1,500 years, it becomes a moot point where history ends and mythology begins. Few people would argue, however, that the greatest Greek historian was **Herodotus** (*ca.* 484–425 B.C.)—Cicero called him the father of history, and Cicero wasn't prone to admitting that anyone was better at anything than he was. Herodotus is said to have been the first to research and verify past events, which lifts him above his predecessors, known as *logographi* ("word writers"), who merely recorded oral traditions, without distinguishing between history and myth.

Most of Herodotus's writing deals with the Persian wars described in this chapter. Sometimes he excuses his many improbable anecdotes by saying, "I am obliged to record the things I am told, but I am certainly not required to believe them." On many occasions, he says firmly, "What I have here mentioned I saw with my own eyes." As I said in the Introduction, anyone who tells you the classics are dull hasn't read Herodotus.

Thucydides (*ca.* 460–400 B.C.): An Athenian who wrote an account of the Peloponnesian wars that some say is one of the greatest works of history ever. It's not an easy read, but it's remarkably unbiased and an astute analysis of the politics and strategy of the wars. Thucydides is also our source for Pericles's *Funeral Oration* (see page 68), though he thought Pericles was the bee's knees and may have spiced the speech up a little.

Xenophon (*ca.* 435–364 B.C.): A contemporary of Plato and pupil of Socrates. He never quite cut it as a philosopher, so he turned to soldiering and writing. His great work is the *Anabasis* ("expedition") *of Cyrus*, an account of the war between two Persian princes, Cyrus and Artaxerxes, when the latter had been chosen to succeed their father and the former was pissed off about it. (This is Cyrus the Younger, not to be confused with Cyrus the Great mentioned on page 64.) Xenophon was one of a force of 10,000 Greeks who supported Cyrus, so this is genuine eyewitness stuff—something that can't be said for all history.

Much later, **Plutarch** (*ca.* 46–120 A.D.) was not so much a historian as a biographer and moralist. Born in Greece, but spending part of his adult life in Rome, he wrote in Greek, as many "cultivated" Romans did at the time.* His *Parallel Lives* consists of twenty-three essays in which he compares a great Greek and a great Roman—Theseus, the legendary founder of Athens, and Romulus, ditto of Rome; the orators Demosthenes and Cicero; the generals Lysander and Sulla. Plutarch is interested in character rather than politics, so he chooses anecdotes "calculated to reveal the nature of the man"—which makes him great fun to read. He is also remarkably even-handed, neither groveling to the Romans (among whom he was living) nor being jingoistic about his fellow countrymen. Plutarch is the main source for Shakespeare's *Coriolanus*, *Julius Caesar* and *Antony and*

---

* He is said never to have mastered Latin, which surely adds to his charm for many of us.

Cleopatra, with lots of sumptuous details about Cleopatra's lifestyle: He describes a treasure consisting of "gold, silver, emeralds, pearls, ebony, ivory and cinnamon," which presumably means Cleopatra liked to look like Fanny Farmer when she was doing her baking.

Cue the beginning of the Golden Age

So, back to Athens, just in time to catch up with **Pericles**. Nothing to do with Shakespeare's *Prince of Tyre*, this Pericles held sway over what is known as the **Golden Age of Athens**, from the 450s B.C. until his death in 429 B.C.

Pericles was responsible for rebuilding the city after it was sacked by the Persians, and most notably commissioned the **Parthenon** (see page 127). He was a great orator, an important ability at a time when swathes of the electorate could neither read nor write, and was apparently incorruptible. He instigated reforms that took Athenian democracy to a new level: One was the introduction of state pay to members of the many juries scattered around the courts, ensuring that it was not only the rich who could afford to sit on them. At a time when Greeks were traveling, settling and intermarrying widely, Pericles also tightened up the definition of an Athenian citizen, encouraging Athenians to marry Athenians and preserve Athenian identity. As a committed enemy of Sparta, he was largely responsible for the outbreak of the **Peloponnesian Wars** (see page 70), which continued for twenty-five years after his death. His great *Funeral Oration*, given at a state funeral for the war dead, isn't really a eulogy at all but a celebration of

Athens and an exhortation to the Athenian people to live up to the standards of honor and courage demonstrated by the dead. Much of the decoration of the Parthenon is about just how honorable and brave the Athenians are, too. A man with a mission, you might say.

About Sparta

The word *spartan* has come into English to mean "restrained and unluxurious."* The Spartans prided themselves on their military prowess: From a very early age (some sources say as young as five), boys lived communally, were taught military discipline and toughened up by not being fed enough and none of this namby-pamby nonsense about asking for more, thank you very much. In the Spartans' own eyes at least, this was in stark contrast to the Athenians, whom they regarded as decadent, self-indulgent imperialists who did nothing but write great plays and produce great philosophers and rubbish like that. The Spartans believed in oligarchy—rule by the few. The needs of the individual were subservient to those of the state, and for a long time this was a genuine ideological difference between the two cities.

The ruling Spartan military class was vastly outnumbered by its one-up-from-the-slaves population, the Helots, a subjugated people from another part of the Peloponnese

---

* Sparta was in the region of Laconia, from which we derive another useful word, *laconic*, meaning never uttering more words than are strictly necessary—a further example of the Spartans' spartan approach to life.

(that bit stuck on the bottom of Greece, joined to the rest of the country by the Isthmus of Corinth). Because the Helots were all of the same race and spoke the same language—which was not the case in Athens, nor later in Rome, where laboring populations came from all over the place—there was always a risk that they would unite to overthrow their masters. This is part of the reason why Sparta never became a great imperial power: The Spartans needed to be on constant military alert, turning themselves into what the world expert on the subject, Professor Paul Cartledge, calls Fortress Sparta, because the risks from within were every bit as great as those from outside.

Sparta was important for about 120 years, between 480 and 360 B.C. At the start of this period it led the Greek defense against Persian invasion, making a name for itself at the **Battle of Thermopylae** (480 B.C.), where a ridiculously small army comprising 300 Spartan champions under **King Leonidas** resisted the massive Persian forces for two days.[*] Although technically a defeat, this heroic stand had a hugely morale-boosting effect on the Greeks and inspired continued resistance.

The Persians thoroughly dealt with, intercity warfare picked up again. From about 461 to 446 B.C., and then again for almost thirty years from 431 B.C., Athens and Sparta fought what are known as the **Peloponnesian Wars**.

---

[*] These were hard men: They thought the Persians were wimps for using arrows in order to avoid hand-to-hand combat.

Sparta emerged victorious thanks, ironically enough, to the support of a Persian fleet.

The defeat of Athens left the way clear for Sparta to attack a few neighbors, but seizing the citadel in Thebes proved a deeply unpopular move. Thebes defeated Sparta at the **Battle of Leuctra** in 371 B.C. and Sparta was pretty much never heard of again. Athens and Thebes then squabbled their way through a few more decades until Philip of Macedon came along and banged their heads together (see page 72).

Apart from Leonidas, practically the only famous person to have come out of Sparta is its naval commander **Lysander**, who crops up in the old patriotic song "The British Grenadiers": "Some talk of Alexander and some of Hercules/ Of Hector and Lysander and such great names as these," and so on. And even he is probably only really famous if you have ever belonged to the British Grenadiers. The young lover in Shakespeare's *A Midsummer Night's Dream* came from Athens and has nothing to do with any of this.

Off with the old...

After being defeated by Sparta, Athens ceased to be an important power, although some of the playwrights were still going strong and the philosophers had hardly started (see Chapters 6 and 9), so we shouldn't write it off altogether. But its fall coincided with the rise of **Macedon** and left the way clear for the conquering achievements of **Alexander the Great**.

One more name before we finish with Athens, though: The orator **Demosthenes** came to the fore at this time, because he was an ardent opponent of any form of appeasement of Macedon. His passionate eloquence persuaded the Athenians to hold out against the proposed **Hellenic confederacy** (that's the formal name for Philip of Macedon's plan for world domination, which we'll come to in a minute) for a while, but more important for our purposes his speeches continued to be studied and rote-learned by anyone interested in public speaking for the next thousand years. He is generally regarded as the greatest orator of all time, no mean feat for someone who started life with a speech impediment and cured it by speaking with stones in his mouth until his diction improved.

Alexander the Great

Reflecting on how little many of us accomplish in life, Tom Lehrer (political satirist) once said that "when Mozart was my age, he had been dead for two years."

If that idea upsets you, don't read this section.

Alexander (ruled 336–323 B.C.) was the son of Philip II of Macedon, who had in the course of his reign subdued the barbarian tribes to the north of his kingdom and imposed his will on the warring Greek city-states to the south by creating the

League of Corinth, of which he proclaimed himself head, and forcing the Greeks to join it. Perhaps unsurprisingly, Philip was assassinated and Alexander became king at the age of twenty.

Macedon or Macedonia comprised the province of northern Greece that stills bears its name, plus what is now the former Yugoslav republic, plus part of modern Bulgaria. Most of the land to the east was ruled by the Persians. So, after quickly checking that the Greeks were under control and could be trusted to behave themselves while he was away, Alexander set off to conquer the rest of the known world.* Some authorities say that his intention was to create a cosmopolitan blend of European and Asian cultures and a multiracial society (he married at least two Asian women and forced his officers to do the same); others suggest this was just an excuse to extend his dominions, besiege or massacre anything or anyone that stood in his way. It could have been a bit of both.

Certainly he was a great general, combining the prudence to consolidate his position and establish adequate garrisons before moving on, with the ability to make quick and ingenious decisions that took the enemy by surprise. He is often compared to Napoleon, and not just because both were vertically challenged egomaniacs.

Having sorted out Asia Minor, Alexander marched south along the east coast of the Mediterranean, successfully besieged Tyre and Gaza and, his reputation going before him, strolled pretty

---

* The term *known world* is a decidedly Eurocentric one in this context. What the Chinese or the Mayans knew at this time is beyond the scope of this book.

much unopposed into Egypt. Turning east, he went through five years of guerrilla warfare in modern-day Iraq and Iran. He eventually destroyed the ancient Persian capital, Persepolis, and, by crossing the River Indus (in modern Pakistan), extended his realm beyond anything that the Persians had conquered.

By this time his men were exhausted and close to mutiny, so Alexander turned back to Babylon, which he had decided to make his capital. He died there of a sudden fever a year later, a month short of his thirty-third birthday.

Alexander's empire fell apart pretty quickly after his death, but he left one lasting legacy—a **Hellenic** or "Grecianized" world (*Hellas* being the Greek name for Greece). Thanks largely to Alexander, the area from the middle of the Mediterranean to the north of modern India, including almost all of what we now call the Middle East and northern Egypt, spoke a common language and shared cultural ideas. The Hellenic period was as rich in the development of arts and science as the Athenian Golden Age: **Archimedes**, **Epicurus** and **Zeno**, founder of Stoicism, all came along at this time (more about them in Chapters 8 and 9), and **Alexandria**, with its huge library,* became the great center for scholarship.

All this lasted for a couple of hundred years until some other conquering power came along and decided that everyone should speak Latin. Now who could that have been?

---

* At its peak it is said to have housed 700,000 volumes, a figure that the Bodleian Library in Oxford didn't match until the early twentieth century.

5
The Old Stuff II: Roman History

We'll see when we get to the chapter on literature that the ancestor of the Romans was a Trojan prince called **Aeneas**. Which will confuse you if you think that Rome was founded by **Romulus** and **Remus**. It's another of those areas where mythology flows into history and you just have to go with it.

Romulus and Remus

The story that links the descendants of Aeneas with Romulus and Remus is a complicated one, but here it is in a nutshell: Numitor, the king of an ancient Italian city called Alba Longa, had a daughter named Rhea Silvia. She became pregnant by the god Mars (don't ask) and produced twin sons, who were thrown into the River Tiber by Numitor's rival. Miraculously washed ashore, the babies were found and suckled by a she-wolf, brought up by a shepherd and eventually recognized by whoever needed to recognize them. At a key moment some birds flew overhead, suggesting that the lads should build a new city and that Romulus should be king of it. Remus was understandably put out by this arbitrary bit of favoritism. In a fit of petulance, and with a deplorable lack of tact considering his brother was about to become king of the most important city in the world, he marched up to the foundations, said "That's not much of a wall"—which it wasn't; the builders had only just started, having been held up on another job—and jumped over. Romulus killed him and carried on building.

In order to provide wives for his followers, Romulus carried off a number of women from a neighboring tribe (famous painting by Poussin, *The Rape of the Sabines*, in the Louvre) and settled down to be the first king of Rome.

The traditional date for the founding of the city is 753 B.C., and Roman dates were calculated based on this: A.U.C. or *ab urbe condita*, "from the founding of the city."

The seven hills of Rome

Pub quiz time. Everyone knows that Rome is built on seven hills. (So is Cincinnati, but for some reason not as much fuss is made about that.) They are the **Palatine**, the **Quirinal**, the **Viminal**, the **Capitoline** (which today encompasses much of central Rome), the **Caelian**, the **Esquiline** and the **Aventine**. Although Romulus's settlement began on the Palatine, the **Capitol** or citadel on the summit of the Capitoline was the site of the most important temple of early times, the Temple of Jupiter Optimus Maximus (that's "the best *and* the greatest," so don't mess with him) and of Juno and Minerva. In 390 B.C., the Gauls invaded Rome in the dead of night. As they were sneaking up the hill, Juno's sacred geese (they lived in the temple) put up such a cacking fuss that they woke the guards. The Capitol was successfully defended, and the geese continued to be sacred (and fed at great public expense) for centuries afterward.

The Capitol was also the location of the **Tarpeian Rock**, from which condemned traitors were hurled to their deaths.

In the early years of the empire, the Palatine was the upscale area—if you climb the hill behind the **Forum,** you can see the ruins of palaces belonging to Augustus and his wife Livia. But that is getting ahead of ourselves. Long before that there was ...

The Roman Kingdom

After Romulus came six more kings:

- Numa Pompilius
- Tullius Hostilius
- Ancus Marcius
- Tarquinius Priscus
- Servius Tullius
- Tarquinius Superbus

Superbus doesn't mean "superb" in this context, it means "proud and tyrannical," and Tarquin was, very; so in 510 B.C. the Romans threw him out and founded a republic. If you are old enough to have read Macaulay's *Lays of Ancient Rome*, you may remember that this is the time when Horatius and two companions "kept the bridge" by holding off the forces of Lars Porsena of Clusium, who was supporting Tarquin, to give the Romans time to chop the bridge down behind them and prevent the enemy from crossing the Tiber and entering Rome. Horatius sent the other two scampering back across the bridge just before it collapsed, then dived into the river and swam back—to mighty cheers from one side and great gnashing of teeth from the other.

About Gaul

Why bother with a bit about Gaul? It's just France, right? Not quite, but don't worry, I won't keep you long.

In the really old days, much of northern Italy was occupied by Celtic tribes known as **Gauls**, and the area was called **Cisalpine Gaul** (meaning it was on this side of the Alps, as far as the Romans were concerned). It was from here that the Gauls raided Rome off and on, including the time they were rumbled by the geese (see page 77), until the Romans finally got fed up and took over the entire area in the first century B.C.

On the other side of the Alps was **Transalpine Gaul** (easy enough, isn't it, once you get the hang of it?). This was one of the first areas the Romans conquered. They called it "our province" or simply "Provincia," a name that lives on as modern Provence.

By the time Caesar wrote that "all of Gaul was divided into three parts," however, he was more or less talking about modern France, with a bit of Belgium, the Netherlands and so forth thrown it. Defining the three parts, he explained that the River Garonne separated the Aquitani from the Gauls, who occupied the area up to about Paris and east into Switzerland; beyond that were the Belgae.* Between 58 and 51 B.C., Caesar conquered all of it. The last general to resist him was Vercingetorix, who won a great victory at Gergovia, not far from Clermont-Ferrand, but succumbed shortly afterward.

The Roman Republic

The Roman Republic† was essentially an aristocracy, in the original sense of the word, which means that it was ruled by the aristocrats—formally known as **patricians**. The rest of the Roman citizens were known as **plebeians**, meaning "of the common people."

The main governing body was the **Senate**, at first made up of 300 patricians (they let plebeians in later) who were in charge of advising the **magistrates** on almost all aspects of civil and military government. The word *advising* is something of a

---

* There is no record that Caesar ever said "If it's Tuesday it must be Helvetia," but it would have been in keeping with this slightly broad-brushstroke attitude to geography.

† The word comes from the Latin *res publica*, meaning "a public matter."

euphemism here, because in reality there had to be a very good reason for a magistrate to go against the will of the Senate.

Sorting out the system didn't happen overnight, but by and large the magistrates were elected by popular vote (of the male citizens, of course) and served for a year at a time. The most important of them were the two **consuls**, who acted as judges, oversaw the civil service and commanded the army (the word for the right to command the army was *imperium*, hence *imperial*, *emperor* and *empire*, of which more later). The two consuls had to agree about any decision and each had the power of *veto* ("I forbid" in Latin) over the other. Their bodyguards, called **lictors**, carried bundles of rods, sometimes containing an axe; these were called **fasces** (which simply meant "bundles," but from which ultimately the word *fascism* derives).

Below the consuls came two **praetors**, who were in charge of civil law but were also entitled to command an army[*]; then a number of **aediles**, who ran all sorts of domestic matters from organizing games to mending the sewers; and **quaestors**, who looked after various bits of public expenditure.

In addition to this group, there were two **censors**, elected for an eighteen-month term every five years, ostensibly to conduct a census and carry out ritual purification. In fact they seem to have spent most of their time punishing people—even

---

[*] Hence the Praetorian Guard, who by imperial times were basically the emperor's bodyguard and an immensely powerful bunch. Tradition has it that it was the guards who placed Claudius on the throne when Caligula was assassinated (see page 97) and the Senate was dithering about what to do.

to the extent of removing someone from the Senate or stripping a man of his Roman citizenship.

And there were two plebeian **assemblies**, one military and one civilian, and two plebeian **tribunes**, who represented the interests of the people and were the only officials to have the power of veto over the Senate.

This basic system held sway for more than 400 years, with the balance of power between Senate, consuls and tribunes teetering back and forth depending on the personalities of the individuals concerned, the economic needs of the moment and whether there was any major fighting to be done. As time went by, the rich-poor divide increased, with powerful plebeians tending to lose touch with the concerns of the less-powerful plebeians, who should have been their primary fan base. Two important names at this point are the **Gracchus** (plural **Gracchi**) **brothers**, Tiberius and Gaius, powerful tribunes of the second century B.C. They instituted reforms to extend land ownership among the poor, which brought them into conflict with the powers that be: Both came to unpleasant ends, but they are celebrated by some as the founders of socialism.

As Rome increased its influence abroad, military campaigns might be fought simultaneously in more than one outpost, so more than one general could be rising to prominence (and wealth and power) while another person was running the show at home.

It's asking for trouble, isn't it? Read on…

About Carthage

Carthage had become such a thorn in the flesh of the Romans by the second century B.C. that the great censor Cato the Elder was going around saying *delenda est Carthago*— "Carthage must be destroyed." So what was that all about?

Carthage was situated on the coast of North Africa, in modern Tunisia (you can visit the remains while you're lapping up some cheap winter sun). It was founded by a people the Greeks called **Phoenicians**, and in mythological times it was ruled over by **Dido**, the queen who features in Virgil's *Aeneid* (see page 117). The name *Phoenician* derives from the Greek for purple or crimson, because the Phoenicians were particularly skilled in dyeing cloth this color. They had another claim to fame, too: The Greek alphabet is based on the Phoenician one, so the Phoenicians were probably the first people to use letters as opposed to pictograms for writing.[*]

By the middle of the third century B.C., Carthage had risen to be a considerable power, the only one in the west that rivaled Rome. Although the Roman Empire *per se* was still over two centuries away, the Romans never missed a chance to annex anywhere that would provide grain, manpower or tax revenue, and a twenty-three-year spat known as the **First Punic War**[†] resulted in the Romans taking control of Sicily.

---

[*] One claim to fame the Phoenicians seem to lack is the invention of the fantastical bird that is reborn from its own ashes. The concept of the phoenix seems to have originated in India, and didn't reach Greece until the first or second century A.D. The Greeks presumably decided that purple was the only color for such a groovy bird and named it accordingly.

[†] The Latin for *Phoenician* is *Punicus*, hence the name.

But the Carthaginians were not crushed by this war, and within thirty years they were back, this time with a great general called **Hannibal** (247–182 B.C.). Hannibal marched through Spain (which was part of the Carthaginian empire), crossed the Alps into Italy and headed for Rome. He'd won a succession of battles in order to get this far, and once he reached Italy he had a great victory at Cannae, but not much after that; he was eventually forced to retreat back to Africa, where he was defeated once and for all at the Battle of Zama in 202 B.C.

Carthage continued to be important, though, at least in Africa, and soon came into conflict with Rome again. The Romans' stated goal in the **Third Punic War** (Hannibal's having been the second) was to destroy Carthage completely, which they did after a siege in 146 B.C.

The city was later restored and it thrived again until the Arabs destroyed it in the seventh century A.D., but 146 B.C. marked the end of it as a world power. Today there are five cities in the United States named Carthage, though, and one named Hannibal, so the memory lingers on.

But, I can hear you saying, "Who cares? What about the elephants?" Well, yes, Hannibal did have elephants. It's one of those urban myths that is actually true. Livy (see page 103) mentions that there were forty of them. In one battle they "terrified the horses not only by their appearance but by their unaccustomed smell, and caused widespread panic."

Marius and Sulla

Marius did well in wars against a North African king called Jugurtha and was elected consul in 107 B.C. His plebeian background led him to support the power of the tribunes, which meant weakening the Senate and the consuls. Despite the fact that his party was allegedly the democratic, "popular" one, he broke a lot of the rules and put his own cronies into office without the formality of elections.

All this brought him into conflict with an aristocrat called **Sulla**, who was busy out east fighting a king named Mithridates, a potentially prestigious gig that Marius had wanted for himself. In 86 B.C., Sulla marched on Rome, forcing Marius to flee to Africa. Sulla then headed back east, but a year or two later, having made peace with Mithridates, he marched his army to Rome, took control of the city and proclaimed himself dictator. Which wasn't exactly in the rule book either.

Marius was dead by this time, but there were enough of his party left to turn the next couple of years into a pretty bloody civil war, from which Sulla emerged triumphant. He introduced massive constitutional reforms, restoring the power of the Senate at the expense of the tribunes. He also popularized a handy way of dealing with opponents, known as **proscription**: He simply stuck their names up on a post in the Forum and decreed that they no longer had any human rights—*ergo* (that's Latin for "therefore" and it seems not too show-offy to throw it in here), it was perfectly OK for anyone to murder them. And believe me, they did. In droves.

Rather surprisingly Sulla died in his bed in 78 B.C.. He merited the first-ever state funeral for a Roman citizen—which puts him on a par with U.S. presidents and Winston Churchill, in that respect if in no other. But he had paved the way for a protégé who took Rome pretty promptly into another civil war.

About Latin names

The Greeks kept names simple, tending to have only one, and to append "son of X" if they needed to distinguish one Aristophanes or one Zeno from another, though when democracy caught on (see page 60), they began to add the name of their deme instead.

The Romans were more orderly about it, and most of them—or at least most patricians—had three names, called respectively the **praenomen, nomen** and **cognomen**.

The **praenomen** (forename) was the personal name— what your mother called you—and there were surprisingly few of these: Marcus, Gaius, Publius; names like Quintus and Sextus (fifth and sixth), which showed that your parents already had lots of sons and were running out of ideas, and not a lot else. No Samuels, Archies or Kevins.

The **nomen** (name) was the name of the clan or gens, effectively an extended family. It always ended in -*ius;* famous ones included Julius and Claudius, a combination of which produced the Julio-Claudian dynasty that was responsible for the first handful of emperors (see page 93).

The **cognomen** (additional name) was initially a nickname but came to be transferred from father to son, so that it became more like a modern surname. It almost always denoted a physical characteristic, but because it stuck to a family through generations, it was not always relevant to the individual who bore it: *Caesar*, for example, probably means "hairy," and we know that Julius Caesar went bald and took great pains to disguise it.

A fourth name, the **agnomen** (another additional nickname), was sometimes added to mark a personal achievement or to signify adoption, so you end up with mouthfuls such as Gaius Julius Caesar Octavianus, which meant Gaius, originally of the Octavian clan, adopted by Julius Caesar (he changed his name to the Emperor Augustus, and who can blame him?). The Emperor Claudius's father was dubbed Germanicus, because he had been victorious in battles against various German tribes; Claudius, his elder brother and his nephew, who became Caligula, all adopted that name to add to the plenty that they already had.

Women at first had only one name, the feminine form of their father's nomen. So Catullus's Lesbia (see page 114) was only ever called Clodia, Octavian's sister who married Mark Antony was Octavia, and so on. Later women also used another name belonging to their husband or one or other parent, but—rather outrageously—there were no female praenomens.

Pompey and Caesar

Pompey* had been a supporter of Sulla and had fought successful campaigns against the Marius faction in Spain, Sicily and Africa. Having served as consul, he was put in charge of the armies in the eastern Mediterranean, where he was immensely successful, but on his return to Rome ran up against that rising young star **Julius Caesar**.

Caesar had had an exciting early life, including being captured by pirates while on the run from Sulla's wrath, but by the time we are talking about—62 B.C.—he was firmly on the political ladder. It was about this time that he divorced his second (or third, depending on whom you read) wife, **Pompeia**. *The Cambridge Biographical Dictionary* says this was because of "a fertility rite scandal in which she had been involved." That's a tantalizing piece of information, isn't it? What happened was that Roman ladies held a festival in honor of the Good Goddess, an otherwise unnamed deity who looked after women. Men were not allowed to attend, but in the course of the celebration, Pompeia had an assignation with **Clodius** (see page 114), who defiled the proceedings just by being there, never mind anything he may or may not have done with Pompeia.

Although Clodius was tried for impiety, Caesar refused to testify against him (perhaps for political reasons, to keep in with the mass of the Roman people, who were very pro Clodius) and

---

* His proper name was Gnaeus Pompeius, and through his various successes in battle he had earned the nickname Magnus—"the Great"—while still in his twenties. Interesting that no one thought *he* was getting above himself and needed to be assassinated.

he got off. When asked why he had nevertheless dismissed his wife, Caesar replied, "I wished my wife to be not so much as suspected." Hence the expression "Caesar's wife must be above suspicion," which has survived long after (the probably very suspect) Pompeia has been forgotten. Subsequent to this Caesar married **Calpurnia** who, according to Shakespeare, had a dream foreseeing his murder and begged him not to go to the Senate that day. Above suspicion she may have been, but she'd have ruined a brilliant play if anyone had listened to her.

Enough of this domestic gossip. The important thing is that Caesar wasn't prepared to kowtow to Pompey, nor Pompey to him. Additionally, there was an immensely wealthy man called **Crassus** who couldn't be ignored—and he and Pompey loathed each other. An awkward situation when all three of them had armies at their backs.

There are a number of good stories about Crassus, one of which is mentioned in the footnote on page 144. He was also the general who finally overcame **Spartacus**, an escaped gladiator who put together a vast army of slaves and runaways, and defeated the Roman army on a number of occasions between 73 and 71 B.C. If you are of the generation that thinks of Spartacus as Kirk Douglas, then Crassus was Laurence Olivier.*

---

* Spartacus himself was killed in battle, not crucified, but apart from that minor detail the last scene in Kubrick's film, with 6,000 of Spartacus's followers nailed up along the Appian Way, has its basis in history. At least, that is what we are told by a later historian named—in one of those happy coincidences that make the study of trivia so rewarding—Appian.

Anyway, Caesar, realizing that trouble was brewing, suggested the three of them divide control of the Roman provinces between them. This was, it has to be said, bypassing the "let's elect someone democratically for a year" principle that was still theoretically in place.

This arrangement—often called the **First Triumvirate**—fell apart when Crassus died in 53 B.C. (The historian Dio Cassius later tells the story that the Parthians defeated Crassus in battle and forced him to drink molten gold as an ironic punishment for his thirst for riches.) By this time Caesar had conquered much of Gaul (see page 78) and tried invading Britain. As his power grew over the next few years, the Senate in Rome became more and more anxious and eventually ordered him to return to Rome without his army. Caesar obeyed only the first part of this command and by crossing the River Rubicon—which marked the boundary between Cisalpine Gaul and the Roman Republic—at the head of an army, committed an act of treason. The Roman forces sent to stop him were commanded by—any guesses?—Pompey.

Battles between them meandered all over the empire (we might as well start calling it that—the republic is on its last legs by now and the first emperor will be making his entrance, admittedly under an assumed name, in a couple of paragraphs' time) until Pompey was finally defeated at the **Battle of Pharsalus** in 48 B.C.; he sought refuge in Egypt and was murdered there on the orders of the Egyptian prince **Ptolemy,** seeking to curry favor with Caesar. Caesar, disgusted by this breach of trust, put Ptolemy's sister **Cleopatra** on the Egyptian throne instead. Pausing only to have an affair with her (see the play by George Bernard Shaw, in which she smuggles herself into his presence rolled in a carpet), Caesar went off to win a quick battle in Asia Minor—after which he declared, *Veni, vidi, vici* (I came, I saw, I conquered)—and a few more in other outposts of the empire. He then returned to Rome to be assassinated.

According to Shakespeare, the motives of Caesar's assassins were entirely honorable. In *Julius Caesar* he shows the conspirators **Brutus** and **Cassius** fearing that Caesar was about to be proclaimed king, which they thought would destroy the liberties that Roman citizens enjoyed under the republic. And speaking of Shakespeare, opinions vary as to whether Caesar actually said, *"Et tu, Brute?"* as he died. There are no reliable eyewitness reports and—as ever—lots of people making up their own versions.

One other thing before we leave Caesar: He found time to reform the **calendar**. Before this, a normal year had been 355 days long, with what are called intercalary months inserted every now and then to bring the calendar into line with the solar year. Caesar's advisers worked out that 365¼ days was nearer the mark, so in 45 B.C. he decreed that most years would be 365 days long and instituted the leap year, which gave an extra day every four years, as it does to this day.

The Roman calendar had had twelve months for a long time, but the year had started around the spring equinox (traditionally, though not accurately, March 25). Caesar decided that the year should start nearer the winter solstice, so January became the first month. Which explains why September, October, November and December—whose names mean the seventh, eighth, ninth and tenth months— became the ninth, tenth, eleventh and twelfth. There also used to be months called Quintilis and Sextilis—the fifth and sixth—but these were renamed in honor of Julius Caesar and his successor, Augustus. By the way, the really imaginative guy who couldn't think of any better names for the months than Fifth, Sixth and so on was Romulus, who must have run out of energy after he had built a city and wrought havoc on the Sabine people.

We now know that Caesar's system wasn't perfect either, but the **Julian Calendar**, as it was called, hung in there until Pope Gregory XIII changed it in 1582. So it couldn't have been all that bad.

About the Roman calendar

The Romans calculated dates by working backward. Each month had three key dates, the **Calends** (hence the word *calendar*), the **Nones** and the **Ides**. The Calends was always on the first of the month, the Nones and Ides usually on the fifth and thirteenth, except in March, May, July and

---

October, when they fell on the seventh and the fifteenth (like so much else in life, it was to do with the phases of the moon). So a date was given as "three days before the Ides" or "ten days before the Calends." And, just to make it more complicated, they counted the days at both ends, so where we would say that March 12 was three days before the Ides (the fifteenth), they would have said it was four.

The Greeks didn't work their dates in this way, so the old-fashioned idiom "the Greek calends" meant never, because there was no such day.*

An interesting footnote to this, courtesy of a wonderful book called *The Calendar* by David Ewing Duncan: This system was still in use a thousand years after the collapse of the Roman Empire. When Shakespeare had a soothsayer warn Julius Caesar to beware the Ides of March, he could safely assume that his 1590s audience would know what he meant.

And after Caesar?

Public opinion quickly turned against the assassins, so Brutus and Cassius fled from Rome. This left **Mark Antony**, Caesar's friend and supporter who had officially shared consulship

---

* The Greek calendar was so complicated that everyone who ever knew anything about it has wiped it out of their memory banks. The Athenians had a civil year and a Bouleutic year, the latter concerned with when the Boule or Senate held office. The two years were calculated in different ways, had different numbers of days, and involved solstices and new moons and intercalary months and goodness knows what else. Plus they applied only in Athens. Practically every city-state had its own system.

with him at the time of the assassination, in charge. However, Caesar had an adopted son and heir, **Octavian**, who was not about to be passed over in the rush for power. He raised an army, defeated Antony and got himself proclaimed consul, but, on Antony's return with another army, backed down and agreed to form a triumvirate.* Antony meanwhile defeated Brutus and Cassius at the **Battle of Philippi** (powerful stuff in Shakespeare's version), and then took time out with Cleopatra in Egypt (Shakespeare covered this, too, in a separate play).

The next ten years were full of quarrels and complications, including Antony marrying Octavian's sister **Octavia** in an attempt to heal the rift, but in the end Octavian managed to turn public opinion against Antony; Antony and Cleopatra were defeated at the **Battle of Actium** (31 B.C.) and both committed suicide, leaving Octavian free to change his name to **Augustus** and get on with the business of being emperor. Augustus later boasted that he found Rome brick and left it marble, but my guess is that it was marble all the time—you just couldn't tell because it was covered in blood.

The Roman Empire

The Roman Empire was a masterpiece of administration, probably the greatest of its kind there has ever been. At its

---

* Because they'd always worked out so well in the past, of course… The third member of this triumvirate was a nonentity called Lepidus, who was basically there to make up the numbers.

fullest extent, it stretched from Scotland to North Africa, from Spain across to eastern Turkey and Armenia, down through Israel and over into Iraq. It was ruled by the same legal system, and its sixty million people all officially used the same language (they didn't all speak it as their mother tongue, but Latin was the language of administration). In a time when it took a minimum of three days to sail from the Roman port of Ostia to Marseille, on the nearest coast of the nearest province, and when if you wanted to travel anywhere by road you probably had to build it first, this was staggering.

And yet it was run by some of the maddest, baddest and most dangerous men ever to have graced the history books. Here's a rundown of some of the most significant of them. The first few were all related and belonged to what was called the **Julio-Claudian line**. A lot of intermarrying went on, which may help to explain why each generation seems to have been more bonkers than the one before.

Augustus (ruled 27 B.C.–A.D. 14): Once things settled down and people accepted the idea of an emperor, Augustus presided over a time of immense prosperity and a damn sight more peace than the Romans had seen for a century. He was a consummate politician and, strangely for a man in his position, had a great respect for the forms of government and for the concept of a budget. Or if he didn't he could certainly talk the talk. He also presided over a Golden Age of literature and the arts (see page 114). The Augustan Age was so, well, august that the term was applied centuries later to the high spot of French drama, and to

English literature in the early eighteenth century, when people such as Alexander Pope were imitating Virgil and Horace. But Augustus's reign was also a time of—how shall I put this?—a certain laxity of morals. The emperor himself was rather austere, approved of marriage and old-fashioned family values, and didn't eat or drink too much, but he was fighting a losing battle where that was concerned. See page 114 for a bit of tabloid gossip about his daughter, for instance.

About Roman citizens and slaves

Unlike the Athenians, the Romans conferred **citizenship** on a lot of the peoples they conquered. Citizenship gave a man the right to vote, to make contracts and to enter into a legal marriage. It also gave him the obligation to pay taxes and to do military service: One of the arguments for making a "barbarian" a citizen was that he could then be co-opted into the army. Women weren't allowed to vote or run for public office, but they had more freedom than in a lot of Western cultures over the ensuing millennia: They could own property and become rich in their own right, and the Roman matron was a respected figure in society.

The poorest Roman citizen might own a slave or two, and rich households had many. Slaves—who were mostly prisoners of war or the victims of pirates' raids—could be freed by their masters, a process called **manumission**, as a reward for loyal service. They could also save up any

---

money that came their way—tips and bribes, presumably—and eventually buy their freedom.

The **freedman** of a Roman citizen was not allowed to hold public office, but many held positions of trust within the home of their previous master or became influential "special advisers": The Emperor Claudius, perhaps not the sharpest knife in the box, was widely criticized for allowing a number of freedmen, nominally his secretaries, to have too much power.[*]

Even so, there was no shortage of slaves in Rome. The figures are vague, but in the time of Augustus thepopulation of the city was probably a bit over a million, and slaves almost certainly made up at least 25 percent and possibly as much as 50 percent of the total number. No citizen was really worried about having to iron his own toga.

Tiberius (A.D. 14–37): The son of Augustus's wife Livia, but not of Augustus; she assured her son's succession by systematically murdering or arranging the disgrace of everyone who might stand in his way, including, rumor has it, Augustus himself. Some say that Augustus suspected she was trying to poison him and refused to eat anything except figs that he had picked himself. Livia, rising to the occasion, painted poison on to the figs while they were still on the tree.

---

[*] One of them, Narcissus, was responsible for the summary execution of Claudius's rampantly unfaithful wife Messalina and one of her lovers, so there may be an element of truth in this.

Anyway, Tiberius became emperor. He was in his fifties by then, with a strong track record in administration and military matters, but he had none of Augustus's flair. His supporters say that he was deeply unhappy because he had been forced, for political reasons, to divorce the woman he loved and marry Augustus's promiscuous daughter Julia. His detractors say he retired to Capri to indulge his loathsome sexual depravities. They may all be right. Anyway, members of the royal family kept dropping like flies—Livia wasn't the only one who went in for poisoning—so that by the time Tiberius died, the most obvious candidate for the throne was his twenty-five-year-old great-nephew...

Gaius Caligula (37–41): A distinguished pedigree—great-grandson of both Augustus and Mark Antony—but crazy despite all that. *Caligula* means "little boot," a nickname he earned as a child because he was brought up in an army camp and wore little boots. He is said to have thought he was a god or the Jews' much-discussed Messiah, to have made his horse a consul,* slept with and impregnated at least one of his sisters, and generally shed blood and wasted money with extraordinary abandon. He came, unsurprisingly, to an unpleasant end.

Claudius (41–54): The "I, Claudius" of the novel and TV series; Caligula's uncle, chosen by the Praetorian Guard (see footnote, page 80) to replace him before the blood was dry on

---

* That happened a lot. It allowed the miscreant (normally an aristocrat) to do the decent thing and, more important, not forfeit his property to the state and leave his family destitute, which is what would have happened if he had been tried and condemned.

the assassins' swords. Suetonius describes Claudius as "so weak in understanding as to be the common sport of the emperor's household"; certainly he was more a scholar than a politician. Nonetheless, he was the emperor who finally made Britain a Roman province, traveling there himself. He entered into a number of disastrous marriages; his fourth wife Agrippina was the mother of…

Nero (54–68): There is no evidence that he fiddled while Rome burned, nor that he started the fire himself, though, as the saying goes, "The rumors persist." *The Cambridge Biographical Encyclopedia* sums him up beautifully: "Nero, more interested in sex, singing, acting and chariot-racing than government, neglected affairs of state [I should think he did—where would he have found the time?] and corruption set in." He was overthrown by the army and forced to commit suicide,* but not before he had found time to have his own mother murdered.

There were no relatives left to succeed him, so, on the one hand, good riddance; on the other, oh dear, there's a vacancy. You might think that anything that happened after Nero would have been an improvement, but you had to get through 69 A.D.—the year of the four emperors—before that turned out to be true. **Galba**, **Otho** and **Vitellius** came and went within a matter of months and were followed by:

---

* That happened a lot. It allowed the miscreant (normally an aristocrat) to do the decent thing and, more important, not forfeit his property to the state and leave his family destitute, which is what would have happened if he had been tried and condemned.

Vespasian (69–79): A successful general, proclaimed emperor by his troops as a way of putting an end to the civil wars of the previous year. One of the few emperors with a modicum of common sense, he presided over a decade of relative calm and started the building of the Colosseum (see page 140). On his deathbed he is alleged to have said, "My goodness, I think I am turning into a god!" So some of the loony Julio-Claudian blood must have rubbed off on him by the end.

Titus (79–81): Vespasian's elder son. During his father's reign he managed to offend the Jews for all eternity by destroying Jerusalem; as emperor he was in charge at the time of the eruption of Vesuvius that buried Pompeii and Herculaneum. Let's be charitable and say that the second part of this wasn't his fault.

Domitian (81–96): Younger brother of Titus. There was a lot of great architecture going on at this time, and Domitian built an immense palace on the Palatine Hill and an arch in memory of his brother. The latter is still more or less intact and is one of the highlights of the Forum (see page 132). However, he turned into a complete tyrant, behaved as if he were a god (yes, another one) and was assassinated. End of another dynasty.

Nerva (96–98): A senator promoted because he was considered a safe pair of hands. He was the first of what the Italian Renaissance writer and politician Machiavelli later called "the five good emperors." They had, Machiavelli said, "no need of praetorian cohorts, or of countless legions to guard them, but were defended by their own good lives, the goodwill of their subjects, and the attachment of the senate." Maybe, but Nerva, well-meaning though he was, didn't win the goodwill of his subjects, and the Praetorian Guard made him adopt Trajan so that they knew they would be happy with what they were getting next.*

Trajan (98–117): Rome still boasts the remnants of Trajan's column, Trajan's baths, Trajan's forum—he was a busy man. A great soldier, he extended the Roman Empire (whose borders hadn't changed much for a hundred years) to its greatest ever area, going as far east as the Persian Gulf. Also, fascinatingly, he had a Beatles haircut, some 1,860 years before Brian Epstein invented it all over again.

Hadrian (117–138): Ah, now, we know about him. The man with the wall, indeed a number of walls. He believed in defending the existing empire rather than trying to extend it. The amazing thing about Hadrian is the way he managed to stay in power while spending almost no time in Rome, and this becomes all the more amazing when you consider that the Roman Senate hated him. At the very beginning of his reign, when Hadrian himself was out east, four senior senators were executed in suspect circumstances, possibly because they had been plotting against the new emperor, and the relationship between emperor and Senate never healed. So Hadrian just

---

* Adopting someone as your chosen successor happened a lot, too. None of the five "good" emperors was the son of his predecessor.

stayed away. He traveled to Britain, he traveled to Greece, he traveled to Africa, he inspected troops and garrisons and reformed anything he thought was too luxurious.

On the rare occasions when he was at home, he continued his practice of consolidation, most notably codifying and humanizing (by the abolition of torture) a pretty haphazard legal system.* He also found time to build the most stupendous villa for himself (an estate of more than 66 acres containing a hundred buildings, many copied from things he had seen on his travels) at Tivoli, just outside Rome, and to commission the Pantheon (see page 129). He had a lover named Antinous, who died young and whom Hadrian subsequently deified (generally frowned upon, but not as bad as making your horse consul, see page 97).

Antoninus Pius (138–161): A fairly uneventful time, but worth mentioning because the Antonine Wall in Scotland is named after him. When Hadrian died, the Senate, which had never forgiven him for the executions mentioned above, tried to prevent him from being made into a god. (Emperors were always made into gods after they died. That was considered absolutely fine.) Antoninus persuaded them to change their mind, which is probably how he earned the nickname Pius.

Marcus Aurelius (161–180): The last of the five good emperors; was also a philosopher and is dealt with on page 170, as is his far-from-good successor, Commodus.

---

* A much later emperor, Justinian, completely revised Roman law, but drew heavily on Hadrian's reforms.

Then followed a number of emperors who have been all but forgotten, including a period of half a century when no one lasted much more than two years. Memorable figures from the later empire are few:

Diocletian (284–305): By this time the empire was not only being torn apart by internal wars and attacks from external tribes; it was also suffering from galloping inflation and was in a financial and administrative mess. How very modern of it. Diocletian finally decided that it was too much for one man to rule and divided the empire in two. He took charge of the eastern part and his friend Maximian took the west.

Constantine the Great (306–337): The one who became a Christian and made Christianity acceptable throughout the Roman world. He also brought the empire back together again, defeating Licinius, who was by that time in charge in the east, and making himself sole emperor. But the damage was done. Constantine made Byzantium (modern Istanbul) his capital, rebuilding it and renaming it Constantinople, and the focus of the empire moved to the east. While Rome remained prestigious and wealthy, it would never again be the political center of the universe.

Rome was finally invaded and sacked by a Germanic tribe called the **Visigoths**, led by **Alaric**, in 410.* Although

---

* You can't mention Alaric the Goth without a quick word on Attila the Hun. Attila came a little later (he died in 453), but he, too, rampaged over the Roman Empire, invading all sorts of places from the Balkans to Gaul. He eventually murdered his brother and became the sort of autocratic ruler that has made his name a byword.

Constantinople went from strength to strength, this date ("the Fall of Rome") is normally regarded as the end of the Roman Empire.*

About Roman historians

Julius Caesar (*ca.* 100–44 B.C.) chronicled his own conquests of Gaul, famously beginning *Gallia est omnis divisa in partes tres*—"All of Gaul is divided into three parts" (see page 78)—and it doesn't get much more exciting than that. The books are mostly straight military history, with some useful historical information on Gaul and its people and perhaps just a glancing reference to what a great general Caesar was.

Most people know of **Livy** (59 B.C.–A.D. 17), perhaps because he wrote 142 books of history and told us practically everything we know about everything that happened *ab urbe condita* (see page 76) to the early years of Augustus. He covered the period of the kingdom, the wars with Carthage, wars in the east, all sorts of stuff about Marius and Sulla, Caesar's invasion of Gaul and his civil war against Pompey—you name it. But he wasn't an accurate historian. Really what he was doing was praising the ancient Roman character and virtues, as opposed to the decadence of his own times. Personally I could never get along with him,

---

* Actually the last Roman emperor in the West wasn't deposed until A.D. 476, but despite his fancy-sounding name—Romulus Augustulus—no one was taking much notice by then.

not because I am a stickler for historical accuracy but because he had a Henry James–like attitude about the length of sentences and paragraphs, and by the time you came to the verb at the end, you had lost all trace of the noun at the beginning.

But give me **Tacitus** (*ca.* A.D. 55–A.D. 117) anytime. His *Annals* and *Histories* start with the reign of Tiberius and go up to his own time, so they include Caligula, Nero and all the fun people who went really off the rails. Tacitus was sharp on character analysis and a superb writer, but what makes him so enjoyable is that he was pretty opposed to the whole concept of emperors, so he tended to believe (and relate) all the bad stuff about them—and there was no shortage of that.

Suetonius (*ca.* A.D. 70–*ca.* A.D. 140) is more a gossip than a historian, so great fun if you are not looking for scholarly rigor. His *Lives of the Caesars* covers Julius and the first eleven emperors, up to Domitian. If what you want to know is that Augustus was careless about his dress, frugal in his eating habits and had eyebrows that met in the middle, or that Nero played with little ivory horses and chariots even after he became emperor, Suetonius is your man.

6
The Posh Stuff: Classical Literature

The one person we've all heard of in Greek literature is **Homer**, who may not have existed or may have been two people.* But worrying about that is like worrying about whether Bacon or Marlowe wrote Shakespeare's plays: Frankly, who cares, they're great stuff, sit back and enjoy. After Homer there is a bit of a blank for a few hundred years, and then we hit a Golden Age in Athens (which you know about already if you've read Chapter 4).

Homer and other Greek literary figures

Homer (probably ninth century B.C.) wrote two great epics, the *Iliad* and the *Odyssey*, almost certainly based on existing ballads.† The story behind the *Iliad* is that Helen was the most beautiful woman in the world and lots of Greek noblemen were after her.

---

* One of the things people do think they know about him is that he was blind, although as there is debate about whether or not he existed at all, this seems to come under the heading of "surmise."

† Another thing people think they know about Homer is that he didn't actually *write* anything; his stories were circulated by word of mouth and only written down centuries later—by someone else.

She married Menelaus, King of Sparta, but all the rejected suitors made a promise that they would come to her rescue should anyone abduct her (a sort of early pre-nup in reverse). And guess what?

Yes, she ran off with Paris, a prince of Troy (see page 47 for the story of the Judgment of Paris that started it all). And all the Greek warriors, including Achilles, Agamemnon, Odysseus (Ulysses in Latin), and Ajax, trotted off and camped outside Troy for ten years to try to get her back.

All this happens before the *Iliad* begins (Ilium or Ilion is the other name for Troy, by the way, hence the title). What mostly happens in the *Iliad* is that Achilles has a hissy fit because Agamemnon has stolen a slave girl of his, sulks in his tent for eight books and spends the ninth telling Agamemnon he's had enough and he's going home. Achilles is a great warrior, so the war is going badly for the Greeks because of his petulance. Achilles's friend Patroclus borrows his armor, goes out to fight on his behalf and is promptly killed by the Trojan prince Hector. Achilles finally bursts out of his tent, kills Hector and turns the tide of the battle. There is no mention here of the Trojan horse; that story crops up in the *Odyssey* but isn't told in detail until Virgil's *Aeneid*, so we'll come to it in about a thousand years' time (see page 117).

So, at long last, the Greeks win and set out for home. But Odysseus takes another ten years to do it, seven of them dallying with the goddess Calypso, during which time he's presumably ignoring his wife Penelope's text messages asking him to pick up a couple of bottles of retsina wine on his way past the liquor store. This is where the *Odyssey* begins: Penelope has been besieged by suitors urging her to marry again on the basis that her husband is surely dead. She delays a decision, saying that she will choose one of them once she has finished a piece of weaving, which she works at during the day and then secretly unravels at night.

Zeus orders Calypso to release Odysseus, but on the next leg of the journey he is shipwrecked. (Poseidon doesn't like him because he has blinded the god's son, the Cyclops Polyphemus—yet another example of how easy and how foolhardy it is to upset Poseidon.) Odysseus is now rescued by a princess called Nausicaa. In her father's palace he recounts the events of his journey: his visit to the land of the Lotus-Eaters (there's a poem by Tennyson about this); his visit to the land of the Cyclops (who by the way had only one eye each and now have a high-tech Wimbledon line-judge named after them); his encounter with the sorceress Circe, who turns his companions into pigs; his descent into the Underworld, where he meets many dead companions; his struggles with Scylla and Charybdis (see page 43)—and on and on and on. Can't you just see the nice people in the palace yawning and wishing they'd left him stranded on the beach so they could go to bed?

Anyway. Odysseus gets home to discover that the suitors are eating him out of house and home, but that Penelope is going to make her choice the next day. He wins the contest Penelope has set for the suitors, kills them all and they live happily ever after. If she has a few harsh words to say because he has been away chasing after other women for twenty years, Homer doesn't mention it.

About Troy

For many years, scholars believed that the city of **Troy** was no more than the basis for the mythical events described in the *Iliad*. But in 1871 the obsession of a self-made German millionaire, **Heinrich Schliemann**, proved them wrong.

Schliemann had fallen in love with the *Iliad* as a child and was convinced that it was a historical account. Homer's writings gave him sufficient information to set up an archaeological dig in northwestern Turkey. Schliemann was no archaeologist and didn't know or care about digging very gently in case you disturbed anything; he also wasn't interested in anything that didn't tie in with his own theories. Despite his bull-in-a-china-shop methods, more delicate digging has since confirmed that a fortified city—or rather a succession of nine cities, one on top of the other—had existed just where Homer said it did, from about 3000 B.C. to A.D. 400. The second layer from the bottom—known as Troy II—had been destroyed by fire, tying in with Homer's account, but scholars now think that the sixth or seventh layer is probably the one that dates from the right period.

But Homer was of course not the only literary figure in ancient Greece...

Sappho (probably seventh century B.C.): The only female writer of classical times whose name means anything to most of us. She lived on the island of Lesbos, surrounded by a community of women, but it is likely that this was for the sake of studying music and poetry rather than for anything, well, sapphic. That said, whether she was thinking of men or women, the fragments of poetry that have come down to us contain some pretty sexy stuff.

Aesop (*ca.* 620–560 B.C.): Wrote fables—stories about animals, with a moral. There are lots of them, but perhaps the most famous are *The Hare and the Tortoise* (slow and steady wins the race) and *The Fox and the Grapes* (in which the grapes are too high up for the fox to reach them, so he turns away, sniffing "I'm sure they are sour"—hence the expression "sour grapes"). Warnings against a wolf in sheep's clothing and the foolishness of killing a goose that lays golden eggs also come from Aesop.

Aeschylus (*ca.* 525–456 B.C.): The first of the three great tragedians of Athens, known as "the father of Greek tragedy" and author of, among others, *Seven Against Thebes* and the *Oresteia* trilogy, *Agamemnon*, *Choephoroe* and *Eumenides*. The story of the *Oresteia* is—roughly—that many years ago, Agamemnon, on his way to Troy, agreed to sacrifice his daughter Iphigenia to the goddess Artemis (Diana in latin) in return for good sailing weather. In some versions Artemis took pity on the girl and saved her, but even so Agamemnon's wife Clytemnestra never forgave him. So she murders her husband on his return from Troy. Their son Orestes in turn kills his mother and is pursued by the Furies (a.k.a. Eumenides; see page 36), who are stirred into action by the ghost of Clytemnestra. The issue is taken to the court of Athena, and Orestes is acquitted. The Choephoroe, by the way, are the women, including Orestes's sister Electra—who pour libations (sacrificial wine) on Agamemnon's tomb.

Sophocles (496–406 B.C.): Came to the fore after he beat Aeschylus in a drama contest in 468 B.C., when doubtless he was the Angry Young Man of Greek tragedy. His great surviving plays are *Oedipus the King, Oedipus at Colonus* and *Antigone.* Oedipus is the one immortalized in song by Tom Lehrer ("His name appears in Freud's index/'Cause he loved his mother"). He is abandoned and left to die as a baby because of a prophecy that he would kill his father and marry his mother, but—as always when people try to get around prophecies like this—he is rescued by a kindly shepherd or some such person,* and brought up by people he assumes are his natural parents. In due course he bumps into his father and, not recognizing him (it's been awhile), quarrels with and kills him. He then goes on to the city of Thebes, which is being hassled by the Sphinx and her riddles. Oedipus solves the riddle,† relieves the city and marries the queen, Jocasta, who just happens to be a teeny bit older than he is…

…and four children later, word gets out that Jocasta is his mother. She hangs herself and Oedipus blinds himself (according to Sophocles, using Jocasta's brooch. Yuck).

---

* Just to be sure that he would die, they pushed a spike through his feet, hence the name Oedipus, which means "swollen foot." But they had not counted on the kindly shepherd.

† What goes on four legs in the morning, two legs at noon and three legs in the evening? Answer: man—as we were allowed to say in those days—who crawls as a baby, walks upright most of his life and ends up leaning on a stick.

That is the background and action of *Oedipus the King*. The remaining two plays deal with Oedipus in banishment, tended by his daughter Antigone, and the subsequent destruction of his family. More corpses than *Hamlet* by the end of it all.

Euripides (*ca.* 480–406 B.C.): His plays *Orestes*, *Electra* and *Iphigenia at Aulis* cover the stories described under Aeschylus above, though in this version no one intervenes to save Iphigenia. Perhaps Euripides's most famous play is *Medea*, about the lady who murders her own children to avenge herself on their father, Jason (see page 49), who has abandoned her. Powerful stuff, especially if you happen to have seen Diana Rigg doing it, but see also page 156 for the philosophical aspect.

Aristophanes (*ca.* 448–*ca.* 388 B.C.): The only comic dramatist of the period whose work survives. His plays include *The Clouds*, *The Birds*, *Frogs* and, most memorably, *Lysistrata*, which is the one where the women on both sides of a conflict between Athens and Sparta refuse to have sex with their husbands until they end the war. *The Oxford Companion to Classical Literature* remarks austerely that "as results from part of the theme of the comedy, there are passages of gross indecency," which may be why the play appeals to modern audiences who don't give a hoot about wars between Athens and Sparta.

The classical theater

Now here's an odd thing. The great classical work of literary theory is **Aristotle**'s *Poetics*, though all the great Greek tragedians were dead before Aristotle was born. But hey, that's Aristotle all over: not inventing, but classifying and organizing. We'll be hearing lots more about him in later chapters.

The *Poetics* deals mostly with tragedy, of which, Aristotle says, the plot is "the first principle, and, as it were, the soul of a tragedy; character holds the second place."

What Aristotle wants is "unity of action"—a single thread running through the entire work: The hero has (or achieves) success, makes a mistake, suffers a reversal and then, in all probability, tears his eyes out or is driven mad by the Furies. This is not the same as "unity of hero": The *Odyssey* may be all about Odysseus, but it wanders around all over the place, in more senses than one. For the audience, what matters is to experience pity and fear, "effecting the proper purging of these emotions." In other words, if you come out of the theater feeling drained, you've gotten your money's worth.

The hero of a tragedy should not be a pre-eminently good or bad man, because although the misfortunes of the one or the downfall of the other might satisfy some moral sense, neither would evoke pity or fear. So the central figure of a tragedy is one "whose misfortune is brought about not by vice or depravity, but by some error or frailty."

The *Poetics* had a great influence on later European drama: Macbeth's "vaulting ambition" and Othello's loving "not wisely but too well" are just the sort of frailty Aristotle was talking about. On the other hand, Shakespeare didn't stick rigidly to unity of action—Edmund's affairs with both Goneril and Regan in *King Lear* must be considered a subplot, and Aristotle might have thought Rosencrantz and Guildenstern were surplus to requirements, too. The French classical tragedians, however, notably Corneille and Racine, not only stuck to unity of action but went a stage further: They introduced unities of time and place, so that the action of the play took place within a period of twenty-four hours (the purists insisted on "real time," i.e., no more than a couple of hours) and all in the same scene. The extreme example is Corneille's *Le Cid*, in which the hero has to defeat a vast Moorish army—off-stage—in the course of a single night in order to make the play fit the rules.

Aristotle's rules aside, Greek drama, whether tragedy or comedy, followed a fairly set pattern. It began with a prologue—an idea borrowed by Shakespeare for *Romeo and Juliet* and Frankie Howerd for *Up Pompeii!**—followed by the entrance of the chorus, then the action of the play, interspersed with commentary from the chorus. Early plays had a lot of chorus and little action; by the time of Sophocles *et al.*, individual actors had become more important, but the chorus was still there to provide a few tunes and point out the moral.

The plays always had a religious background, so very often a god was brought on at the end to sort things out. The actor playing the god was carried by a crane (*mechane* in Greek,

---

* Mentioning *Up Pompeii!* gives me an excuse to bring in the word *innuendo*, which comes from a Latin gerund or verbal noun, meaning "that which must be conveyed by a nod."

machina in Latin) to give the impression that he was descending from the sky. Hence the expression *deus ex machina*—"a god from a machine"—to mean some unexpected intervention that resolves an apparently hopeless situation. A classical variation on "with one bound he was free."

The Romans weren't as hot on theater as the Greeks, and a lot of Roman plays are adapted from Greek originals. **Seneca the Younger** (*ca.* 4 B.C.–A.D. 65, see page 157) wrote tragedies, **Plautus** (*ca.* 254–184 B.C.) produced some raunchy, crowd-pleasing comedies (Frankie Howerd quoted him a lot too), and **Terence** (*ca.* 190–159 B.C.) wrote comedies for a more refined audience, but for the most part the Romans seem to have preferred chariot races and people being torn apart. See Chapter 10 for more about that.

Roman literature

After Aristotle we can skip forward a few hundred years to the **Golden Age** of Roman literature. If you look at the dates—and see Cicero on page 115 and the historians on page 103—you can see why it was called a Golden Age: Practically everyone you have heard of was born within a couple of generations of each other.

Catullus (*ca.* 84–54 B.C.) addressed his best poetry to a lady he called Lesbia. This was meant to be a compliment, likening her to the poet Sappho, who lived on Lesbos (see page 108); Lesbia's real name was Clodia, and she was the sister (and some say lover) of the Clodius mentioned under Cicero. Whether or not she slept with her brother, Clodia did sleep with a lot of other people and gave Catullus a rotten time—as a result of which he wrote some beautiful, passionate poetry, so it's an ill wind...

About Cicero

It's difficult to know where to put **Cicero**—politics, literature, even philosophy—so let's give him a box of his own.

Born in 106 B.C., he studied law and made his first great speech at the age of twenty-seven, successfully defending one Sextus Roscius on a charge of parricide (killing one's parent). This brought him fame as an advocate; at the same time he started moving up the political ladder, becoming consul in 63 B.C. He then foiled a revolutionary plot by a corrupt patrician called Catilina, which produced some of his greatest speeches (*In Catilinam*). This was a time of great political in-fighting in Rome, and Cicero, who was notoriously pleased with himself and had a habit of making enemies, fell out big time with the unscrupulous but influential Clodius and to a lesser extent with Julius Caesar, and found himself exiled. Caesar forgave him a year later and Cicero returned to Rome to continued success as an advocate, a position that was consolidated after Clodius was murdered (which had only been a matter of time).

Cicero then sided with Pompey during the civil war (see page 87), but was again pardoned by Caesar and was able to live peacefully in Rome until the latter's assassination.

Cicero was a staunch defender of the republic and although he admired Caesar the man, he was horrified at the power he wielded, and even more horrified at the additional power that Rome wanted to give him. For much of this he blamed Mark Antony; his late great speeches, the *Philippics*, are diatribes against Antony and his policies. There are fourteen *Philippics*, so Antony can have been in little doubt of Cicero's views. Antony had Cicero murdered in 43 B.C., and his head and hands were displayed on the Rostra, the platform in the Forum from which orators addressed the people.

For a bit more about Cicero's speeches, see page 164. He also wrote works of philosophy and books about oratory and kept up a remarkably frank lifelong correspondence with his friend Atticus, which gives great insight into his own vanity, wavering moods and political indecision. He wrote and wrote and wrote: It is no surprise that his secretary Tiro should be credited with having invented shorthand. He was pompous, fantastically fond of the sound of his own voice and tireless in the pursuit of his own ambition. But he died because he wouldn't give up on his own ideals of liberty, and you can't make cheap jokes about that.

Virgil (70–19 B.C.): Author of the great Latin epic, the *Aeneid*, the story of how the Trojan prince Aeneas escapes from Troy and makes it to Italy to found Rome. Taking a break from his journey in Carthage (see page 82), he becomes involved with the queen, Dido, and tells her about the fall of Troy and his journey so far. This is where the details of the Trojan Horse come from (see *Homer*, page 105): The war was at a deadlock and one of the Greeks—possibly Odysseus, he was normally the one with the bright ideas—suggested that they build an enormous wooden horse and then withdraw from the siege, leaving behind a man named Sinon. Sinon would go to the Trojans pretending to be a traitor and giving them the horse as an offering to Athena (who had not hitherto been on the Trojans' side, having been passed over in the Golden Apple awards; see page 47). The Trojans fell for it, bless them, not realizing that the horse was full of soldiers who would leap out at night once the horse was inside the walls, and sack the city.

Other key events of the *Aeneid* are Aeneas's desertion of Dido—he abandons her after being scolded by the gods for dallying in Carthage when his destiny is to get off his backside and found Rome, and she commits suicide—and his descent into the Underworld to meet his dead father (see page 35). The rest is about his arrival in Italy and his (surely not unexpected) war with the people who are already there. Frankly this second half goes on a bit, but in the end Aeneas wins, marries the local king's daughter and is all set to be the ancestor of the Romans (see *Romulus and Remus*, page 75).

Virgil also wrote a collection of pastoral poems called *Eclogues*, and a long poem called *Georgics*, about farming and with advice on raising crops, rearing cattle, bee-keeping and planting herbs on land unfit for anything else. Who said the classics were no use to anyone nowadays?

Horace (65–8 B.C.): Mostly wrote odes, but also a longer poem called *Ars Poetica*—"On the Art of Poetry"—which includes the famous words (I'm translating loosely here) "Even the great Homer sometimes has an off day." Lots of Latin "tags" come from Horace: *nil desperandum* ("never despair"), *carpe diem* ("seize the day") and the one that First World War poet Wilfred Owen called "the old lie," *dulce et decorum est pro patria mori* ("it is sweet and honorable to die for one's country"). Horace's poems are full of robust common sense, advocating moderation and simple pleasures, with the occasional glass of good red wine thrown in. *Nunc est bibendum* ("now is the time for drinking," motto of many an oenophile society) is also one of his.

Ovid (43 B.C.–A.D. 18): Lived in fashionable circles at the time of Augustus, so it was almost inevitable that he should have an affair with the Emperor's daughter Julia (everyone else did), as a result of which he spent the last ten years of his life in exile in a gloomy area near the Black Sea. Actually, the part about Julia may be scurrilous rumor; Ovid himself seems to have thought that he was exiled because he wrote a poem called *Ars Amatoria* ("The Art of Love"), a racy guide to promiscuity and adulterous "love," written in a mock-serious elegiac form. Something in it to offend everyone, particularly the rather prudish Augustus.

Chief among Ovid's other works is the *Metamorphoses*, an important source of our knowledge of ancient myths. He focused on stories in which one of the protagonists ended up turning into an animal, plant or other non-human form. You might think this was a specialist area, but he got fifteen books out of it. The *Metamorphoses* contains the stories of Pyramus and Thisbe, which later turn up in Shakespeare's *A Midsummer Night's Dream* (the "metamorphosis" in the original is that a mulberry tree grows from the blood of the dead lovers); Echo and Narcissus (Narcissus rejects the love of Echo, and in punishment Aphrodite makes him fall in love with his own reflection in a fountain; he pines away and turns into the flower that bears his name); and Arachne, who challenged Athena to a weaving contest and ended up being turned into a spider. There are lots more, but you get the gist.

Pliny the Elder (*ca.* 23–79 A.D.): Incredibly prolific, but his main contribution to posterity is a massive work of what he called natural history, but which covers much more than we understand by that term. Its thirty-seven books (!) cover the composition of the universe, geography, zoology, botany (including a lot of the medicinal properties of plants), metallurgy and lots more.

Pliny's nephew, known as **Pliny the Younger** (61 or 62–*ca.* 113 A.D.), wrote volumes and volumes of letters that tell us a lot about the life of a wealthy Roman during this comparatively placid period of the empire. Toward the end of his life, he became governor of the province of Bithynia, now part of Turkey. His final book of *Letters* contains those addressed from Bithynia to the Emperor Trajan, asking advice on many trivial matters and showing how very hands-on the central government of the empire was at this time. But Pliny also consulted the emperor on what he was to do with a group of Christians who had been denounced to him: If a man had "repented" of being a Christian, could he be excused, or did having once committed the offense tarnish him forever? Trajan replied that such a person could be forgiven, provided he went back to worshipping the right gods, but he also came down hard on the idea of anonymous informers: "For this is both a dangerous kind of precedent and out of keeping with the spirit of our age."

Juvenal (*ca.* 55–130 A.D.): His *Satires* were so, shall we say, earthy that my school edition was censored. It was one of those books where the lines were numbered and sometimes it skipped from line twenty to line forty, and you knew that you were missing the part about it being more difficult to get an erection as you got older. In fact, Juvenal was a harsh moralist, and his theme is really the vice and depravity to which Rome had sunk by this time. What he's saying is that it is crazy to pray for a long life, because of all the indignities that go with age, including it being more difficult… You get my drift. The maxim *Mens sana in corpore sano*—"a healthy mind in a healthy body"—comes later in the same poem. Juvenal is known to have influenced lots of English writers who later wrote raunchy and/or satirical stuff, including Chaucer, Donne, Swift, Pope and Samuel Johnson.

7

The Fancy Stuff: Architecture and Art

We all know what classical buildings look like. They're those big chunky things with lots of columns, and they're all over the place. The White House, the Pentagon and the Capitol in Washington, D.C., the National Gallery and Somerset House in London; most of the city of Bath, England; and almost every civic building in the Western world that is over a hundred years old. They are all inspired by the designs established by the Greeks well over two thousand years ago.

As in many cultures, the oldest buildings we know about are temples, for the simple reason that anything built to honor the gods was more important than anything built to house mere mortals, and therefore made to last. As early as the seventh century B.C., the Greeks (following the example of the Egyptians) were using stone for temples; by the sixth century they were using it for public buildings as well.

Doric, Ionic and Corinthian

There are three principal styles or orders of classical architecture, defined largely by the type of **column** they use and more specifically by the style of the top (properly called the **capital**, which is the part that joins the column to whatever it is supporting, the **entablature**). Such things as the ratio of the diameter of the column to its height (1:6 in the purest Doric form) and the distance that each column stood from the next went a long way toward dictating the proportions of the whole building.

The oldest and simplest of these orders is the **Doric**, which emerged on mainland Greece. The Dorians were an ancient people who had settled in the Peloponnese some time before the beginning of this book. Ethnically the Spartans were Dorians, so it'll come as no surprise that the Doric column is sturdy with no adornment and, in the early days, no base.

The fancier **Ionic**—originating in Asia Minor, where all the decadence came from[*]—is slimmer and has four spiral scrolls on the capital. These two orders were kept strictly separate for a couple of hundred years (this was the time when the mainland Greeks were fighting the Persians for control of the Greek-speaking towns in Ionia, so it's not surprising that an "us and them" attitude spilled over into architecture). By Hellenistic times this had relaxed a little, so that the styles were allowed to develop: Doric columns tended to become

---

[*] Well, that's what the Spartans thought, anyway. See the footnote on page 70 about the Persians using arrows.

slimmer and more widely spaced, creating less severe buildings that let in more light. The two styles occasionally even appeared on the same building. Purists maintained that this was heresy, but—a bit like those of us who still argue in favor of the apostrophe—they had to accept that they weren't going to win every battle.

The time was ripe for the emergence of the third great order, the **Corinthian**. If you have ever had occasion to read a gardening book that mentions the cottage-garden plant called bear's breeches, you will know that its opulent leaves inspired the design of the Corinthian capital. (The plant's Latin name is *Acanthus mollis*, but it wouldn't have been called that even in Roman times, because it wasn't the Romans who invented Latin names for plants as we know them.)

Anyway, the Corinthian order was generally a lot fancier than anything that had gone before and reflected the "art for art's sake" attitude that was a feature of the Hellenistic world.[*]

The Romans adopted and adapted these architectural orders, introducing two of their own—the **Tuscan**, which was their equivalent of the Doric, and the **Composite**, which was basically a mixture of the Ionic and the Corinthian. Why these names haven't caught on in the same way as the Greek ones is a matter for speculation for anyone who cares to speculate about it.

---

[*] Sparta had ceased to be a force to be reckoned with by this time. The concept of "art for art's sake" would really have been Greek to them.

If you want to see these columns *in situ*, the Parthenon and the Temple of Hephaestus, both in Athens, are good for Doric, or there is a lovely temple at Segesta in Sicily; many of the Deep South plantation houses of the Antebellum style have Ionic ones; and the Pantheon in Rome and the Capitol in Washington, D.C., have Corinthian columns.

About the Seven Wonders of the World

The **Seven Wonders of the Ancient World**, chosen by an otherwise forgotten Greek poet called Antipater of Sidon in the second century B.C. as being "remarkable for their splendor or magnitude," were:

- **The Hanging Gardens of Babylon**
- **The Mausoleum of Halicarnassus**
- **The Pharos** (lighthouse) **of Alexandria**
- **The Colossus of Rhodes**
- **The Temple of Artemis at Ephesus**
- **The Statue of Zeus at Olympia**
- **The Great Pyramid of Cheops** (or **Khufu**)

Of the seven, only the pyramid is still in existence, but there is talk about rebuilding the Colossus—a gigantic statue of the sun god Helios—at the entrance to Rhodes harbor. The original was toppled by an earthquake, and the plan is that, rather than attempting to replicate it, the architect will create a massive light sculpture. The mind boggles.

On a more banal note, the ruins of the Mausoleum are just outside Bodrum in Turkey, and if you drive there from Istanbul or Izmir, you pass what is left of the Temple of Artemis on the way. The temple was vandalized and rebuilt a number of times over the centuries, before being destroyed for the last time in an act of anti-pagan violence by Christians in around A.D. 400. The Statue of Zeus was probably destroyed by fire or earthquake, but no one seems to be sure. The Pharos of Alexandria was weakened by a series of earthquakes, but lasted into the Middle Ages.

Oh, and it is just possible that the Hanging Gardens of Babylon never existed at all. If they did, there is a rather sweet story attached to them. Babylon, for all its magnificence (and it was the most magnificent city in the world at one time), was flat and arid. King Nebuchadnezzar was married to a lady who came from a green and mountainous place and he created a vast, terraced garden to make her feel less homesick. Aww. Impressively, given that this was the sixth century B.C., he installed a pump that brought water from the River Euphrates all the way up to the top of the artificial hillside so that it could irrigate the plants on its way down. And yes, it is the same Nebuchadnezzar who appears in the Old Testament, gaining notoriety for destroying Jerusalem.

Some important buildings

There are remnants of Greek temples all over the place. In addition to the one that became a wonder of the world (see page 135), there is the fantastic **Temple of Apollo** in Didyma, in southwestern Turkey. It took something like 700 years to build, ran monumentally over budget and was never actually completed. *Didyma* means "twins," and this temple is not a million miles from the **Temple of Artemis** (Apollo's twin sister) at Ephesus. It was 360 feet (110 m) long with over 120 (mostly Ionic) columns, each intended to be almost sixty-five feet (20 m) high. It's an impressive ruin by any standards, but its real selling point is that there is a scale drawing of the temple scratched into a marble wall; the architects knew it was going to take more than a lifetime to build and wanted the next generation to know what the plan was. Ironically, if the temple had ever been finished, this would have been polished over and lost forever. Another ill wind, eh?

Most people nowadays would say that the most important building in ancient Greece was the **Parthenon** in Athens. Certainly it is the most iconic, using *iconic* in the sense of "we all know what it looks like." So let's give it a moment or two.

First off, the Parthenon is not the same as the **Acropolis**; it is *part* of the Acropolis. *Acropolis* means "high town," and Athens, like many historic towns all over the world, was built on a hill or rocky plateau that was difficult to attack. So the word has come to mean the citadel—the central, usually fortified, part of the city where the important religious and civic buildings were. It was all rebuilt under the auspices of Pericles after the Persians destroyed Athens (see page 60), and the Parthenon—a temple dedicated to Athena, but also a symbol of the invincibility of the Athenians—is the most important of a number of buildings that survive.* It only ever had forty-six outer columns, about 36 feet (11 m) high—no big deal by Didyma and Ephesus standards—but it was dedicated to the most important goddess of the most important city in the world, so deserves some respect. It is also a highly sophisticated piece of architecture in that it allows for some oddities in our visual perception. For example, to counteract "imperfections" caused by optical illusions and the laws of perspective, the Parthenon's base slopes downward very slightly at the corners, and the columns lean ever so slightly inward.

The Parthenon was, like many important buildings of the period, sculpted all over. There were ninety-two panels (called **metopes**) along the **architrave** (the bit just above the columns, part of the **entablature**); sculptures on the **pediments** (the triangular gable-like parts at either end) and over 492 feet (150 m) of **friezes** around the central chamber, all carved with stories about the gods and Athenian victories over various enemies. The chamber also contained a 42-foot (13-m) gold and ivory statue of Athena.†

---

* Other buildings of the Acropolis included an *asclepieion*—see page 142.

† The original statue had disappeared by A.D. 400, but a replica exists in a replica of the Parthenon in, of all places, Nashville, Tennessee.

So all in all, the place was well worth looting. Which is why you can see chunks of it in the British Museum. In the early nineteenth century, Greece was controlled by the Turks, who were allies of the British in the war against Napoleon. A certain Lord Elgin was the British Ambassador to Turkey and inveigled the Turks into giving him permission to take a few souvenirs. Whether they realized he was going to hack off big chunks of marble is a cornerstone of the debate that has raged ever since as to whether or not the so-called Elgin Marbles should be "sent home."

Roman buildings

You could write a whole book about the fabulous buildings in Rome—indeed, plenty of people have. Here is a note about just two of the most remarkable.

The first **Pantheon** in Rome was built in 27 B.C. to commemorate Octavian's victory over Antony and Cleopatra at the Battle of Actium a few years earlier. The current version was commissioned by Hadrian (he of the wall—see page 96) in the second century A.D. The name means that it is dedicated to all (*pan*) the gods (*theos*),* although it became a Christian church in A.D. 609 (the first pagan temple to be taken over in this way).

It is remarkable in all sorts of ways. Mostly because it is nearly 2,000 years old and has survived virtually intact, so it is

---

* Yes, both of those words do come from Greek rather than Latin.

probably the best-preserved building of its age in the world. Its height, 142 feet (43.3 m), is the same as the diameter of its dome, which makes it "feel" perfect the moment you walk in. Until the twentieth century it was the largest vault ever built, and it remains the largest unreinforced concrete dome, weighing over 4,960 tons. When the door is closed, the only light comes from a massive hole in the ceiling called the *oculus* ("eye"), which also acts as a sundial, telling the time and doing clever things with equinoxes and solstices. And, just in case you are wondering, the floor slopes gently toward a central drain, so that any rain that comes in quickly flows away. In other words, it is just amazing.

So is the **Colosseum**, which dates from about fifty years earlier and is the largest Roman amphitheater ever built. Although not on a par with the Pantheon, it is still in pretty good condition and you can see that, as so often, the Romans thought of everything when they built it. It was four stories high, decorated with Doric, Ionic and Corinthian columns, had a huge awning to keep the sun off the more important members of the audience, and could accommodate 50,000 people. The seats were steeply banked so that—and I am not making this up—*everyone could see:* an innovation that many modern theaters should really consider next time they have a makeover. Numbered arches made it easy to find your seat.

All this was supported by eighty walls that radiated from the arena. (The name comes from the Latin word for sand, *harena,* because the area was scattered with sand after each round of combat to soak up the blood.) Beneath the wooden floor of the arena was a network of cages, rooms and passageways for the people and animals that took part in the "games" (more about them on page 166), plus lifts and trapdoors to get them up into the arena. A fence about 5 feet (1.5 m) high separated the arena from the lowest tier of spectators and was topped with wooden rollers to stop the wild beasts climbing over it.

The Colosseum was also a masterpiece of crowd control. A system of corridors called—rather too graphically perhaps—**vomitoria** opened out into the tiers of seats. Each efficiently "spewed" its section of the crowd into their places and equally effectively vomited them out into the streets at the end of the performance. It is said that the Colosseum could be emptied in a quarter of an hour.[*]

Amphitheaters caught on in a big way after the Colosseum opened and some are remarkably well preserved. The one in Verona is still used for spectacular opera productions and the one in Arles for bullfights.

On a smaller scale

It's worth a quick mention here of the private house of a wealthy Roman, because some of the terms they used are still familiar. By the fourth century B.C., Rome

---

[*] Contrary to rumor, there was never a room—in a Roman house or anywhere else—called a *vomitorium*. If you wanted to throw up after overindulging at a banquet, you went outside with everyone else.

had become very crowded, and building technology involving a sort of concrete made from volcanic ash allowed the Romans to erect high-rise apartment buildings to house the poor.

However, those who could afford it had more luxurious homes in town and probably villas in the country as well. Obviously there were variations on the basic theme, but most such houses were built around a central **atrium**, wholly or partly open to the sky, and a **peristyle**—a covered colonnade a bit like a cloister. Entrance to the house was through a **vestibule**; the atrium acted as a reception room; bedrooms, dining areas, kitchens, etc. were built off it. The dining room was known as the **triclinium**, because couches were arranged on three sides of the central dining table. Diners reclined, three to a couch, while eating, and there was a strict protocol about who lay where.

About the Forum

Originally the marketplace in a large Roman town, the **forum** developed into the focus of political, religious and social life. All the main civic buildings surrounded it, debates took place inside it, and important public notices were posted there. The main Forum in Rome (known as the **Forum Romanum**, imaginatively enough) contains the remains of the Curia or Senate House, the Rostra from which speeches were made,

---

the House of the Vestals, various temples and the triumphal arches of Titus and a later emperor, Septimius Severus. It's open to the public, and it's free, which means that you can wander in at lunchtime and have your sandwiches within inches of where Julius Caesar was murdered or Cicero made his greatest speeches. Or you can say, "It's just a pile of old ruins," and go to McDonald's.

A bit of etymology: The word *forensic* comes from *forum*, because the forum was the focus of so many things to do with the law. The Greek equivalent was the *agora*, whence the word *agoraphobic*, meaning "afraid of open spaces." And Septimius Severus won his great victory over the Parthians, a people of southwest Asia who could twist around in the saddle and fire their arrows backward while they were retreating—hence the expression "a Parthian shot," meaning a final remark to which the hearer has no chance of replying. Most people would now say "a parting shot," because they're a bit vague about who the Parthians were, so there's a chance for you to show off at dinner parties.

Finally, a bit about triumphal arches. They were freestanding monuments—as opposed to being built into a wall and serving as an entrance—erected to celebrate an emperor's victory in battle. A triumph—that is, a triumphal procession—had, in Republican times, been a serious thing, awarded by the Senate to a victorious general. He could then put on a laurel wreath and a gold-trimmed robe and parade through the streets of Rome at the head of his army, displaying his prisoners and the spoils of war, accompanied by trumpeters and other musicians and generally making no secret of the fact that he had done something to shout about. Later on, you won't be surprised to learn, emperors awarded triumphs to themselves because they felt like it. And presumably built themselves arches for similar self-aggrandizing reasons. The other great surviving arch is Constantine's, near the Colosseum. Like those of Titus and Septimius Severus, it may not have led anywhere, but that doesn't stop it from being pretty impressive.

Greek art

Sculpture was the great classical art form, predating even architecture: The Greeks first made images of the gods, then built temples to house them. But lots of even more ancient people produced sculptures. In Egypt, Ramses the Great was having colossal statues of himself built in the thirteenth century B.C., 400 years before Homer. What really made the Greeks stand out from the crowd was their **vase painting**.

They did this in Crete way back in time, but the art died out when the Minoan civilization collapsed. It is likely that there were still skilled craftsmen farther east—among the Phoenicians, for example—and sooner or later the know-how drifted back to Greece.

Like everyone else the ancient Greeks had pots for all sorts of purposes, from cooking and water-carrying to storing perfume or keeping the ashes of the dead. At a very early stage people began decorating their pots with geometric shapes* or representations of humans and animals, with special imagery for special pots, such as mourners on funerary urns. Initially (till about 530 B.C.) the decorating was done by incision and was mostly in black, with the occasional dab of red or white on the background clay color. Then the Athenians invented the technique of **red figure**, and also learned to paint. Now the figures could be drawn in outline, the background painted black and the base color left to show through. This allowed for more detail, so that the figures became more than mere silhouettes. The pictures grew more complicated, too, with scenes from mythology and also from daily life. A lot of what we know about life in those days is deduced from vase painting. Or, as Keats put it in his "Ode on a Grecian Urn":

> What men or gods are these? What maidens loth?
> What mad pursuit? What struggle to escape?
> What pipes and timbrels? What wild ecstasy?

---

* Including the swastika; it was perfectly respectable, once upon a time.

8

The Clever Stuff I: Math, Science and Inventions

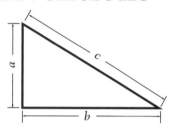

The things that the ancient Greeks invented, developed, classified and first thought of stagger the imagination, and they are basically the subject of this chapter and the next. We've already mentioned that Herodotus is considered the father of history; in this chapter we'll mention the father of mathematics (most say Archimedes, although he had two famous predecessors who might argue with that) and the father of medicine (Hippocrates). In the next chapter we can debate who deserves the title "father of philosophy," though one thing we can't deny is that it is an ancient Greek. And while we're at it, we'll look at some of the many ideas that the Romans took from the Greeks and improved upon.

So—no groans, please—let's start with the people who may have made you miserable in school: mathematicians and scientists.

Math and science

Pythagoras (sixth century B.C.): Most people remember Pythagoras because of his theorem (the square of the hypotenuse is equal to the sum of the square of the other two sides), even if they aren't sure what a theorem or a hypotenuse is. In fact, the theorem was probably developed by followers of Pythagoras, who was first and foremost a philosopher.

Euclid (fourth to third centuries B.C.): Credited with inventing geometry, for which I am sure we are all very grateful. In fact, his masterwork, *Elements*, organized the work of earlier mathematicians such as Eudoxus and Theaetetus and formalized the proofs of propositions that they had initiated. So if you spent part of your childhood proving that there were indeed 180 degrees in a triangle and writing "QED" (see page 25) at the end, Euclid is the man to blame.

Aristarchus of Samos (310–230 B.C.): Never heard of him? Neither had I. But would you believe that all those years ago he hypothesized "that the fixed stars and the sun remain unmoved, that Earth revolves about the sun on the circumference of a circle, the sun lying in the middle of the orbit," and that as a result the universe was vastly bigger than most scientists then thought? The quote is not from Aristarchus himself but from Archimedes (see next entry), who went on to trash the idea, with the result that Earth remained officially at the center of the universe for something like another 1,800 years. It would have saved a lot of trouble for Copernicus, Galileo *et al.* in the Middle Ages if Aristarchus's theories had caught on.

Aristarchus also made a brave attempt to calculate the distance from Earth of both the sun and the moon, and their respective sizes. I don't pretend to understand the calculations, but apparently his reasoning was sound; his instruments just weren't accurate enough to get it just right.

Archimedes (*ca.* 287–212 B.C.): Quite something. In addition to being the first man in recorded history to have really bright ideas in the bath, he was an expert in astronomy; he developed theorems for calculating the volume of geometrical shapes; he invented a water-lift known as Archimedes' Screw, which is still used to draw water from the Nile; and he may also have been the engineer behind the Romans' road-building scheme. At the end of his life, when no longer so friendly with the Romans, he was able to fortify the city of Syracuse in Sicily so powerfully that the mighty Roman army couldn't get in. He had concocted catapults that fired stones; cranes that dropped timbers over the battlements; and a claw-like device that pulled ships out of the water. Yet legend has it that he was killed during this very siege, by a Roman soldier whose challenge he ignored because he was engrossed in a mathematical problem.

Going back to the part about the bath, Archimedes is said to have been sitting there when he noticed that the level of the water was higher than it had been before he got in—that is, his body had displaced a volume of water, and therefore the volume of his body could be calculated. He may or may not then have leapt out and run naked through the streets crying "Eureka!" ("I have found it!") What he undeniably did was calculations about the water he had displaced. This turned into Archimedes' Principle: "An object immersed, whether wholly or partly, in a fluid is buoyed up by a force equal to the weight of the fluid displaced by the object." Or, if you prefer, $W = pVg$ (weight = density x volume x gravity). It's important. Take my word for it.

Ptolemy (*ca.* A.D. 85–*ca.* A.D. 165): A Greek-born Roman subject working in Alexandria. The first thing to say about him is that he wasn't a pharaoh, although lots of pharaohs also were named Ptolemy. This one was, however, a great astronomer and mapmaker, and he did a lot of work on the supposed movement of the sun, moon and planets around Earth, so he must share the blame with Archimedes for consigning Aristarchus to near oblivion. Ptolemy also identified (or at least systematically recorded) most of the constellations we still recognize in the skies and produced an atlas of the world, which introduced the concepts of latitude and longitude to a wider audience. And if we had known that he also invented trigonometry, he would have been someone else we hated in school.

About numbers

Greek numerals seem to have been so complicated that it's a miracle the people using them managed to count at all, never mind invent all that math.

For a start there were two systems, the **Acrophonic** or **Attic** and the **Alphabetic** or **Ionic**. The Acrophonic took the initial letter for the name of a number and used that to represent the number. In other words, the word for 10 was *deka*, which began with a delta (Δ), so Δ was used to mean 10. This system had symbols for 1, 5, 10, 50, 100, 500, 1,000, 5,000 and 10,000, and mixed them together to make other numbers.

In the Ionic system, all twenty-four letters of the alphabet plus three more were allocated values ($a = 1$, $b = 2$ etc. up to 9, then $i = 10$, $k = 20$ and so on[*] up to 90, then $r = 100$ and so on. Then variants on these symbols were used to mean 1,000, 2,000, up to 100,000. So again, you put a string of symbols together to make any number you wanted.

Roman numerals derived from the Acrophonic system and consisted of:

I = 1	C = 100
V = 5	D = 500
X = 10	M = 1,000
L = 50	

Roman numerals introduced the refinement that you didn't only add numbers together, you also could use subtraction. In other words, whereas the Greeks counted

I = 1	III = 3
II = 2	IIII = 4,

---

[*] There was no *j* in the Greek alphabet.

the Romans decided that IIII was getting a bit cumbersome and substituted IV (one-before-five) to mean 4. Similarly more complicated combinations made up larger numbers, such as XCIX (ten-before-a-hundred, then one-before-ten) to make 99. Limited though it was, this system prevailed throughout Europe until the twelfth or thirteenth century, when it was supplanted by the so-called Arabic system we use today.

Medicine

The **Hippocratic Oath** used to be taken by doctors when they graduated and were about to go out into the world of practical medicine, but as it required the speaker to swear by Apollo, Asclepius, Hygieia and Panacea, it has rather fallen into disuse. It does, however, contain the still-relevant promise that a doctor will always do his best for his patients and not seduce them. I'm not joking—it does. Be they women or men, free or slaves. Anyway, I mention this because the Hippocratic Oath was probably invented by a man called...

Hippocrates (*ca.* 460–*ca.* 377 B.C.): The "father of medicine." Apart from the oath, his claim to fame is that he collected together a body of works known as the Hippocratic Corpus, which contained more or less all the medical knowledge that anyone had up to that point. His practice was based on the belief that all matter was made up of four elements—fire, earth, air and water—each of which had its own characteristics, later associated with the four bodily fluids or "humors": blood, phlegm, yellow bile and black bile. These in turn became associated with dispositions known as sanguine, phlegmatic, choleric and melancholic, respectively. The idea was that the four humors had to be kept in balance, so an excess of any of them led to ill health. This system was codified in the second century A.D. by **Galen**, a Greek-born, Egyptian-educated physician living in Rome; it was kept alive by the Arabs after the fall of Rome and formed the basis of Western medical practice for another thousand years, pretty much until the medieval Italians started studying anatomy and William Harvey discovered the circulation of the blood in the 1620s.

Going back to the oath, **Asclepius**, the son of Apollo, was the Greek god of medicine. (Apollo is also regarded as a god of medicine, but he had a pretty broad portfolio; see page 37.) Asclepius's symbol was the snake (because snakes slough off their skins and are thus rejuvenated), which is why a snake winding round a staff is still widely used as a symbol of medicine.

The cult of Asclepius came into its own in around 300 B.C. If Greeks were feeling unwell, they'd go and spend the night at an **asclepieion**, a sort of healing center. While they were sleeping, Asclepius would come in and heal them with the help of his snakes[*] and his daughters, **Hygieia** and **Panacea**, who were responsible for cleanliness and healing. And yes, their names are indeed connected with the word hygiene and with the synonym for a cure-all.

---

[*] Some *asclepieia* had actual live snakes slithering around on the floor to get people in the healing mood.

So what about the Romans?

The Romans were not only exceptional engineers and organizers, they were also fantastic developers and improvers. They didn't invent glass, for example, but they took up the technique of glass-blowing where the Phoenicians left off and were probably the first to put glass in windows. They didn't invent the spear or the javelin, but they improved upon them by making the shank out of a softer metal than the point, so that it bent on impact and couldn't just be chucked back by the enemy. They didn't invent armor, but they developed an articulated form that was both lighter and more flexible than anything that had gone before. And they didn't invent roads, but they invented the road system, so that they could get anywhere they wanted throughout their empire and keep tabs on any restless natives. Roads were built by legionnaires—soldiers who went everywhere on foot—so it was in their interests to keep them straight and make the route from anywhere to anywhere else as short as it could be. Being able to achieve this meant that the Romans were also pretty clever surveyors.

The structure of the army was brilliant, too, with the possible exception of calling a unit of eighty men a **century**, which was surely somebody's idea of a joke. Six centuries made a **cohort** and ten cohorts made a **legion**, which therefore consisted of 4,800 men under normal circumstances.* It

---

* In fact the first cohort was often larger, consisting of five double-sized centuries, i.e., five lots of 160, and one normal century, which meant that a legion could equally well consist of 5,400 men. Which is just what you might expect from a system that puts eighty men into a century.

sounds formulaic, but in fact the subdivision into small units made it very flexible: Soldiers marched and went into battle in strict formation, but each century could be redeployed quickly if conditions changed.

But they did invent some things…

One of the great inventors of the Roman period was a man known as **Hero** (or Heron) of Alexandria. Although he probably spent his entire life in his hometown, the existence of the Roman Empire gave his inventions the chance to travel throughout the known world.

Hero invented some pretty cool stuff for a dude you've never heard of. Some were really important to the future of civilization, such as an "inexhaustible goblet" that regulated the level of wine in it, or a mechanical theater with its own fire, thunder and drunken dancing girls; others were kind of transient, including an early steam engine (yes, really; forget England's *Rocket* from 1829; Hero was way ahead of him) and the first "fire engine."* This consisted of a hand pump that forced water out through a nozzle that could be adjusted to point in the direction of the fire. Hero also developed—but

---

* In the first century B.C., Crassus (he of the First Triumvirate, see page 88) became the richest man in Rome by the simple expedient of employing a fire brigade that would rush to the scene of a fire, buy the property at a knock-down price and only then put the fire out. This was before Hero's time, though, so Crassus's fire brigade relied on buckets and ladders. A system that was only faintly more sophisticated developed in London after the Great Fire of 1666 and led eventually to the emergence of both insurance companies and an official fire department.

probably didn't invent—a water organ that boasted the world's first keyboard (so forget Steinway and Moog, too) and the first coin-operated vending machine. It gave out holy water rather than condoms or multicolored candy, but that's probably because condoms and multicolored candy hadn't been invented back then.*

Another useful thing to emerge from this period is the odometer or "milometer." It was first described by **Vitruvius**, who wrote a ten-volume work on architecture in the first century A.D., but he suggests that it dates back to an earlier generation. Vitruvius's odometer (from the Greek, meaning "measuring the way") had a gear that turned another gear and dropped a stone into a box every time you had traveled a mile.

Vitruvius also wrote interesting stuff about **acoustics**, advocating the arranging of bronze vessels in a particular way around the theater to improve the sound. And, on the subject of theaters, the Greeks had already invented the proscenium arch, separating the audience from the stage and used in theaters to this day; the "wings" that hid performers from the audience when they were offstage; and the orchestra, originally a circular area in which the chorus sang and danced, refined by the Romans to a semicircle.

---

* The first recorded use of condoms in Europe comes in the sixteenth century, when the Italian scientist Gabriello Fallopio wrote that they helped guard against syphilis. Natural food coloring was probably in use in around 1500 B.C., but for the artificial stuff designed to attract children we have to wait until the early nineteenth century, when anything bright green probably contained both copper and arsenic.

Back to basics

Just as they were organizers and improvers rather than inventors, so the Romans were practical rather than high falutin'. So they made some pretty good **sewers**. Sewers and halfway decent toilets had existed in Knossos, Crete (see page 55), in 2000 B.C., but the Romans made theirs well, and they made them to last. The Pont du Gard in southern France is surviving evidence that they gave a lot of thought to transporting water—eleven **aqueducts** supplied water to Rome in the time of Augustus—and the Cloaca Maxima (literally "greatest sewer") existed as early as 600 B.C.

Most of the water supply went to—and the sewers came from—the houses of the rich, public baths, and public lavatories, where communal toilets sat over a channel that was flushed out by a constant supply of running water. You can see excavated examples of all this in York, England, and Pompeii.

Then there were the **baths**: hot baths, cold baths, something-in-between baths. They were a focal point of Roman social intercourse—and not always just social, if you believe all you read. The important thing here is the **hypocaust**, from the Greek, meaning "burning below." It was a form of underfloor heating that, among other things, heated the water for the tepidarium and the caldarium (think *caldo*—"hot"—rather than *cold* here). The idea was that you created a shallow basement under the room you wanted to heat and connected this to a furnace that produced a flow of warm air. A more sophisticated version also pumped hot air through tiles in the walls. Luxury.

9

The Clever Stuff II: Philosophy and the Liberal Arts

The word *philosophy* means "love of wisdom," and as a concept—understanding the meaning of life, and of right and wrong, and of what we can know about knowledge*—it seems to have emerged in ancient Greece, principally Athens, in the sixth century B.C. Vaguely remembered names from this period include **Parmenides**, who was overzealous about the concept of being and not being; and **Heraclitus**, who came to the not-very-helpful conclusion that everything was in a state of flux: Even the ancient Greeks called him "the obscure one." The first celebrity philosopher, however, appeared about a hundred years later. He never wrote a book, but he did do a lot of talking and his influence on later philosophers was immense.

---

* *Knowledge* in this context doesn't mean knowing the way to the supermarket or knowing how to boil an egg or change the tire on a car. We are in the realm of life, the universe and everything here.

The father of philosophy I: Socrates

We know—because everybody who wrote about him mentioned it and because there is a pot-bellied statuette of him in the British Museum—that **Socrates** (*ca.* 469–399 B.C.) was short, fat and ugly, but for the next few pages we are going to be above worrying about that sort of thing.

Socrates specialized in dialogues in which he challenged whoever he was talking to to justify their position on a given subject and then gently tore them apart. He never put forward a firm point of view of his own, but instead asked question after question in order to show the lack of wisdom (*sophia*) of his interlocutor. To be any good at talking to Socrates, you had to have a really deep, coherent understanding of your point of view, and be able to justify it rationally. So this questioning shouldn't be seen as negative and destructive; underlying it was a search for truth.

The way it began was that somebody had asked the Oracle at Delphi (always a bad idea) whether there was anyone in Greece wiser than Socrates.

"'No,' came the answer. (Less obscure than many Delphic pronouncements, but troublemaking nonetheless.)

Socrates was shocked, because he knew that he wasn't wise, so he set about looking for people who were wiser than he was. He asked an important priest to define piety.

"It means honoring the gods and doing their will," said the priest.

"But we have lots of gods," said Socrates, "and our myths say that they often quarrel among themselves. If two gods are quarrelling, which of them do I honor?"

There was, of course, no answer to that.

Proceeding down this perhaps rather tactless path, Socrates questioned some of the most influential men in Athens, and came to the conclusion that perhaps he was quite wise after all, because at least he knew he was a fool. Unsurprisingly, this approach made him some powerful enemies, and he was eventually indicted for "not recognizing the gods which this city recognizes and introducing other gods" and for corrupting the young. He was sentenced to death and executed by being forced to drink hemlock. But his memory lingers on.

The father of philosophy II: Plato

Socrates's most famous pupil was **Plato** (*ca.* 429–347 B.C.), who founded a school called the **Academy,** where for the first time students were able to come together and study philosophy as a subject. Plato's approach broadly followed that of Socrates's dialogues, forcing people to think for themselves rather than simply accepting Teacher's point of view.

Plato is never a participant in his own published dialogues, so he always appears as one step removed from any views that are being put forward. This doesn't mean that he didn't have any ideas of his own, but they didn't really become famous until his philosophical descendants starting writing about them after his death. Perhaps the most important thing that Plato did was lay out a system of philosophy, based on rational argument.

Plato's own teaching (as opposed to that perpetuated by later followers) was in the Sceptic tradition. Different branches of **Scepticism** developed from this, the most important of them founded by **Pyrrho of Elis** (*ca.* 360–270 B.C.), who had traveled in India and may have been influenced by Buddhism. His stance was to refute as dogmatic any branch of philosophy that claimed to have found answers, because philosophical questions are so complex that suspending judgment and living by appearances is the only rational way. The cynical, taking-it-to-its-logical-conclusion approach to this point of view is that that big yellow buslike thing coming down the road may not be a bus at all, so you can cross the road anytime you like; the "living by appearances" part means that if it looks as if there is a bus coming, it's probably better not to walk under it. Even if it's an illusion.

Back to the man himself. His best-known and most controversial work is *The Republic*, which describes, among other things, his vision of an ideal city-state run by Guardians, whose lives were entirely devoted to the common good—they had no family life and no possessions. The concept was adopted by the Victorians to encourage young men (or at least the sort of privileged young men who were reading Plato) to devote themselves to public life, but in the twentieth century *The Republic* fell from grace and was criticized as proposing a totalitarian state that had uncomfortable resemblances to Nazism or Cold War–era Communism.

To treat *The Republic* exclusively as a political tract, however, is to miss the point, because Plato was also concerned with the idea of what makes a virtuous citizen, and indeed a virtuous person. The concept of virtue is an important one here, and we'll come back to it once we have touched on a few more schools of thought.

The Master: Aristotle

Plato's most important "descendant" was **Aristotle** (384–322 B.C.), who was born in Macedon, came to Athens and joined the Academy, then returned to Macedon on Plato's death and became tutor to the young Alexander the Great (see page 72). Once Alexander became king, Aristotle came back to Athens and founded a "research community" called the **Lyceum**, from which a lot of his research and lecture notes have survived.[*] For a thousand years (until Plato's work was rediscovered during the Renaissance), he dominated western philosophy: For example, in *Inferno* (written around 1307), the poet Dante meets a number of philosophers, including one "who is called Master of those who know." This Master is surrounded by, and being admired by, Plato and Socrates and all sorts of other people whom Dante names, but there is no need to name the Master—in those days it could only have been Aristotle.

---

[*] Aristotle's followers were also known as the Peripatetics, from his habit of walking around and around the garden while lecturing.

Aristotle's philosophical approach was to solve problems: to take questions that puzzled mankind and find ever more complex answers to them. He was interested in everything from metaphysics to biology, invented formal logic (see page 159), and viewed the adaptations of plants and animals to their way of life as an argument against a random creation of the universe. One book I read about him says that Aristotle's life was "ruled by an overwhelming desire to know." In short, he was a man who simply wouldn't have understood the words "Should I care?", even if you'd spoken them in ancient Greek.

He also had that rare commodity among philosophers: a smattering of common sense. Most of the others lived in and wrote about some sort of ideal world. Aristotle acknowledged that, although virtue was essential to happiness, it had to be considered in a concrete situation and as a mean point between two opposite evils. Courage, for example, should be seen as a sensible position somewhere between cowardice and foolhardiness. Virtue—and therefore happiness—comes from an individual practicing those qualities in a way relevant to his own circumstances. An oft-quoted example is that of the shoemaker who may be judged to have fulfilled his function in life if he makes the best shoes he can with the leather available to him.

Part of Aristotle's thinking is sometimes labeled **empiricism:** He believed that the active intellect (*nous,* a word the British still use to mean common sense or alertness) was somehow divine and, properly used, enabled us to understand universal truths. The empirical approach, however, made generalizations from the information available—through experience and the senses—and allowed you to get on with life while you struggled with universal truths. Plato didn't approve of this at all, but it worked for a lot of other people.

And just in case you want to quote him at a dinner party, here is my favorite Aristotle line: "Probable impossibilities are to be preferred to improbable possibilities." Perhaps best to wait until everyone is a bit drunk, though.

Other schools of thought

Also floating around in ancient Greece were:

- **Stoics**—so called because they met under a *stoa* or colonnaded porch—whose school (in both the physical and the intellectual senses) was founded by **Zeno of Citium** and taken over and developed by **Chrysippus**. The Stoics took a holistic approach to the universe, which they believed had been created by a rational god, and maintained that the wise man lived in harmony with nature (the stern commitment to duty that has given them a rather bad name came later).

- **Hedonists**, founded by a friend of Socrates named **Aristippus**, who believed in the pursuit of pleasure and the limitation of pain.

- **Epicureans**, founded by **Epicurus**, who developed his own form of hedonism by equating the concept of happiness with that of pleasure. This was at total variance with almost everyone else; we'll come back to these terms in a moment. He also differed from the others in rejecting the power of reason, which, he said, could lead you into error (in other words, even if you thought carefully about something, you could be wrong); only things experienced by the senses were reliable. That's empiricism again.

- **Sophists**, who weren't a philosophical entity as such, but traveled around "selling" intellectual skills such as rhetoric, grammar and ethics (which were certainly saleable, as they would be of great use to anyone intending to enter public life; more about them later in this chapter). Plato hated— and lampooned—the Sophists because he felt that by doing what they did for mere money, they were debasing the previously unsullied coinage of philosophy. The fact that Plato was rich and didn't at first take payment from his students may have had something to do with this. His view has stood the test of time, and we now define *sophistry* as "plausibly deceptive or fallacious reasoning."

That's probably enough schools of thought for now.

So what's all this about virtue, happiness and pleasure?

Well, lots of philosophers maintained that the purpose of life was **happiness**. They differed in how they defined the term. In fact, people still argue about the translation—the Greek word is *eudaimonia*, and there are those who think that "human flourishing" is a better way of rendering it. However, it's a bit of a mouthful, so let's stick to "happiness."

The important distinction is between the lasting quality of happiness and the transitory feeling of **pleasure**. Happiness meant a happy life, not a happy day or hour; and the road to it might involve sacrificing the (pleasurable) whim of the moment. The hedonist approach ran contrary to this: It advocated living in the moment—in other words enjoy the wine now, worry about the hangover tomorrow—which really wasn't a very philosophical approach to philosophy. Epicurus tried to get around this by defining two sorts of pleasure: the short-term kind we all understand (it tends to have booze/sex/chocolate in it) and the longer-term or "static" kind, which didn't get much more exciting than seeking tranquillity and a lack of pain. This may be why the word *epicurean* has come down to us as meaning "devoted to sensual pleasures, especially food and drink," because nobody was very interested in the more serious side of what he had to say.

The way to lasting happiness—at least according to Socrates—was through **virtue**. This was a powerful word that covered much more than sexual restraint. It meant an ingrained morality. Again, it's a distinction between the permanent and the temporary, between reason (always being a good person) and desire (only occasionally resisting temptation). And in the Socratic/Platonic tradition there is—crucially—a rational argument in favor of virtue: The virtuous person is a model citizen, and Plato's idealized *Republic* is an analogy for the internalized state in which a moral person can aspire to live.[*] In this ideal situation, the person's soul or psyche is under control and reason prevails over emotion.

A much-quoted example that may be of interest here is the story of Medea in Euripides's tragedy (see page 111). For revenge on her faithless husband, Jason, she murders their children—because, however horrific this may be for her, it is the worst possible punishment she can inflict on him.

In the play, she debates with herself: "I know that what I am about to do is bad, but anger is master of my plans." And indeed anger (emotion/desire) wins out over reason, and the children are duly murdered.

Now the Stoics, who saw the human soul as one united thing, would say that Medea had made a rational decision here—she acted premeditatedly, not out of blind passion. Plato, on the other hand, considered humans as tripartite beings in whom reason was always fighting to control desire and emotion (he uses the image of the charioteer—reason—struggling to control two horses, one of whom—emotion—will listen to reason while the other—desire—can be restrained only by force). So a Platonist would say that Medea's reason had lost the battle with her emotions, and she had acted irrationally.

You may say it doesn't matter much—the kids are still dead—but that is not an attitude that will get you very far with philosophy.

---

[*] This may be one of the ideas the antitotalitarians latched onto in the twentieth century.

Roman philosophers

There were other philosophers in the classical Greek period, but most of those who came after the ones mentioned above were followers of an existing doctrine rather than great innovators. The ideas were eventually picked up by the Romans, and it was common for a patrician Roman boy to have a Greek tutor, one of whose subjects would be philosophy. So the concept continued to be important.

Seneca the Younger (*ca.* 4 B.C.–A.D. 65): Son of, you'll be amazed to hear, Seneca the Elder, known as "the Rhetorician"; the Younger is known as "the Philosopher." He was a senator under Caligula but fell out with him (easily done), held a position at court under Claudius, was banished for allegedly having an affair with Claudius's niece Julia,* and then recalled to be tutor to Claudius's stepson Nero, over whom he briefly exercised a restraining influence once Nero became emperor (for more about all these emperors, see page 105 or just watch *I, Claudius*—it's available on DVD and worth every penny).

A life crowded with incident, you might say, but it didn't stop there. Nero, as every schoolchild knows, went more and more bonkers, and there was a plot to overthrow him. Seneca, accused of involvement, was ordered to commit suicide, which Tacitus tells us he did with extreme calmness, dictating a last few lines of philosophy to his secretaries after he had cut his own wrists. His parting words to his friends and family urged

---

* This is not the Julia with whom absolutely everyone had an affair; it's a couple of generations away, but they were still very active.

them not to mourn but to remember their maxims of philosophy.*

Marcus Aurelius (A.D. 121–180, emperor from 161): His philosophy survives in a book of *Meditations,* a collection of short pieces of self-scrutiny and "practical ethics." Marcus is full of advice to himself on how to be a virtuous person while performing his social role, that is, being a good emperor. He warns himself against "turning into a Caesar" and "being stained with the purple"; his aim is to be "good, sincere, dignified, free from affection." The Stoics were also hot on keeping emotions under control, and one of Marcus's observations on this theme refers to sexual intercourse, rather unsexily, as "the friction of a piece of gut and, following a sort of convulsion, the expulsion of some mucus."

It's ironic that Marcus, who worked so hard to be a Good Thing, should have produced a son who was so Bad that he (the son) was eventually assassinated. That was Commodus, played by Joaquin Phoenix in *Gladiator,*† the one who was so mean to that nice Russell Crowe.

A classical education

Yes, I know that's the title of the book, but it's also a useful way of introducing the three topics that, along with four

---

* Yes, really. Tacitus, *Annals* Book 15, if you don't believe me. Though to be fair, Tacitus was ten years old at the time of the incident, so possibly not an eyewitness.

† Marcus himself was played by Richard Harris, slumming it a bit before he was promoted to be headmaster of Hogwarts.

branches of mathematics, made up a liberal arts education in Greek and Roman times. These three topics—**logic** or dialectic, **rhetoric** and **grammar**—persisted into the Middle Ages and came to be called the **trivium** or "three ways," a word that was later devalued in English because these "trivial" subjects were regarded as the lowest common denominator of any school syllabus. It just shows how times change, because if you study philosophy at a university these days, you will come across logic and rhetoric.

Logic

I've mentioned elsewhere that there was almost nothing that didn't interest Aristotle. Whatever the subject, he liked systems and he liked classifying things, and one of the things he systematized was logic. He worked out a way of distinguishing between an argument that persuaded the hearer, and one that genuinely proved a point. Aristotelian logic relies on a **deductive inference** or **syllogism**, with the form:

All A's are B.

C is an A.

Therefore C is a B.

Aristotle was the first to use letters in this context to produce a general principle that could be applied to any proposition. The first two statements of the syllogism are called **premises**, the third is the **conclusion**.

For example:

> Blondes have more fun.
> Marilyn is blonde.
> Therefore, Marilyn has more fun.

Similarly, you can have the negative form:

> No man is an island.
> Peter is a man.
> Therefore, Peter is not an island.

If you want to convince someone that you know what you are talking about here, you can throw in the phrases **major**, **minor** and **middle terms**. The minor term is the subject of the conclusion, the major term is the predicate of the conclusion, and the middle term occurs in both premises but not in the conclusion. So, in my first example, "have more fun" is the major, "Marilyn" the minor and "blondes" is the middle term.

But your premises must be absolute; if they are not, the syllogism becomes what logicians call a **false deduction** or **fallacy**, that is, illogical:

> No man is an island.
> Helen is not a man.
> Therefore, Helen is an island.

This example doesn't work because, although you have stated that no man is an island, you haven't specified that everything that *isn't* a man *is* an island, so the move from premise two to the conclusion isn't logical.

The **undistributed middle term** is another example of a fallacy. In this instance, the second premise is not distributed in such a way as to make the conclusion logical:

> Dogs have four legs.
> My kitchen table has four legs.
> Therefore, my kitchen table is a dog.

In order to be logically correct—admittedly while demonstrating an alarming grasp of natural sciences—the last two lines of this syllogism would need to state that my kitchen table is a dog, ergo my kitchen table has four legs.

The best kind of fallacy, however, is called **post hoc propter hoc**. Yes, really. It translates as "after it, therefore because of it," meaning that if something has happened after you did something completely unrelated, you can take the credit. Praying for rain just before Wimbledon starts, for instance.

Most of this is laid out in Aristotle's treatise *Prior Analytics* (although he didn't use the Marilyn or Wimbledon examples). Then he came up with *Posterior Analytics*,* which is an analysis of the premises or "first principles" on which his syllogisms are based. There is a lot of complicated debate about the nature of knowledge (which blurs the already indistinct

---

* Sadly this title isn't remotely smutty in ancient Greek.

boundary between logic and philosophy), but what it boils down to is that the first principle or axiom must satisfy certain conditions if it is to be a basis for scientific knowledge. To quote the great man himself, "The premises of demonstrated knowledge must be true, primary, immediate, better known than and prior to the conclusion, which is further related to them as effect to cause."

For example, take the statement "Chocolate is good for you." Most women would treat this as an axiom: It is so universally known and glaringly, obviously true that it needs no further analysis. The occasional man, though, might say, "Well, that's because chocolate releases endorphins, which make you feel better." Pushing his luck, perhaps, he might then go on to say that "chocolate releases endorphins" is the axiom and "chocolate is good for you" an inference drawn from it. And actually a scientist would be able to demonstrate *how* chocolate releases endorphins, so that would become the axiom.

Oh, enough about that. St. Thomas Aquinas, one of the greatest of medieval scholars, wrote a treatise on the *Posterior Analytics*, and that's where you should go if you want to know more. He wrote it in Latin, but if you are the sort of person who wants to know more about the *Posterior Analytics*, I'm sure that won't put you off.

Rhetoric

The *Oxford English Reference Dictionary* defines *rhetoric* as "the art of effective or persuasive speaking or writing; language designed to persuade or impress, often with an implication of insincerity or exaggeration." It is really the first part of that definition that concerns us here.

Recognition of the importance of public speaking coincided with the emergence of democracy (see page 60), when being able to persuade a magistrate in a court of law or sway the crowd in a political debate suddenly had the power to make or break a man's career. (Before that, in the days of the tyrants, eloquence wasn't much of an issue; if the tyrant didn't like you, you'd had it, whether you had the gift of the gab or not.) So around the fourth or fifth century B.C., rhetoric became a subject of study, an accomplishment that could be taught and practiced in the same way as a language or a musical instrument.

It will come as no surprise—if you have been paying any sort of attention—to learn that Aristotle wrote a treatise on it. He considered three methods of persuasion: a) relying on logic, i.e., facts and inference; b) appealing to or playing on an audience's emotions; and c) convincing the audience that one is a trustworthy character and thus to be believed. Most rhetoricians would agree that logic is less important in oratory than the other two ways of swaying your audience.

This was precisely the skill that the Sophists peddled and that was so despised by Plato (see page 159): Rhetoric had nothing to do with a regard for the truth; indeed, you were a more skilled rhetorician if you could make the worse cause seem like the better one.

But if you really want to learn about rhetoric in the sense of swaying an audience's emotions, regardless of the facts, skip forward a couple of hundred years and read Cicero (see page 115). Cicero's speeches are wonderful and very readable examples of rhetoric and of the way in which Roman trials differed from ours—personal abuse of the accused (or the accuser, if Cicero was defending) and everyone and everything associated with him was a major and, to modern eyes, outrageous feature. Almost everything he said would have had Perry Mason on his feet yelling, "Objection, Your Honor!" Cicero was a great believer in oratorical training and technique; he rehearsed and rehearsed to perfect his delivery. As I said earlier, he was in many ways a man of great integrity. But once you got him into the courtroom, he really didn't give much thought about evidence—which is one way of defining rhetoric.

Grammar

Grammar as we know it was invented by Greeks from the Hellenistic period onward. Aristotle didn't write a treatise on it, for the simple reason that he was dead by then, but other people did, laying down the laws of syntax, parts of speech and the use of accents. Accents must have been pretty important in ancient Greek, because a man called Herodian wrote a treatise in twenty-one books about them, most of which, you'll be happy to know, are now lost. These Greek writers inspired the Latin grammarian Priscian, whose works, along with those of a later writer called Donatus, formed the basis of grammar teaching well into the Middle Ages. So all in all they have a lot to answer for.

10

A Bit of Light Relief: The Games

Gymnastic exercises, specifically running, jumping and wrestling, were an essential part of a Greek boy's education and—just to get it out of the way—yes, *gymnasium* does mean a place for exercising in the nude, and yes, that is what they did.

The Olympics

The original Olympics, which according to tradition date from 776 B.C. but are probably not as old as that, were part of a festival in honor of Zeus. They took place every four years at **Olympia**, on the Peloponnese—the place where the massive Statue of Zeus became a wonder of the world (see page 125), but not the same as Mount Olympus where the gods lived, which was way up in the northeast. As time went by, the games grew in importance and the program expanded from just sprinting to include long-distance running, the pentathlon, boxing, two- and four-horse chariot racing and more.*

---

* Mule-cart racing was featured briefly but was abolished as "possessing neither antiquity or dignity." Softball and baseball, which first entered the modern Olympics in the 1990s, have both been axed from the 2012 London program, though it isn't clear whether antiquity and dignity had anything to do with the International Olympic Committee's decision.

There were other pan-Hellenic games (meaning that people from all over Greece stopped fighting each other for a while so that they could compete), but none that rivaled the Olympics in importance. The Olympics themselves waxed and waned for financial reasons from about the first century B.C. and were finally banned in A.D. 393 by the Christian **Emperor Theodosius the Great**, whose greatness evidently didn't extend to allowing naked men to compete in athletic events.

By the time of the first modern Olympics, which took place in Athens in 1896, someone had found a way around the problem by encouraging the competitors to keep their clothes on.

Here's a little gem, courtesy of my beloved *Oxford Companion to Classical Literature:* Olympia is said to have been founded by **Hercules** (see page 44), and its stadium, like all the others in Greece, should have been 600 feet long (the word comes from *stade*, a measure of about 600 feet, which is a bit over 180 meters). This particular stadium was in fact a little longer because the great Hercules had paced out the 600 feet himself, and his feet were, naturally, larger than those of ordinary men. As Herodotus said (see page 65), "I am obliged to record the things I am told, but I am certainly not required to believe them."

And, just in case you were wondering, the Olympic torch isn't an ancient Greek invention: Every Greek city-state had a temple with a sacred flame that was never allowed to go out, and the Greeks held torch relay races, originally as a religious rite, and later as an athletics competition. But these weren't specifically to do with the Olympics.

In 1936, however, a man named **Carl Diem**, who was in charge of the forthcoming Berlin Olympics, came up with the bright idea of reviving the tradition. He proposed having a team of 3,422 young runners pass the flame from torch to torch along the 2,126-mile (3,422-km) route from the Temple of Hestia at Olympia to the Olympic stadium in Berlin. The lighting ceremony—with the flame lit by the rays of the sun—would be supervised by a High Priestess, as it had been in the good old days, and it would have acquired a vaguely sacred mystique by the time the flame reached Berlin. The PR man for these Olympics, by the way, was one Josef Goebbels— yes, him—and you can imagine that he loved the idea.

Roman games

"Now that no one buys our votes, the public has long since cast off its cares," wrote Juvenal in around A.D. 100. "The people that once bestowed commands, consulships, legions and all else, now meddles no more and longs eagerly for just two things—bread and games." The Latin *panem et circenses* ("bread and games")—an expression used to denote vote-winning freebies—is sometimes translated "bread and circuses," but *circenses* doesn't mean clowns and trapeze artists; it's something more like the World Series, or at least a high school track meet.

What Juvenal meant was that the people had lost interest in matters of state and had become fickle and irresponsible, and the only way to stop them from getting into mischief was to keep them well fed and amused, which is what the games were about.

The public (i.e., state-funded) Roman games were initially dedicated to a god, as the Greek games had been; later they were also held to celebrate an emperor's birthday or as part of the funeral of an important man. Private games—often on an obscenely lavish scale—might also be given by a political candidate looking to improve his standing with the electorate.

Unlike the Greek games, the Roman ones weren't full of naked athletes. In the early days, the main feature was a chariot race; later there were wild beasts and the gory stuff you see in the movies. The number of animals slaughtered was horrendous and only got worse under the empire; at a time when murdering emperors was commonplace, you couldn't expect many people to balk at the violent slaughter of a few lions and elephants.

The men who fought the animals were condemned criminals, prisoners of war, slaves or others hired for the occasion. **Gladiators** were drawn from the same apparently limitless pool of expendables, and their task was to fight each other. The name comes from *gladius*, meaning a sword, but only a few gladiators actually fought with swords. Most famously the **retiarius** carried a net (*rete*) in which he tried to tangle his opponent, and a dagger with which he could then finish him off.

Once a gladiator was floored by his opponent, he would appeal to the crowd for mercy, and this is where the much-maligned "thumbs down" comes from. In fact, turning the thumb down granted mercy; if the audience turned their thumbs up or inward, toward their chests, it meant "fight on," which was probably a bad sign for the guy who was already on the deck.

The **Colosseum** (see page 130) was the main venue for Roman games, but the **Circus Maximus**—which means "the biggest circus," or arena or stadium or whatever you want to call it—was the place for chariot races. The course was oval rather than circular, with a low wall down the middle and pillars at either end that the charioteer had to drive around. There might be as many as six chariots in a race, so there were plenty of opportunities for crashes and professional fouls. But you know that; you've seen *Ben-Hur*.

A final word

The 1959 film *Ben-Hur* won eleven Oscars, a feat that was unequaled until *Titanic* came along nearly forty years later. And why was the *Titanic* so named? Because she possessed titanic strength, an attribute of the Titans of Greek mythology, who existed even before the gods. As I said about 200 pages ago, the classics really are everywhere.

Cut.

Bibliography

Julia Annas, *Ancient Philosophy: a very short introduction*
(Oxford University Press, 2000)

————, *Plato: a very short introduction*
(Oxford University Press, 2003)

Marcus Aurelius, *Meditations*
(Wordsworth, 1997)

John Boardman, Jasper Griffin & Oswyn Murray,
The Oxford History of the Classical World
(Oxford University Press, 1986)

Thomas Bulfinch, *The Age of Fable*
(1855, Harper & Row Perennial Classics edition, 1966)

Paul Cartledge, *The Spartans*
(Channel Four Books, 2002)

David Crystal,
The Cambridge Biographical Encyclopedia, second edition
(Cambridge University Press, 1998)

David Ewing Duncan, *The Calendar*
(Fourth Estate, 1999)

Robin Lane Fox, *The Classical World*
(Penguin, 2006)

Robert Graves, *I, Claudius*
(Penguin, 1941)

Sir Paul Harvey, *The Oxford Companion to Classical Literature*
(Oxford University Press, 1940)

Jacquetta Hawkes, *Atlas of Ancient Archaeology*
(Rainbird, 1974; reprinted Michael O'Mara, 1994)

Herodotus, *Histories*, trans. George Rawlinson
(Quality Paperback Book Club, 1997)

Ted Hughes, *Tales from Ovid*
(Faber, 1997)

Peter James & Nick Thorpe, *Ancient Inventions*
(Michael O'Mara, 1995)

Alta Macadam, *Blue Guide: Central Italy*
(Somerset Books, 2008)

Nick McCarty, *Troy: the myth and reality behind the epic legend*
(Carlton, 2004)

Judy Pearsall & Bill Trumble,
The Oxford English Reference Dictionary, second edition
(Oxford University Press, 1996)

Nick Sekunda & John Warry, *Alexander the Great*
(Osprey, 2004)

Dava Sobel, *Longitude*
(Fourth Estate, 1996)

John A. Vella, *Aristotle: a guide for the perplexed*
(Continuum, 2008)

Virgil, *The Aeneid*, trans. W. F. Jackson Knight
(Penguin, 1956)

Philip Wilkinson, *What the Romans Did for Us*
(Boxtree, 2000)

All the classical texts I have referred to in this book (and many more besides) are available in translation on the Internet. Try http://www.fordham.edu/halsall/, www.tertullian.org or http://penelope.uchicago.edu/Thayer/E/Roman/Texts and just play around until you find what you are looking for. I also found a number of interesting things (by no means all of them relevant to what I was looking for) at itotd.com, where *itotd* stands for "interesting thing of the day." In addition, www.dl.ket.org/latin1/mores/law/citizenship.htm told me more than any of my reference books about Roman citizenship.

Dramatis Personae

Many of the people, historical or mythological, who appear in this book could have been included in more than one section—I chose, for example, to put Marcus Aurelius in the Philosophy chapter, despite the fact that he was also an emperor and could have gone under History. So this isn't intended as a comprehensive index (it's not that sort of book); it's just a list of the principal entries to the principal characters, because most of the ones most of us have heard of are in here somewhere.

My Grammar and I...
Or Should That Be Me?

How to Speak
and Write It Right

CAROLINE TAGGART
J. A. WINES

English language is sometimes more than mere taste, judgment, and education—sometimes it's sheer luck, like getting across the street.

—E. B. White

INTRODUCTION

It is in the nature of a living language to evolve, since new inventions require new words, foreign influences enliven the vocabulary, and social changes give people more or less leisure to write at length. The monks who copied out medieval texts invented short forms to save themselves time, which passed into the language as ligatures in words such as *mediæval*, which we now deem archaic. In our own time great revolutions have occurred because of e-mailing and texting, and who knows: a standard dictionary of 2028 may well contain the word *gr8* (great).

We cannot stop English from changing—and only the most ardent, dyed-in-the-wool pedants waste their time trying—but we can do our best to ensure that it does not become compromised along the way, and to preserve its best features. Since linguistic sloppiness often leads to ambiguity—one of the things that grammar rules try to avoid—a few rules are surely a good thing. And frankly, if you can't bring yourself to agree with that, you might as well stop reading now and get your money back before the book starts to look tattered.

Rules were very much in the minds of the sticklers of the eighteenth century, who, fearing for the health of the English language, decided to impose on it a grammar system that would fix it "good and proper." Unfortunately for us, these scholars were specialists in ancient Greek and Latin—not German, the language from which English is derived—so they imposed a number of Latin rules that didn't fit too comfortably with English, thereby creating all manner of unnecessary complications.

GRAMMAR RULES (TO AVOID)

1. Verbs has to agree with their subjects.
2. Remember to never split an infinitive.
3. Parenthetical remarks (however relevant) are (usually) unnecessary.
4. Never use a big word when a diminutive one would suffice.
5. Use words correctly, irregardless of how others elude to them.
6. Use the apostrophe in it's proper place and omit it when its not needed.
7. Eliminate unnecessary references. As Ralph Waldo Emerson once said, "I hate quotations."
8. Who needs rhetorical questions?
9. Exaggeration is a billion times worse than understatement.
10. Last but not least, avoid clichés like the plague.

Ignoring this major flaw in the plan, in 1762, an Oxford professor called Robert Lowth produced a prescriptive text titled *A Short Introduction to English Grammar*, a publication so influential that it dominated grammar teaching into the twentieth century (and indeed is quoted in this book). Over time, one no longer dared to end a sentence with a preposition, to split an infinitive, or to say "between you and I."

> 🐄 **Teacher's Corner:** When grammar became a required subject in many U.S. schools in the mid-nineteenth century, teachers complained that they knew no more about it than their pupils.

Grammar lessons began to fall out of favor as the twentieth century progressed. This book aims to fill in some of the gaps that the education system may have left you with, but remember that English is a rich and fluid language and that one person's unbreakable rule is another person's insufferable pedantry. Knowing the rules—and breaking them because you feel like it, not because you don't know any better—will make you a more confident, creative, and entertaining writer and speaker.

If your reaction to that is along the lines of "Yeah, right," consider this: When you're chatting among friends, it may not much matter how you express yourself, but what about when you are applying for a job? Language is as much a part of how you present yourself—and how other people react to you—as the way you dress. if we alwez rote howeva we pleazd itd b like showing up 2 an interview in ript jeanz n a scruffy t-shirt, y'know?

1
Spelling and Confusables

ABC: Easy as 1, 2, 3 (or, Spelling)

"My spelling is Wobbly. It's good spelling but it
Wobbles, and the letters get in the wrong places."
—A. A. Milne, *Winnie the Pooh*

In the late-1500s, the state of English **spelling** and the "invasion" of foreign words was so troubling to scholars and teachers that some of them took it upon themselves to harness the language by compiling dictionaries. But even if we have the help of education and dictionaries, spelling can still be an uphill climb.

> ✋ **Smart Aleck:** More than one-tenth of English words are not spelled the way they sound.

We have an overwhelming tendency to leave letters in words even though they are no longer pronounced (think of the *g* in *weight* or *daughter*, for example, or the *b* in *subtle*, or the *p* in *pneumonia*). And we are surely the only language to have nine ways to pronounce a single four-letter combination:

A rough-coated, dough-faced, thoughtful ploughman strode through the streets of Scarborough; after falling into a slough, he coughed and hiccoughed.

Then we have things called **eye rhymes,** which are words that look alike and perhaps used to rhyme but which, due to shifts in pronunciation, no longer do. In Shakespeare's day, for example,

Blow, blow thou winter wind
Thou art not so unkind

would probably have rhymed, as would have

I am monarch of all I survey…
From the centre all round to the sea

when poet William Cowper wrote those lines nearly two hundred years later. Then there is another problem. Many words that sound the same are spelled differently:

aloud/allowed	*fair/fare*	*pale/pail*
beach/beech	*knot/not*	*plane/plain*

which makes English a wonderful language for puns but a nightmare for non-native speakers and for those who aren't confident in their spelling (or who rely on their spellcheckers).

"They went and told the sexton, and
The sexton toll'd the bell."
—Thomas Hood

🖐 **Smart Aleck:** A **homophone** is a word that is pronounced the same as another word but differs in meaning. The words may be spelled the same or differently.

It's My Bizness to Be Definate

Here are the correct spellings of a random selection of commonly misspelled words:

accidentally	*cemetery*	*liaison*
accommodate	*definite*	*millennium*
allege	*diarrhea*	*necessary*
avocado	*ecstasy*	*niece*
association	*embarrass*	*privilege*
broccoli	*grammar*	*separate*
business	*height*	*sincerely*

Take My Advice

In these commonly confused noun/verb pairs, the noun has a *c* and the verb has an *s*.

Noun	**Verb**
advice	*advise*
device	*devise*
prophecy	*prophesy*

Useful mnemonic: *I'd advise you not to give advice.*

☛ **Teacher's Corner:** Until the eighteenth century, English spelling was not standardized on either side of the Atlantic. Then, in 1755, Samuel Johnson published his *Dictionary of the English Language,* and in 1828, Noah Webster published *An American Dictionary of the English Language.*

Webster was an orderly minded man who disapproved of a lot of the spelling that Johnson had recorded. (Indeed, he disapproved of a lot about Johnson, saying that he was "naturally indolent and seldom wrote until he was urged by want. Hence…he was compelled to prepare his manuscripts in haste.")

Webster's dislike of words that weren't pronounced the way they looked led him to decree that words such as *centre* and *theatre* should be spelled *center* and *theater;* he also dropped the silent *u* from words such as *colour, favour,* and *honour.* In fact, Webster was singlehandedly responsible for most of the differences between British and American spelling that survive to this day.

Seize the Sieve: A Spelling Rule

The most famous **spelling rule** is *i before e except after c,* although this does not work for *ancient, foreign, neither, protein, science, seize, species, vein* or lots of other words. It really applies only to certain words in which the *ie* or *ei* makes an *ee* sound: *achieve, receive, deceive.*

So even the most famous spelling rule works only in a very limited set of circumstances. There is really no way around this other than reading a lot, taking note of unfamiliar words, and investing in a good dictionary.

One Word or Two?

As a general rule, one word tends to be an adjective, while two words form the noun. Here are some common confusions:

alot/a lot

There is no such word as *alot. A lot* of people know that *a lot* should be two words. If you mean to write the verb *allot,* however, you should allot it two *l*s.

alright/all right

According to *Merriam-Webster's Dictionary*, the term *alright* has had its critics since the early twentieth century. Although *alright* is less frequent than *all right*, it is still commonly used.

> Useful mnemonic: *don't worry about getting it all right, alright?*

altogether/all together

> ***Altogether***, *it's sixty miles.*
> ***All together*** *now: "sixty miles to go…"*

anyone/any one

> *Does this bag belong to **anyone**?*
> *It could belong to **any one** of those tourists over there.*

always/all ways

> *I **always** get lost in Rome.*
> ***All ways** lead to Rome.*

cannot/can not

Either is acceptable, but *cannot* is more common. Sometimes *can not* may be the better choice if you want to be emphatic: *No, you **can not** speak Swahili.*

everyday/every day

> *His **everyday** life is very dull, but at night he's in a cabaret act.*
> ***Every day** I dream of becoming a showgirl.*

everyone/every one

> ***Everyone** has a guilty secret.*
> ***Every one** of you pretends not to like Barry Manilow.*

into/in to

> *I can't seem to get **into** the office.*
> *I was hoping to go **in to** use the free Internet.*

maybe/may be

> ***Maybe** you'll remember what I tell you in the future.*
> *Although it **may be** that I forgot to tell you in the first place.*

nobody/no body, somebody/some body, anybody/any body

> ***Nobody** was at the crime scene, so I assumed they'd all gone home.*
> *There was a lot of blood at the crime scene, but **no body**.*
> *I think **somebody** is trying to break in.*
> *Gosh, that burglar has quite **some body**.*
> *Will just **any body** suffice for the bikini advertisement, or does **anybody** here happen to have Pamela Anderson's address?*

sometimes/some times

> ***Sometimes** trains arrive on time.*
> ***Some times** on that train schedule I gave you are wrong.*
> *I'll give you a call **sometime**.*
> *Perhaps we can arrange **some time** for ourselves.*

I'll Get My Coat

When two words are combined to form a single word, the new word is called a **portmanteau**. As Humpty Dumpty tells Alice in *Through the Looking-Glass*, "There are two meanings packed into one word." For example:

breakfast and lunch	*brunch*
French and English	*Franglais*
guess and estimate	*guesstimate*
information and commercial	*infomercial*
motor and hotel	*motel*
smoke and fog	*smog*

> ✋ **Smart Aleck:** *Portmanteau* is itself made up of
> two words, the French *porter* (to carry) and *manteau*
> (cloak or mantle).

What's the Word I'm Looking for?

abuse/misuse/disabuse

To *abuse* something means "to treat it so badly that you damage it."

To *misuse* something means "to use it wrongly."

To *disabuse* someone of something means "to show them that their thinking is wrong."

acute/chronic

An *acute* illness is one that is sudden and severe but short-lived.

A *chronic* illness persists for a long time.

> Useful mnemonics:
> *acute: children are short, a pain, and not cute for long.*
> *chrOnic = Old (lasting a lOng time).*

affect/effect

Affect is a verb and *effect* is a noun. So you *affect* something by having an *effect* on it. (The exception is if you *effect* a change; that is, cause a change to happen.)

Useful mnemonic: **RAVEN, that is:** *Remember Affect-Verb Effect-Noun.*

aggravate/annoy

Aggravate means "to make worse." Therefore, while you can *aggravate* a situation, a problem or a condition, you irritate or *annoy* people.

alternate/alternative

An **alternate** *plan* would be wrong. The verb *alternate* means going back and forth between two things, and thus you have *alternate* letters of the alphabet (a, c, e, g, for example). If you mean "another plan," it should be *alternative.*

among/between

Use *between* for two things; *among* for more than two.
Between *you and me, there's no way we can divide these five loaves and two fishes* **among** *our five thousand guests.*

Useful mnemonics:
beTween = Two
aMong = Many

amount/number

Use *amount* for things involving a unified mass—bulk, weight, or sums. In general it is safe to use *amount* to refer to anything that can be measured. *Number* is used to refer to anything that can be counted in individual units.

*That's a large **amount** of sugar for one cup of tea.*

*What is an acceptable **number** of sugars for one cup of tea?*

Useful mnemonic: *use **amount** for things we **cannot count**.*

as if/like

Something looks *like* something else—they physically resemble one another.

*He looks **like** his mother and she looks **like** Margaret Thatcher.*

However:

*It looks **as if** a storm is coming.*

*Teenagers use words **such as** "like" far too often.*

***As with** all homework, students can now research geography topics online.*

"Dream as if you'll live forever;
live as if you'll die today."
—James Dean

---

complement/compliment

*May I **compliment** you on your new hairstyle? The color **complements** your dress beautifully.*

Useful mnemonics:

*A compl**E**ment adds something to make it **E**nough.*

*A comp**LIME**nt puts you in the **LIME**light.*

continual/continuous

Continual means "happening over and over and over again"; *continuous* means "happening constantly without stopping." You may *continually* receive unwanted telephone calls from telemarketers. However, if this were happening *continuously*, you would never be able to put the phone down.

Useful mnemonics:

continuAL = Able to Leave off

continuouS = never Stopping

defuse/diffuse

You *defuse* a situation, by (metaphorically) taking the *fuse* out of it before it catches fire.

Diffuse means "to spread out" if it is a verb, or "already spread out" if it is an adjective.

due to/owing to

Due to means "caused by."

Owing to means "because of."

To determine which to use, decide whether you would replace *due to* or *owing to* by *caused by* or *because of.*

*The collapse of hundreds of buildings was **due to** the earthquake.*

***Owing to** collapsed roads and bridges, it was impossible to get outside help.*

elude/allude

*Your meaning **eludes** me. I do not understand to what you are **alluding**.*

farther/further

This is another example where the difference between words is becoming blurred, but generally speaking *farther* relates to a physical distance, *further* to metaphorical distance.

*Before we travel any **farther**, let's have a **further** look at the map.*

*Before we take this argument any **further**, how much **farther** is it to the hotel?*

Useful mnemonic: ***FAR**ther is about how **FAR**.*

fortuitous/fortunate

Fortuitous means "happening by chance" but not necessarily a *fortunate* chance.

forward/foreword

Useful mnemonics:

*Forw**Ard** means to **Advance**.*

*Foreword: the **WORD**s that come be**FORE** the main text*

hear/here

Useful mnemonics:

*One h**EAR**s with one's **EAR**s.*

*I want **HER** to come **HER**e.*

hanged/hung

Pictures or jackets are *hung*; criminals used to be *hanged*.

imply/infer

Speakers *imply* something by hinting at it; listeners *infer* something based on the information they hear.

*I **infer** from your tone that you are angry with me.*

*I didn't mean to **imply** that.*

lay/lie/laid

You ***lie*** in bed but *lay* the book on the table or (if you are a hen) *lay* an egg.

In the past tense, you *lay* in bed all day yesterday, but you *laid* the book or the egg.

So *lie* is the present tense of an intransitive verb that means "to put oneself or to remain in a more or less horizontal position."* The present participle is *lying,* the past tense is *lay,* and the past participle is *lain.*

Lay is the present tense of a transitive verb whose basic meaning is "to place something in a more or less horizontal position." The present participle is *laying;* the past tense and the past participle are *laid.*

In the sense of telling an untruth, the forms are *lie*, *lying*, and *lied.*

lend/loan

Lend is a verb, *loan* is normally a noun.

> *If she asks me for a **loan**, I will **lend** her the money.*

> Useful mnemonics:
> *People will gr**OAN** if you ask them to l**OAN**.*
> *People will s**END** if you ask them to l**END**.*

Increasingly *loan* is used as a verb: *the bank will **loan** you the money if you have enough security.* Not everybody likes this, but it's in the dictionaries.

less/fewer

Less means "not as much." *Fewer* means "not as many."

Or, if you prefer, *fewer* is used to denote things that can be counted and *less* to describe things that can't. Never refer to *less people*. People should stand up and be counted!

---

*For more on verbs, see page 238. For more on tenses, see page 246.

loose/lose

Count the *os* and remember: *if I **lose** any more weight, my clothes will be too **loose**.*

older/elder

An *elder* is a person in old age or a tree. As an adjective, it means *older*, but it is sometimes used to denote respect: *an **elder** statesman* or even *my **elder** sister* may be assumed to have attained a certain amount of wisdom.

Older just means "more old," the way you sometimes feel in the morning, or when you are talking to someone who's never heard of Bob Dylan.

oral/aural/verbal

Oral pertains to the mouth, *aural* to the ears, *verbal* to words. An *oral statement* means one that is not written down. An *oral examination* may be one that is not written down, or it may be performed by a dentist. An *oral/aural examination* may be in a foreign language to test how well you understand what you are hearing as well as how well you speak. A *verbal statement* is a tautology (unnecessary repetition of meaning): how would you make it without using words?

principal/principle

Useful mnemonic: *the princip**AL** is your **PAL**; she makes ru**LE**s called princip**LE**s.*

rob/steal

You *rob* a person and *steal* a thing, but not the other way round.

Useful mnemonic: *you can **rob** Rob, and you can **steal** steel, but you can't **steal** Rob and you can't **rob** steel.*

stationary/stationery

Stationery is sold at the bookstore. The store is likely to be *stationary.*

their/there/they're

Their means "belonging to them."

There means "in that place."

They're means "they are."

> Useful mnemonic:
>
> *They left tHEIR money to their son and HEIR.*
>
> *WHERE shall we place ourselves, HERE or tHERE?*
>
> *THEY'RE mad at THEIR son, who is standing over THERE.*

weather/whether

I do not know whether he is weather-wise.

"Whether the weather be fine,
Whether the weather be not,
We must weather the weather,
Whatever the weather,
Whether we like it or not."
—Unknown

THAT WHICH COMES FIRST (OR, PREFIXES)

A **prefix** is a group of letters added to the beginning of a word to change its meaning. Common ones include:

anti	*extra*	*mono*	*pseudo*
auto	*hyper*	*multi*	*re*
circum	*inter*	*omni*	*sub*
demi	*intra*	*photo*	*tele*
dis	*mega*	*pre*	*trans*

Rule: Adding a prefix does not change the spelling of the original word, nor usually the spelling of the prefix, even when the last letter of the prefix and the first letter of the original word are the same: *disservice, dissimilar, unnerve, unnecessary.*

> ✋ **Smart Aleck:** What of *dispirited*? And *transubstantiation*? **Answer:** There are always exceptions. *Always* being one of them.

All's Well That Starts Well…

Rule: When *all* and *well* are used as prefixes, take away one *l*—*altogether, welfare.* But note that this is not the case with hyphenated words: *all-embracing, well-adjusted, well-bred.*

The prefixes *dis-, il-, im-, in-, ir-, mis-,* or *un-* create words that mean the opposite of the root word (*il-, ir-,* and *im-* are all variants of *in-*, used respectively in front of words beginning with *l*, *r*, and *b*, *m*, or *p*): *disobey, illogical, impossible, inapplicable, irresponsible, misunderstood, unattainable.*

But be careful when a root word can take two or more of these prefixes, since the resulting words will have subtly or completely different meanings: *do I **disremember** or **misremember**? I can't remember.*

> *The loss of paid overtime left most of the workers **dis**affected. The only ones who were **un**affected by this decision were those who never worked overtime.*

> *I collected my children's **dis**used toys, intending to donate them to the fundraiser. However, years of **mis**use had left many of them fit only for the trash.*

> *He was a **dis**interested lawyer and therefore **un**interested in taking a bribe.*

HAPPY ENDINGS (OR, SUFFIXES)

Suffixes are added to the *end* of a word to change its meaning. Common ones include:

-ant	*-ise*	*-ful*
-ent	*-ist*	*-ness*
-ible	*-fy*	*-ism*
-ing	*-ly*	*-ment*
-ize	*-able*	*-ation*

Adding a suffix may alter the spelling of the preceding word. If a word ends in a *y* that is preceded by a consonant (*happy, beauty*), the *y* changes to *i*:

happy	*happiness*
beauty	*beautiful*

But if the *y* is preceded by a vowel, the *y* remains: *I envy your enjoyment of the situation. It obviously caused you much merriment.* And if the original word ends in an *e*, this is usually dropped: *You are most **lovable** but not at all **sensible**.*

> ✋ **Smart Aleck:** Hold on to the *e* if dropping it would alter pronunciation. *Pronouncable* would be pronounced *pronounkable*, but *pronounceable* is quite *manageable*. Actually, both *aging* and *ageing* are correct. As are *likable* and *likeable*.

"-able" and "-ible"

It's not easy to remember which words end in *–able* and which in *–ible*, and there certainly isn't a hard and fast rule. Too much of it depends on the Latin root and whether the word comes to us directly from Latin or via French. Wouldn't you rather just invest in a decent dictionary and look each word up as the necessity arises?

☛ **See Me after Class:**

She stopped using a curling iron because she kept singing her hair.
I don't think I know that tune.

Romeo was dyeing to see Juliet.
Did she insist on a new color?

Toad was carless to wreck his car.
He was afterward!

LIVING LARGE (OR, CAPITALIZATION)

A **capital letter** is the Large Letter that is used at the beginning of a sentence and as the first letter of certain words. The word comes from the Latin *capitalis*, derived from *caput*, a head.

Use a capital letter…

- for the first word of a sentence

- for the first word in a line of poetry (usually)

- for the major words in the titles of books, plays, films, works of art: *Death of a Salesman, The Catcher in the Rye, Casablanca, The English Patient, Starry Night*

- for proper nouns: *James, Dad* (but *my dad*), *the Queen*

- for place names and the names of buildings: *London, Paris, Easy Street, the Taj Mahal, the Sears Tower*

- for adjectives derived from proper nouns: *English, Shakespearean, Victorian*

- for the pronoun *I*
- for personal titles that come before a name: *Mr., Ms., Mrs., Dr., Captain, Reverend, Senator*
- for most letters in words that are acronyms: *NASA, NATO*
- for the months of the year, days of the week, and special occasion days: Christmas, Easter, Thanksgiving, Happy Birthday (but *in the new year* or *his birthday seemed to come around faster each year*)
- for brand names: *Kleenex, Mars, Cadillac*

Do Not Use a Capital…

- after a semicolon
- when talking about kings, queens, presidents, and generals in general, rather than a specific individual
- for the seasons—spring, summer, autumn, winter
- for compass points: *north, south, east, west, going north, heading south.* However do write *the South*, as in *the Civil War was fought between the North and the South* or *the South Pole*

> ➤ **Teacher's Corner:** Capital letters are sometimes referred to as "upper case." This is because manual typesetters kept these letters in the upper drawers of a desk—the upper type case. More frequently used letters were stored on a lower shelf, thus "lower case" letters.

TAKE A LETTER
(OR, VOWELS AND CONSONANTS)

"Always end the name of your child with a vowel,
so that when you yell, the name will carry."
—*Bill Cosby*

The word *vowel* derives from the Latin word *vox*, meaning "voice." The dictionary definitions of a **vowel** are a bit scary: "a voiced speech sound whose articulation is characterized by the absence of a friction-causing obstruction in the vocal tract, allowing the breath stream free passage" or "a speech sound made with vibration of the vocal cords but without audible friction, more open than a consonant and capable of forming a syllable." But actually, that "capable of forming a syllable" part is what matters. You can't form a syllable—and therefore can't make a word—without a vowel.

There are five vowels in English: *A, E, I, O,* and *U.*

Useful mnemonic: ***An Elephant In Orange Underwear***
But the letter *y,* although classified as a consonant and used as one in words such as *yellow, young,* and *beyond,* is often used as a vowel (with an *i* sound) in words such as *cry, fly, lynx,* and *rhythm.*

Consonants, by the way, are all the letters that aren't vowels.

2
Parts of Speech

SAY WHAT?
(OR, THE 8 PARTS OF SPEECH)

Every word in every language can be categorized according to its grammatical function, which is what we mean by **parts of speech**. As with so many other things, this system was invented by the ancient Greeks, copied by the Romans, and later adopted into English by scholars who were well versed in Latin, whether it was appropriate or not. (In many cases it was not appropriate, but we're stuck with it now, and that's what this book is all about.)

In English there are generally considered to be eight parts of speech: *noun, pronoun, adjective, verb, adverb, preposition, conjunction,* and *interjection,* and you may once have learned this useful piece of doggerel to help you remember what each did:

Every name is called a NOUN,
*As **field** and **fountain**, **street** and **town**;*

In place of noun the PRONOUN stands
*As **he** and **she** can clap **their** hands;*

The ADJECTIVE describes a thing,
*As **magic** wand and **bridal** ring;*

The VERB means action, something done -
***To read, to write, to jump, to run**;*

How things are done, the ADVERBS tell,
*As **quickly, slowly, badly, well**;*

The PREPOSITION shows relation,
*As **in** the street, or **at** the station;*

CONJUNCTIONS join, in many ways,
*Sentences, words, **or** phrase **and** phrase;*

*The INTERJECTION cries out, "**Hark!***
I need an exclamation mark!"

Through poetry, we learn how each
of these make up THE PARTS OF SPEECH.

We say "generally considered" because there are also three little words—*the, a* and *an*—and a few others that are categorized as **articles** or **determiners** and you can't really ignore them. We'll come back to them in a minute (see page 209), but first let's have a quick look at what parts of speech are all about.

It's Just One Thing After Another

Words from each of the parts of speech are used as **building blocks**: they add to meaning by modifying or qualifying one another. Consider this sentence:

A brown cow in a great, green field ate grass greedily.

By painting a more detailed picture, words limit (modify, qualify—you'll come across all these words to describe the same sort of thing) and thus clarify meaning. In the above sentence, for instance, we are not talking about cows in general; the article *a* tells us we are talking about one specific cow. The cow is not any color; it is brown. The cow is not just standing there; it is eating grass. Where is it eating grass? In a field. Not any old field; but a great, green one. How is it eating? Greedily.

In fact, that sentence doesn't cover all the parts of speech, so let's add another few words:

A brown cow in a great, green field ate grass greedily,
and gosh it grew fat!

The conjunction *and* tells us that we are joining one thought to another. The interjection *gosh* gives us an excuse to write an exclamation mark at the end of the sentence. And *it*, of course, is a pronoun that refers back to the cow.

So let's now look at each of these building blocks in more detail.

DEFINITELY INDEFINITE (OR, ARTICLES)

"A horse, a horse, my kingdom for a horse."
—Shakespeare, *Richard III*

An **article** is any one of a group of things. *I have lost an article of luggage*, for example, means you have lost only one bag of several. In grammar an article is any one of the words *a*, *an*, and *the*.

A and *an* are known as **indefinite** articles because they describe nouns in general. *The* restricts the meaning of a noun to make it more specific. Or definite. It is therefore known as the **definite article.**

A drunk man	any old drunk man (he could be anyone—we haven't mentioned him yet)
The drunk man	a specific drunk man (someone we are already talking about)
A drunk man was lurching down the street.	This implies the man is a stranger to all.
The drunk man was crawling down the street.	This implies the speaker/writer or listener/reader already knows something about this man—he has already cropped up.

Bizarrely, however, when speaking in very general terms, *the* can be used instead of *a* to make something less specific:

There was a tiger in my garden.	an individual animal
The tiger is an endangered species.	that is, all of them
I bought a ukulele.	one specific instrument
I play the ukulele.	I can pick up any ukulele and strum away happily on it.

> ✍ **Smart Aleck:** *The* is the most common word in the English language.

Absolute Zero

Another way to make a statement more general is to use no article at all. This is sometimes referred to as the **zero article** and it usually applies to plurals or to mass nouns (see page 216).

Children *are not good with **maps**.*
Shorts *are not suitable office attire.*
Cats *are thankless creatures.*
Grammar *is hard to learn.*

No Need for Introductions...

Pronouns and proper nouns do not require articles. They stand by themselves.

I *am not good at grammar.*
Ms. Banks *is better at grammar than **I** am.*

A or *an*?

Rule: Nouns or adjectives beginning with a vowel usually take the article *an*, while nouns or adjectives beginning with a consonant take the article *a*.

For example:

an orange, a peach
an octopus, a squid
an ax, a chopper
an island, a continent
an orange peach, a red apple

However, as usual there are exceptions to the rule, because some vowels are sometimes pronounced as if they were consonants, and some *h*s aren't pronounced at all:

a *unique event, **an** unusual event*
a *horrid man, **an** honorable gentleman*
an *hour, **an** hour and **a** half*
a *European, **an** Eskimo*
a *eulogy, **an** epigram*

We say *a* unique event because we pronounce the letter *u* in *unique* as a hard *y* sound—*yoonique.* We pronounce the *h* in *horrid,* but not in *honorable.*

Similarly, abbreviations such as *MGM* or *SEC*—pronounced respectively *em gee em* and *ess e see,* sound as if they begin with vowels, and so we say *see an MGM film, it was an SEC regulation.*

> ☛ **See Me after Class:** There is no *h* at the beginning of the word *aitch.*

An Historical Note

Here's a hypothesis—or rather four separate but vaguely related hypotheses—on words beginning with *h* and an unstressed syllable (or why some people say *an history, an hotel,* and *an hypothesis*):

1. Once upon a time all educated English speakers learned French and so pronounced *history,* such as the French word *histoire,* with a silent *h.* Appropriately they gave it the article *an.*

2. Some—less well-educated and therefore non-French-speaking—people spoke badly, were lazy about pronouncing their *aitches,* and so got into the habit of saying *an 'istory.*

3. Educated people disliked dropping aitches, so they began to pronounce them in French words that traditionally used the article *an: an history.*

4. People spoke too quickly, running together the words *a* and *history*, so that it became pronounced *anistory*. When they paused for breath and separated things out a bit, they thought the word must be *an history*.

Note the inherent snobbishness of these hypotheses. It crops up a lot in the study of language. But whatever the origins of the practice may be, the rule is: if the *h* is pronounced (as in *history*, *hotel*, and *hypothesis*), the correct article is *a*; if it is not pronounced (as in *honor* and *hour*), use *an*.

> ☛ **Teacher's Corner:** Some of those old grammarians who decreed that *an* should be used before an *h* did so because we aspirated less in those days. Aspiration is the release of air that comes out of our mouths when we speak. If you try talking to a candle flame, you should notice that the flame definitely flickers when you say *hotel* or *history* (aspirated), but much less so when you say *'otel* or *'istory* (unaspirated).

Demonstrate Your Determination (or, Determiners)

In fact articles are a subdivision of a class of words called **determiners,** which include **possessive adjectives**, **demonstratives,** and **quantifiers**.

Possessive adjectives—*my, his, her, its, our, your, their*—perform the useful task of telling us what belongs to, or is related to, something else.

> *The captain stood firm at the bow of **his** ship as **its** deck was consumed in flames.*
>
> *The bemused sailors redoubled **their** efforts and extinguished the blaze without **his** assistance.*

Used carelessly, however, they can cause confusion:

> *Both the fashion editors liked her new hat.* (Whose hat? If you mean that each fashion editor had a new hat that she liked, try, *each of the fashion editors liked her new hat*, and if you mean there was only one new hat, be specific: *both the fashion editors liked Susanna's new hat*.)
>
> *Mrs. Jones and Mrs. Brown disliked their neighbors.* (Whose neighbors? Did Mrs. Jones and Mrs. Brown cohabit and dislike the same neighbors? Or did each woman dislike her own neighbors? Or possibly her own neighbors and the other woman's neighbors, too?)

Demonstratives are the words *this/that, these/those* (which may also be demonstrative pronouns; see page 65). When used as determiners, they precede the noun in much the same way as *the* or *a* but are used to differentiate between things that are near at hand (*this, these*) and things that are farther away (*that, those*). The nearness or farness may refer to time or space:

> *Do I look fat in **this** dress* (the one I have on)?
>
> *Ah, do you remember **that** weekend in Paris* (back in the day)?
>
> *I have never seen **these** people before* (though they are standing in front of me now).
>
> *If I had known **those** chocolates* (the ones I ate earlier, so

they are now in the past) *had nuts in them, I would have left them alone.*

Quantifiers are words such as *no, none of, either, neither, any, both, few, little, half,* and so on. Again, some of these words may serve as other parts of speech—*either* or *neither* as conjunctions, for example (see page 270) or *little* as an adjective (see page 254). In this context, however, they go before the noun and tell us the number or quantity of something:

Which of the candidates will I back? **None of the** *above.*

Neither *politician has* **any** *charisma.*

Every one of the *candidates is a crook.*

It would be completely hypocritical of me to vote for **any of** *those people.*

Half the *problems of modern life can be blamed on people like that.*

There is **little** *chance of anyone decent winning.*

WHAT'S IN A NAME? (OR, NOUNS)

There are various categories of **noun**, but they are all "naming words." They just name different types of things.

Common noun: a word used to name a person, animal, place, thing or abstract idea, such as *book, smell, dog, forest, leg, delight, boredom, success* and *failure.* Common nouns can be further subdivided into:

Concrete noun: used to name something you can identify with one or more of the five senses *(book, leg,* for example*).*

Abstract noun: names something that has no physical existence *(delight, failure,* for example*)*.

Proper noun: used to name a specific person, animal, place, or thing. It is usually written with a capital letter to show its importance, such as *President Obama, the Statue of Liberty, Monday, Christmas, Ibiza, and Rolls-Royce.*

Compound noun: a noun made up of more than one word, usually (but not always) two nouns or a noun and an adjective, to make something with a meaning of its own, such as *apple tree, lion tamer, feel-good factor, tan line, lawsuit, science fiction* (or indeed *science fiction writer*), and *will-o'-the-wisp.*

Wikipedia says that English has a habit of "creating compounds by concatenating words without case markers," which is a wonderfully nonsensical way of saying that we just put words together to make other words or phrases: thus a *science fiction writer* is a *writer* who writes *fiction* based on *science*, but there is nothing in the form of the words to tell us whether they are adjectives or nouns or whatever. And as you can see, these compounds may end up as a single word, two or more separate words or two or more words with one or more hyphens. But let's not get into hyphens just yet.

The Numbers Game

Another way of categorizing nouns is to divide them into **countable** and **mass** (or **non-countable**) nouns.

Countable nouns are (reasonably enough) used to name something that can be counted, such as *one plate, two eggs, three sausages*. It's countable if you can ask ***how many*** *are there?* or state *there are **a number of** men/chairs/staplers*—because you can easily count the specific number of items.

A **mass** or **non-countable noun** refers to something that cannot reasonably be counted and therefore has no plural, such as *air, art, milk, money, stupidity, sand,* and *wisdom*. Quantities of non-countable nouns are described as **an amount of** *hair/sand/ garbage*, either because they refer to an unspecified *amount* of stuff or because there are too many individual pieces (of hair or sand, for example) to number. We can't ask *how many?* with non-countable nouns (how many milk, how many traffic); it's simply *how much?*

Twelve Items or Less (Less What?)
A common mistake is the confusion of *less* and *fewer*. Supermarkets almost always get it wrong.
Use *fewer* with countable nouns: *12 items or fewer*.
Use *less* with non-countable nouns: *less traffic than yesterday*.

We're All in It Together

A **collective noun** is one that refers to a group or number of individuals; common examples include *audience, class, family, flock, group, jury, orchestra, parliament, staff,* and *team*, and there are many more.

Strictly speaking, all of these words are singular and take a singular verb. Straightforward enough, you might think. The problem is that a collective noun can refer to a whole group acting as a single entity and also to all the members of that group, acting as individuals. Are you still with me?

Rule: We use a singular verb with a collective noun when we mean the whole group acting as one; we use the plural verb when we are referring to the actions of the individuals within the group.

For example:

The battalion lost all its men in that battle.	All of the men died in the battle.
The battalion lost their lives in that battle.	All of the men died but not necessarily all at once.
The group was waiting in the airport bar.	All members of the group were at the bar.
The group took so long drinking their cocktails that they nearly missed their flight.	But they did not all drink the same cocktail at the same time.
The staff has gone crazy.	All employees are acting strangely.
The staff have locked themselves into their offices.	But they are not all locked in the same office.

Some people call this **formal agreement**—when you say *the staff is*—and **notional agreement**—*the [members of the] team are.*

A related source of confusion lies in the names of sports teams. *The New York Yankees*, for example, is not technically a collective noun. It's a proper noun (hence the capital letters; see page 202), and it should strictly speaking—those words again—be treated as singular. So, bizarrely, should *Manchester United*, *Toronto Maple Leafs*, and the *Boston Red Sox*. On the other hand, there is no denying that lots of people say *the New York Yankees* **are** *in the World Series*, and frankly only the most pedantic among us (and Red Sox fans) are likely to be offended.

Adjectives treated as collective nouns—*the rich, the homeless, the lonely*—are always plural and require a plural verb: *the rich are getting richer.*

> ☛ **Teacher's Corner:** To avoid confusion with collective nouns, it is often sensible to reword a sentence. Try *The hotel manager is offering members of the wedding party a discount on their rooms* instead of *The hotel is/are offering the wedding party a discount on its/their rooms.*

I'm the Leader of the Pack/smack/shiver

There are scores of collective nouns to describe parts of the animal (and particularly bird) kingdom. Some of them are genuinely useful (a flock of sheep and a herd of elephants, for example, if sheep and elephants crop up in your conversation to any great extent). Others are obscure or just plain silly, but the following pages provide a small sample of them.

What Do You Call a Group of...?

Ants	*A colony*	Dolphins	*A pod*
Apes	*A shrewdness*	Ducks	*A flock, brace (in flight), raft (on water), team, paddling (on water), badling*
Bats	*A colony*		
Bears	*A sloth, sleuth*		
Bees	*A grist, hive, swarm*	Eagles	*A convocation*
		Elephants	*A herd*
Birds in general	*A flight (in the air); flock (on the ground); volary, brace (generally for gamebirds or waterfowl)*	Fish in general	*A draft, nest, school, shoal*
		Flamingos	*A stand*
		Flies	*A business*
Buzzards	*A wake*	Frogs	*An army*
Caterpillars	*An army*	Geese	*A flock, gaggle (on the ground), skein (in flight)*
Cattle	*A drove, herd*		
Clams	*A bed*	Giraffes	*A tower*
		Goats	*A tribe, trip*
Cockroaches	*An intrusion*	Grasshoppers	*A cloud*
Cranes	*A sedge*	Gulls	*A colony*
Crocodiles	*A bask*	Hawks	*A cast, kettle (flying in large numbers), boil (two or more*
Crows	*A murder, horde*		

Herring	*An army*	Seals	*A pod, herd*
Hippo-potamuses	*A bloat*	Sharks	*A shiver*
		Sheep	*A drove, flock, herd*
Hornets	*A nest*		
Jellyfish	*A smack*	Snakes, vipers	*A nest*
Kangaroos	*A troop*	Sparrows	*A host*
Lions	*A pride*	Squirrels	*A dray, scurry*
Locusts	*A plague*	Starlings	*A murmuration*
Mules	*A pack, span, barren*	Storks	*A mustering*
		Swallows	*A flight*
Owls	*A parliament*	Swans	*A bevy, wedge (in flight)*
Oysters	*A bed*		
Peacocks	*A muster, an ostentation*	Tigers	*A streak*
		Toads	*A knot*
Penguins	*A colony*	Trout	*A hover*
Pigs	*A drift, drove, litter (young)*	Turkeys	*A rafter, gang*
		Turtles	*A bale, nest*
Porcupines	*A prickle*	Whales	*A pod, gam, herd*
Ravens	*An unkindness*		
Rhinoceroses	*A crash*	Wolves	*A pack*
		Woodpeckers	*A descent*

Is It Common or Proper?

Lots of words have come into English because of the man (with the honorable exception of Mrs. Amelia Bloomer, it was usually a man) who invented or popularized the item concerned. At some stage in the evolution of all these words, they would have been proper nouns, and thus spelled with a capital, but as the word became more commonplace and the association with a person was forgotten, the capital tended to be abandoned, too.

The only one on the list below that merits a capital in the dictionary refers back to an inventor who lived in the twentieth century. We give that capital ten years.

boycott   Captain Charles C. Boycott, Irish land agent ostracized by his neighbors in 1880.

cardigan   The 7th Earl of Cardigan (1797–1868), after whom the garment is named. He was clearly a fashion icon of his day.

dunce   The blessed John Duns Scotus (died 1308), one of the most important theologians and philosophers of the Middle Ages, later accused of unsound reasoning. And presumably made to stand in a corner wearing a pointy hat.

leotard   Jules Léotard, nineteenth-century French acrobat after whom the garment is named.

lynch mob   Captain William Lynch (1742–1820), Virginia justice of the peace at the time of the American Revolution; had a fondness for summarily executing people with whom he disagreed.

maudlin   Mary Magdalene, biblical figure often shown weeping in scripture, to describe the excessively sentimental.

mausoleum	King Mausolos of Caria (died 353 B.C.), whose tomb was one of the Seven Wonders of the Ancient World.
shrapnel	Major-General Henry Shrapnel (1761–1842), English artillery officer, who designed a new type of artillery shell.
silhouette	Etienne de Silhouette (1709–67), unpopular finance minister of Louis XV who imposed harsh economic demands upon the French people. His name became associated with anything done cheaply—particularly the simple form of portraiture that became popular at the time and enabled people to joke that the finance minister was saving money on color paints as well as on everything else.
Zamboni	Frank J. Zamboni (1901–88), ice skating–rink owner who invented an ice resurfacing machine.

ONE DIE, TWO DICE (OR, SINGULAR AND PLURAL)

When a noun means only one thing, it is **singular**. When it is more than one, it is **plural**. The rules on how to change a noun from singular to plural start simply but then tend to head out into left field.

1. Most singular nouns are made plural by adding the letter *s*: *book, bell, candle = books, bells, candles.*

2. However, if you add an *s* to such nouns as *church, bus, fox, bush, bench, Jones,* and *waltz,* they become difficult to pronounce. Which is why we add *-es* and create an extra syllable: *churches, buses, Joneses…*

3. If a noun ends in *y* and the letter before the *y* is a vowel, again just add an *s*: *key* = *keys*. However, if a noun ends in *y* and the letter before the *y* is a consonant, the *y* must be changed to an *i* and followed by *es*: *lady* = *ladies, gallery* = *galleries*. But, wait, there's an exception: This rule does not apply to proper nouns: *one penny, several pennies*, but *Mr. and Mrs. Penny* become *the Pennys*.

4. To form the plurals of nouns ending in *ff*, add that *s*: *cliffs, bailiffs*, and so on. However, words ending in a single *f* or in *fe* need to have these letters replaced with a *v*—oh, and then add *es*: *leaf* = *leaves, wife* = *wives*. Got that? Good, because there are exceptions.

Exceptions to Rule 4

Dwarfs and chiefs
Will cause you griefs.
As will proofs, roofs, safes, beliefs.
Hooves and hoofs can either be,
So, too, scarfs and scarves, you see.
To wharfs and wharves, you may refer,
And turfs and turves, as you prefer.

And just when you thought you were getting the hang of it, humans have one *life*, cats have nine *lives*, but artists can paint as many still *lifes* as they like.

5. Many words ending in *o* can be made plural by adding *-s*: *zoos, kangaroos, igloos, solos, sopranos,*

discos, photos, Eskimos, infernos. Others—seemingly chosen at random—need *-es:* **Buffaloes** *have trampled my* **potatoes** *and* **tomatoes***. If we sit outside to play* **dominoes,** *we shall be plagued by* **mosquitoes***.*

6. A number of nouns have irregular plurals, which is why we do not say *Are you mouses or mans?* and why the plural of *house* is *houses,* but the plural of *louse* is *lice.* Then there's *goose/geese, tooth/teeth, child/children, ox/oxen* (but not *box/boxen*).

> ☛ **Teacher's Corner:** The plural of *talisman* is not *talismen* but *talismans.* Why? Because its origins have nothing to do with *man* or *men.* The word comes to us from Arabic and medieval Greek via French or Spanish.

Rule: The rules always apply, except when they don't. With irregular forms such as *child/children,* sorry, you just have to learn them.

Sorry, Don't Know the Plural...
Dear Sir,
Please send me a mongoose.
Oh, by the way, send me another one, too.

In big-game hunting it appears to be fair game to dispense with the usual plurals. Hence we might shoot *several gazelle, two leopard, three lion, three elephant,* and *six wild pig.* This has a slightly old-fashioned feel and does somehow suggest that you are going out to kill the poor beasts and hang their heads on your wall.

And on the Agendum Today

Some nouns have no (or a rarely used) singular form:

alms	*marginalia*	*tidings*
bellows	*oats*	*tongs*
billiards	*pants*	*trousers*
braces	*pliers*	*tweezers*
clothes	*scissors*	*vespers*
dregs	*shorts*	*victuals*
eaves	*thanks*	*vittles*

Note: Nouns such as these require a **measure word**; for example, *a pair* of trousers, *some* thanks. You cannot say *one scissors*. Nor, happily, can you sow *just the one wild oat*.

"Singularity Is Almost Invariably a Clue"

No, it isn't. That was just Sherlock Holmes being a smart aleck. With some nouns, singularity is more trouble than it's worth.

Such nouns have a plural form but do what the dictionaries describe as "functioning as a singular." Others can function as either a singular or a plural. Which is, frankly, no help at all to those of us who like rules. Still others function as a singular in some senses and as a plural in others.

If the rules don't help, let's try a few examples.

> *Mumps **is** nasty, measles **is** measly* is perfectly correct. But so too is *mumps **are** nasty, measles **are** measly.*

Sports with a plural form tend to take a singular verb when we mean them generically, but a plural when we mean something more countable, such as *exercises*. So:

> *Athletics **is** tiresome.* meaning the whole concept
>
> *Gymnastics **are** a great way* meaning gymnastic exercises
> *to start the day.*

Pilates, by the way, is the name of the man who invented it, so it is singular. And harder than it looks.

A similar distinction can be made with academic subjects. *Acoustics* is singular when we mean the study of sound, but plural when we mean sound qualities: *the acoustics **were** dreadful.* Similarly, if you study *ethics* or *politics*, it is a singular subject, but if you bring a person's *ethics* into question or complain about company *politics*, they are plural.

One Sheep, Two Sheep…

The following nouns take the same form whether they are singular or plural. What would Sherlock Holmes have to say about that?

aircraft	*kudos*	*shambles*
cannon	*means*	*sheep*
deer	*offspring*	*species*
haddock	*series*	*trout*

Take Your Pick…

All self-respecting pedants know about **Latin plurals**; a smattering (and rapidly diminishing number) of older ones know about Greek, too. But here a little learning can be a dangerous thing, because it is easy to assume that a word ending in -*us* is Latin second declension and therefore has a plural ending in -*i*: *abaci, cacti, incubi, succubi*. Then along comes a word such as *platypus*, whose origins are Greek, and whose plural is strictly speaking *platypuses*, to catch you just when you thought you were being clever. A number of words ending in -*on* are derived from Greek neuter nouns and have a plural form ending in -*a*: *criterion/ criteria, phenomenon/phenomena*, and so on.

Some words ending in -*is* are Latin third declension in origin and have a plural form -*es*: *crisis/crises, thesis/theses* (pronounced -*eeze* as in *cheese* or *sneeze*).

And then there are those that have decided to ignore their classical background altogether and allow us to choose between two (or even more) plural forms, some of them rather suspect:

hippopotamus	hippopotamuses, hippopotami
necropolis	necropolises, necropoles, necropoleis, necropoli
octopus	octopi, octopodes, octopuses
oxymoron	oxymorons, oxymora
rhinoceros	rhinoceroses, rhinoceros, rhinoceri, rhinocerotes
syllabus	syllabuses, syllabi
terminus	termini, terminuses
uterus	uteri, uteruses

🐄 **Teacher's Corner:** *Octopus* is a one-word minefield, because it is a Latinized form of the Greek word *oktopous*, whose "correct" plural form would be *octopodes*. But according to *Merriam-Webster's Dictionary*, today the correct form of the plural is *octopuses* or *octopi*.

Keeping Up with the Joneses

When we talk about a family in the plural, we need to add an *s* to the **family name**; for example, *the Smiths, the Windsors*. However, if the family name ends in *s, x, ch, sh*, or *z*, we add -*es*: *the Joneses, the Foxes, the Bushes*.

☞ **See Me after Class:** *The Venables's came to our house this weekend.*
Do not make a family name plural by using an apostrophe.

Exceptions: When a name ends in an *s* with a hard *z* sound, we don't add any ending to form the plural. *We have the Morrises and the Richards coming to lunch.*

Compounding the Problem

The rule with **plural compound nouns** is to pluralize the base element of the compound noun—that is, generally, the most important element of the word or phrase:

> *We have our **mother-in-laws** staying with us, so we stepped out for a beer* is wrong.

> ***Mothers-in-law*** and ***daughters-in-law*** *don't always get along* is right.

because the key element of the phrase is *mother* (or *daughter*). Ask yourself *What sort of mother? A mother-in-law.* Similarly:

> *The role of **Secretary of State** varies among countries, and in some cases there are multiple **Secretaries of State.***

Doctors Payne and Betterman *were speaking at the conference* (there is more than one doctor, but only one called Payne and only one called Betterman).

> *Bert and Benny were both idle but amiable **men-about-town.***

The Media Is the Message

In addition to those mentioned above, here are a few more words whose origins we seem to have forgotten, but in these cases—because the plural forms don't end in *s*—we are beginning to use them as singulars. Lots of perfectly literate people now say (and some even write) *The data **was** incorrect* or *The media **is** very hostile to government policy*, but the purists still cling to the distinction between singular and plural.

Plural	Singular
bacteria	*bacterium*
candelabra	*candelabrum*
data	*datum*
dice	*die*
formulae	*formula*
genera	*genus*
graffiti	*graffito*
loci	*locus*
media	*medium*
opera	*opus*
paparazzi	*paparazzo*

One plural that has lost the fight is *pease*, which used to be the regular plural of *pea*. Now *peas* is found pretty much everywhere except in the phrase *pease pudding* and the nursery rhyme about whether it is hot or cold.

> ✋ **Smart Aleck:** If you add an *s* to the plural words *adventures, bras, cares, cosines, deadlines, millionaires, ogres, princes* and *timelines*, they revert to a singular form: *adventuress, brass, caress, cosiness, deadliness, millionairess, ogress, princess*, and *timeliness*.

By the way, *genie* and *genius* have the same plural: *genii*.

THOU AND THEE (OR, PRONOUNS)

Going back to our poem (see page 37), "In place of noun the pronoun stands," a **pronoun** is used to avoid repeating a noun over and over again. Imagine if you were writing a summary of this book and had to say, *Many people find grammar difficult. Lots of people were never taught grammar at school. Grammar has therefore become a source of anxiety. Indeed, some people might call grammar a minefield.* Just because nobody had thought to invent the words *it* or *them*.

The noun to which a pronoun refers is sometimes called the **antecedent**.

> *Many people find grammar difficult. Lots of them were never taught it at school.*

The antecedent of *them* is people and *grammar* is the antecedent of *it*.

"The masculine pronouns are he, his, and him,
But imagine the feminine she, shis, and shim."
—Anonymous

There are various categories of pronoun, depending on the function they perform in a sentence. The **subject pronouns** are *I, you, he, she, it, we, they,* and the equivalent **object pronouns** are *me, you, him, her, it, us, them.* If we've lost you here, see page 115 for an explanation of subject and object. But it boils down to the difference between *I love him* and *He loves me,* which could be quite significant.

> ✋ **Smart Aleck:** Since *pronoun* is a noun,
> why isn't *proverb* a verb?

The Part about Sex

Ahem. The English language does not have a **singular pronoun** that encapsulates both genders. It used to be that "the masculine was deemed to embrace the feminine," but 1960s feminism put a stop to that sort of hanky-panky and has left us with a grammatical problem ever since. Some people meticulously write *he or she, his or hers,* wherever it crops up, but this quickly becomes cumbersome and tedious. Others go for *s/he,* but that still leaves them with the his/her dilemma. Still others go to the opposite extreme and use *she* or *her* throughout (so the feminine is now embracing the masculine, as it were).

Lots of people nowadays fudge this by using *their* as a non-gender-specific singular, as in *the judge* (who may be a man or a woman; we don't know and it would be sexist to assume either) *adjusted their robe.* It isn't pretty, but sometimes being a purist is no oil painting either.

It's All Relative

The **relative pronouns** are *who, what, whom, that, whose,* and *which,* and their role is to introduce subordinate clauses that tell us more about the noun that precedes them. For example:

> The waiter **who** served you may remember what time you left.
> The girl **whose** name was Sue made a lot of money at her
>   garage sale.
> He **whom** the gods love dies young.
> He was disturbed by the email, **which** he received this morning.
> He was disturbed by the email **that** he received this morning.

Which can also be used to refer back to an entire clause:

> The sun was shining throughout the rainy season, **which** didn't
>   seem right at all.

Excellent Reflexes

> "And not in me: I am myself alone."
> —Shakespeare, *Henry VI*

Reflexive pronouns are formed by adding *self* or *selves* to the basic pronoun: *myself, oneself, yourself, himself, herself, itself, ourselves, yourselves, themselves.* They are used when the subject and object of a verb are the same person or thing:

*I can look after **myself**.*
*Speak for **yourself**!*
*We enjoyed **ourselves** immensely.*
*The kids can never be trusted to behave **themselves** when the
babysitter is there.*

They can also be used to avoid ambiguity. Compare these
sentences:

*Tom had done surprisingly well on his exams. The teacher was
very pleased with **him*** (that is, pleased with Tom).

*Tom had done surprisingly well on his exams. The teacher was
very pleased with **himself*** (that is, the teacher was pleased
with the teacher).

These pronouns can also be used for emphasis, or to mean "alone,
unaided": *I can't see what anyone sees in* Big Brother, ***myself**.*
Or: *Did you really do all of the decorating **yourself**?*

Overuse of reflexive pronouns in this emphatic sense is one of the
banes of modern speech. *I think* is just as persuasive as *I myself think*
(we're sorry to be dogmatic, but please bear with us this once).

"Every one to rest themselves betake."
—Shakespeare, *The Rape of Lucrece*

Let's Reciprocate

The **reciprocal pronouns** are *each other* and *one another. Each
other* refers to two people or things; *one another* to more than two.

*The two candidates who were still in contention congratulated
each other. The others adjourned to the bar to commiserate
with **one another**.*

What's Mine Is Yours

The **possessive pronouns** are *my, mine, your(s), his, her(s), our(s), their(s)*, and *its* (and note that they never—repeat never—need an apostrophe: see page 325 for some common confusions). *Mine, yours, his, hers, ours, theirs,* and *its* tend to be used after the noun to which they refer and mean "the thing belonging to or associated with me/you/whoever":

> *He had forgotten his gloves again, so I gave him* **mine***.*
>
> *Put that book back where you found it: it isn't* **yours***.*
>
> *We were madly envious because their house was much nicer than* **ours***.*

I Don't Want to Be Specific…

There are a number of useful pronouns that we can use when we don't want to or are unable to specify exactly what we are talking about: *all, another, any, anyone, anything, each, everybody, everyone, everything, few, many, no one, nobody, none, nothing, one, several, some, somebody, someone.* These are called **indefinite pronouns**.

> *I think* **someone** *is in the house.*
>
> *You've eaten most of the chocolates; there are only* **a few** *left.*
>
> *In space,* **no one** *can hear you scream.*

By the way, there is no difference in grammatical terms between *no one* and *nobody, someone* and *somebody, anyone* and *anybody.* For once you can just use whichever you like.

Talking about This and That

The **demonstrative pronouns** are *this, that, these,* and *those*— the same words as the demonstrative determiners we met earlier but used in a slightly different way.

*Please take **this** home with you and study it.*	meaning, perhaps, **this** book
*Take **that** to the cleaners, will you?*	**that** jacket
*I want **these** removed at once.*	**these** dirty dishes
***Those** are no good to anybody.*	**those** old clothes

Let's Investigate…

Interrogative pronouns take the place of a noun in a question.

***Who** is that?*	The answer might be: That is Homer Simpson.
***What** is that?*	That is a picture of Homer Simpson.
***Which** is that?*	Which of the many pictures of Homer Simpson in the world are you talking about?
***To whom** should I give the doughnuts?*	It's pretty obvious, really.

Some Common Confusions

their/theirs/there/there's/they're

Their is a possessive pronoun, showing ownership. *It was **their** version of the story that was reported on the news.*

Theirs is also a possessive pronoun indicating that something belongs to more than one person. *That version of the story is **theirs**.*

There is an adverb that indicates a place or position. *My new car is over **there**. **There** is a monkey in that tree.*

There's means *there is*. ***There's** that ring you were looking for.*

They're means *they are*. ***They're** a very happy couple even though they fight all the time.*

its/it's

Its is a possessive pronoun. *We thought the cat was lost, but it somehow found **its** way home.*

It's means *it is*. ***It's** not fair.*

whose/who's

Whose is a possessive pronoun. *The boy **whose** pants were flown from the flagpole.*

Whose can also be an interrogative pronoun. ***Whose** pants are those?*

Who's means *who is*. *The boy **who's** being told off for putting them there.*

Who or That?

Rule: Use *who* to refer to people.

Use *that* to refer to animals or inanimate objects.

> *The people **who** matter will be impressed by this.* (*The people **that** matter* is not incorrect, but is less formal.)
>
> *The tigers **that** come from Siberia have thick fur to protect them against the cold.*
>
> *The house **that** we used to live in has been knocked down to make way for a supermarket.*
>
> *The song **that** he wrote never made it onto the charts.*

In the last two examples, the antecedent is the object of the following clause (we used to live in the house, he wrote the song). In these cases, another option is to omit the relative pronoun altogether:

> *The house we used to live in…*
>
> *The song he wrote…*

And, on the subject of which and that, don't miss the exciting installment on restrictive and non-restrictive clauses later in the book (see page 139).

WHAT A TO-DO (OR, VERBS)

> ✋ **Smart Aleck:** When somebody greets us with *How do you do?* why don't we ever reply, *Do what?*

A **verb** is an "action word": *I **do**, you **go**, he **runs**, we **sleep**, they **sneeze***. A verb also expresses a state of being: *I **am**, it **is**, we **live***.

Verbs have a lot of clout. They make things happen.

I books
You grammar
We money

mean nothing without a verb.

*I **write** books*
*You **learn** grammar*
*We **earn** money*

make perfect sense and are good things—particularly the last one.

To Be or Not to Be

With verbs, we start with the **infinitive**, which is made up of the preposition *to* and the basic form of the verb:

***To be**, or not **to be**, that is the question.*
***To sleep**, perchance **to dream**.*
***To have** and **to hold**.*

These verbs have meaning—we know what *to be, to sleep, to dream, to have, to hold* mean—but they don't tell us anything specific about the action that is being performed, the time it is (or was or will be or may have been) being done, or the number of people doing it. For that, we need either:

to **conjugate** the verb—that is, change the ending to show a change of meaning (*he laughs, I laughed*)

or

to add an **auxiliary** or helping verb to specify time and number (*I **will** laugh, you **are** laughing, he **has** laughed*).

Once you have conjugated a verb and added any auxiliaries you want to make the action complete, you have a **finite verb**. (As in, not an infinitive, you see? Clever, right?)

To Boldly Split

The old rule was simple*: never split an infinitive*—that is, on pain of death, never put a word between the *to* and the rest of the verb. The example everyone trundles out at this point is *Star Trek*'s "To boldly go…"

It is, however, probably one of the sillier rules to come out of the old grammarians' insistence on applying Latin rules to English: Latin infinitives are one word—*amare, potare, studere*—so they couldn't be split anyway. Modern scholars believe that splitting an infinitive is perfectly acceptable if the alternative would be clumsy or ambiguous. In the following sentences, for example, we think that the non-split version is more elegant, and the meaning is equally clear, so it is preferable. But it is surely preferable *because it is more elegant*, not because the infinitive is unsplit.

> *Many people choose **to incorrectly split** an infinitive in everyday speech.* ☒
>
> *Many people **incorrectly choose to split** an infinitive in everyday speech.* ☑
>
> *They decided **to quickly devour** the pie.* ☒
>
> *They decided **to devour the pie quickly**.* ☑
>
> *She put aside extra time **to closely mark** the exam papers.* ☒
>
> *She put aside extra time **to mark the exam papers closely**.* ☑

On the other hand, this fragment (from the British newspaper the *Daily Telegraph*) scrupulously avoids splitting the infinitive and in so doing sacrifices clarity: *A family doctor who installed a camera **secretly to film** a woman using his bathroom…* What was it that was done secretly? The installation or the filming? (Or, given the context, perhaps both?)

> "The English-speaking world may be divided into
> (1) those who neither know nor care what a split infinitive
> is; (2) those who do not know but care very much;
> (3) those who know and condemn; (4) those who know
> and approve; (5) those who know and distinguish...
> Those who neither know nor care are the vast majority,
> and are a happy folk, to be envied by
> most of the minority classes."
> —H. W. Fowler, *Modern English Usage*, 1926

A Few Irregularities

Regular verbs—those that follow the rules—are conjugated as follows:

Present tense:	*I love, you love, he loves, we love, they love*
Past tense:	*I loved, you loved, he loved, we loved, they loved*
Present participle:	*loving, biting.*

(Note that if a verb ends in *e*, we drop the *e* to form the present participle. If not, we just add *-ing*: *wanting, hanging, staggering*, for example.)

Because this is English, however, there are inevitably lots of **irregular verbs**. Some past tenses and past participles are formed by adding *-t* instead of *-ed* (see below). Then we have *to drink*, which becomes *I drank, you drank*, and so on, in the past tense, whereas *to think* becomes *I thought. To speak* becomes *I spoke*, but *to squeak* and *to sneak* are regular and become *I squeaked* and *I sneaked.*

The most thoroughly irregular verbs of all are the common ones *to be* and *to go*: *I am, you are, he is, we are, they are, I was, you were*. *To go* is OK in the present tense, but *I went?* What's that all about?

Again, it's the irritating feature of irregular forms; there's no apparent logic to them, and you just have to learn them.

Back Me Up, Will You?

Auxiliary verbs are used "to indicate the tense, voice, mood, and so on, of another verb where this is not indicated by inflection." Don't you just love dictionaries? It means they are the little words you stick in the front of verbs. There are 23 of them, which can be learned by singing them to the tune of *Jingle Bells*.

> *may, might, must*
> *be, being, been*
> *am, are*
> *is, was, were*
> *do, does, did*
> *should, could, would*
> *have, had, has*
> *will, can*
> *shall*

So they can express simple things such as *I am coming*, slightly more complicated ones such as *it will be done*, or even more complex ones with up to three auxiliaries attached to one main verb: *He must have been feeling unhappy for some time.*

Must and *may*, along with *should and ought*, are also called **modal verbs**: they give information about the mood of the verb (see page 79), expressing such things as obligation (*you must be home by midnight, he ought to pay before leaving the restaurant*), recommendation (*you **should** call and apologize*) or possibility (*I **may** do as you ask, but then again I **may** not*).

May or Might? Can or Could?

Strictly speaking, *may* and *can* operate in the present tense, *might* and *could* in the past or in the conditional (see page 248).

***Can** you lend me 20 dollars?*	Do you have the money?
***Could** you lend me 20 dollars?*	Would you be so very kind as to entrust me with this sum, secure in the knowledge that I will pay it back?

However, this is another distinction that is beginning to be lost in modern-day speech and writing.

Can/could also indicate *capability* or *possibility*, whereas *may/might* grant us *permission* to do something.

***Can** I drive your Rolls-Royce?*	Well, yes, if your feet can reach the pedals and you understand the concept of a steering wheel.
***May** I drive your Rolls-Royce?*	Over my dead body.

Most people in the English-speaking world seem to have had a schoolteacher who, in response to the question *Can I go to the bathroom?* would raise an eyebrow and say, *I don't know—**can** you?*

☛ **See Me after Class**

Could have/could of

There is no verb *to of. He could've told me* is a short form of *He could **have** told me.*

Try and/try to

Try and is wrong. *Try to* get it right.

About Whom Are We Talking?

For the purposes of grammar, there are only three **persons** (not people, there are loads of them) in the world:

first person: the speaker (*I, me, we, us*)

second person: the hearer (*you*)

third person: the person or thing spoken of (*he, she, it, they, him, her, them*)

In modern English, *you* serves as both singular and plural, but always takes a plural verb—***you are** my lucky star,* ***you were** made for me,* ***you drive** me crazy*—even when only one person is being addressed. *Thou* and *thee* were once the singular forms, but they are now never used except as deliberate archaisms, in church and in some dialects.

✋ **Smart Aleck:** Many languages have both informal and formal words for *you:* the French *tu* and *vous* and the German *du* and *Sie,* for example. English only has *you,* having done away with *thou* centuries ago. But did you know that *thou* was in fact the more informal of the two? English has preserved the impeccably polite word rather than the chummy one. Now why should that be?

The Voice of Reason

And there are two voices: **active** and **passive**.

Rule: With the active voice the subject acts; with the passive voice the subject is acted upon.

Active: *The teacher reprimanded the boy because he spilled milk on his notebook.*

Passive: *The boy was reprimanded because milk was spilled on his notebook.*

The two sentences say the same thing but with different emphasis. Using the passive voice too often can make writing dull (let's get on with some action!). However, consider:

> *If **it were done** when 'tis done then 'twere well **it were done** quickly.*
>
> *Should auld acquaintance **be forgot**, and never **brought to mind**?*
>
> *Yossarian **was moved** very deeply by the absolute simplicity of this clause of Catch-22.*
>
> *The stars **are not wanted** now.*

The passive should not be ruled out altogether. It may be found to have its uses.

"We have not passed that subtle line between childhood and adulthood until we move from the passive voice to the active voice—that is, until we have stopped saying, "It got lost," and say, "I lost it."
—Sydney J. Harris, *On the Contrary*

It's Raining Pronouns

In English we use a little-known thing called the **weather verb** an awful lot.

It is raining.

It is freezing.

It is in the nineties.

What is this nameless, shapeless *it* that is doing all these things? Well, it is known simply as the **dummy subject,** a handy little word that enables us to get to the part we all love: describing the weather. Without it we'd be going around saying, *The sky is raining, the sun is hot,* and so on, which might—perish the thought—make talking about the weather boring.

Getting Tense

> "They said: 'You're Laurie Lee, aren't you? Well just you
> sit there for the present.' I sat there all day but I
> never got it. I ain't going back there again."
> —Laurie Lee, *Cider with Rosie*

Tenses add time to verbs. They put actions into the past, present and future, the may-yet-be or the might-have-been.

*I **do** ballet on Tuesdays.*	I do this habitually, and will continue to do this.
*I **am doing** ballet at the moment.*	I am doing this either right at this moment—so I can't come to the phone—or over a longer but current period of time: perhaps I used to do salsa but have changed.

*I **have done** ballet for years.*	I did ballet in the past and up to and including the present, but I may be getting bored with it now.
*I **have been doing** ballet for years.*	I did ballet in the past and have continued it until the present time and probably will continue in the future. I haven't finished with it yet. Ballet is here for the duration.
*I **did do** ballet once upon a time.*	I did ballet at some indefinite time in the past. It belongs there. I have given it up in the present.
*I **used to do** ballet, but now I do jazz.*	I no longer do ballet.
*I **was doing** ballet on Tuesdays, but now they've changed it to Fridays.*	I was doing ballet on Tuesdays until recently. I may or may not be doing it on Fridays.
*I **would do** ballet if they hadn't changed the class to a Friday.*	If it could be changed to suit me, I would consider doing ballet in the future.
*I **had done** ballet for years, before I switched to jazz.*	I had given up ballet before I took up jazz. There is nothing to suggest whether or not I am still doing jazz.
*I **had been doing** ballet for years before anyone told me I had a crooked spine.*	I was still doing ballet—the action was ongoing—at some time in the past when something else happened.
*I **will do** ballet again one day.*	I intend to/predict that I will do ballet in the future.

*I **will have done** my ballet exam by the time we go on vacation.*	A future action will be completed by or before a specified time in the future.
*I **will be doing** the ballet recital on Saturday.*	It is definitely going to happen at this specific point in the future.

Exactly how many tenses there are in English is arguable. Some grammarians claim that there are only two: the present and the past. (Presumably they let the future take care of itself.) Some say the traditional number is twelve, though others have described as many as thirty and, just to confuse us, some tenses have more than one name. But here are fourteen that should get you through most situations (or ballet positions).

present simple	*I pirouette*
present continuous	*I am pirouetting*
present perfect	*I have pirouetted*
present perfect continuous	*I have been pirouetting*
past simple (also known as **preterite**)	*I did pirouette, I pirouetted*
imperfect	*I used to pirouette*
past continuous	*I was pirouetting*
conditional	*I would pirouette*
pluperfect/past perfect	*I had pirouetted*
past perfect continuous	*I had been pirouetting*
future	*I will pirouette*
future perfect	*I will have pirouetted*
future continuous	*I will be pirouetting*
future perfect continuous	*I will have been pirouetting*

░░

Famous Last Words

"I am about to—or I am going to—die.

Either expression is correct."

—French grammarian Dominique Bouhours,

who died in 1702

░░

Judging by Your Mood...

Verbs, like the rest of us, act differently depending on which **mood** they are in. There are three moods: **indicative, imperative,** and **subjunctive**.

The **indicative mood** makes a statement or asks a question:

I'm wet, I'm cold, and I'm hungry.

Winter is almost here.

He will come.

Is that the best you can do?

The **imperative mood** gives us a command:

Chill out!

Do as I say!

Don't eat the daisies!

And even the more politely phrased: *Please look after this bear.*

Easy! Unfortunately the **subjunctive mood** is so complicated that it deserves a subheading of its own.

If Only It Were That Easy

The **subjunctive** sounds scarier than it is and has a tendency to fill people with horror. Let's start with a couple of examples:

*I wish it **weren't** going to snow again* (but it is).

*If it **were** to snow* (which it may or may not do, but we don't know yet), *they would not be able to get home.*

I were or *it were* may sound odd, but they're right when you are using the subjunctive.

Rule: If you know something for a fact, use *was*. If something is contrary to fact, or if you are imagining a future or different situation to the one you are in, use *were*.

> *When I **was** young* (fact: I *was* young once), *I was taught Latin* (it's true, I *was* taught Latin).
>
> *When he **was** young and handsome* (he *was* young and handsome once), *he was also arrogant.*
>
> *I **was** that man* (you *were* indeed).
>
> *When I was poor (I once was indeed poor), I wasn't unhappy.*

but

> *If I **were** you* (but I'm not), *I should teach myself Latin.*
>
> *If I **were** to teach you Latin* (supposing that I taught you Latin), *would you study hard?*
>
> *If I **were** to be young and handsome again* (but I can't be, alas), *I wouldn't be so arrogant about it.*
>
> *If I **were** that sort of man* (but I'm not), *you might find me there.*
>
> *If I **were** rich* (but I might never be rich), *would I be happier than I am now?*
>
> *I wish I **were** taller (but I am currently stuck at this height).*

A number of **set phrases** in English—*come what may, far be it from me, the powers that be*—use the subjunctive, but the joy of set phrases is that you don't have to think about them.

"If I were reincarnated, I'd want to come back as a buzzard. Nothing hates him or envies him or wants him or needs him. He is never bothered or in danger, and he can eat anything."
—William Faulkner

Sic Transit Gloria...

A **transitive verb** allows the subject to perform an action on an object (see page 281 for more on subjects and objects):

She slapped his face.   She *slapped* what? His face.

He pulled the   He *pulled* what? The cord.
communication cord.

> ✋ **Smart Aleck:** Transitive verbs with one object only are called **monotransitive** (*I corrected my teacher*). Verbs with both a direct object and an indirect object are called **ditransitive** (*The teacher threw me an eraser*).

An **intransitive verb** acts by itself:

I sleep.   I cannot *sleep* something.

I fall.   I cannot *fall* something.

Famous Intransitives
"Jesus wept."
—*Saint John's Gospel*

*

"Thus with a kiss I die."
—Shakespeare, *Romeo and Juliet*

Just to confuse things, some verbs can be transitive when used in one sense and intransitive in another. These are known as **ambitransitive verbs**.

Transitive	Intransitive
He **drank his coffee**.	He **drank** *like a fish*.
She **read the menu**.	She **read** *during dinner*.
I **gave up cigarettes**.	I **give** *up*.
He **kissed her hand**.	They **kissed**.

Tip: To check whether a verb is intransitive, place a period directly after it and see if it makes sense: *He died. You survived.* But *he hit.* (*Hit* what?) *She threw.* (*Threw* what?) A transitive verb needs an object to complete its action.

Verbal Warning

Verbal nouns or **adjectives** are formed from verbs, but they perform the function of nouns or adjectives, and there are three kinds: **participles, infinitives,** and **gerunds**. None of these can act on its own as a verb. Instead, each helps a verb to do its job.

Participles

A **participle** is a non-finite form of a verb used with an auxiliary verb to form some compound tenses. It can also be used in **noun, adjectival,** or **adverbial phrases** such as:

Going to the casino *is a surefire way of losing money.*	**noun phrase**, the subject of the sentence
*The horse **favored by the tipsters*** *seemed to lose interest at the second fence.*	**adjectival phrase**, describing the horse
*She stormed out, **slamming the door*** *so hard that the mirror fell off the wall.*	**adverbial phrase**, describing *how* she stormed out

Infinitives

As we saw on page 239, this is the basic form of the verb preceded by *to*, but it is also used in some **compound verb forms** such as:

*I **was going to send** you my address.*

*I **used to go** to a lot of concerts.*

Or following verbs expressing feelings, or to give a reason for an action:

*I **would love to see** her again.*

***Don't forget to wash** your hands.*

*We **built** a fence around the backyard **to keep** the dog under control.*

Gerunds

> "What are all these **kissings** worth,
> If thou kiss not me?"
> —Percy Bysshe Shelley, *Love's Philosophy*

A **gerund** is a noun formed from a verb by adding *-ing*, so it looks exactly like a present participle, but is used in a different way. *When **the going** gets tough, the tough get going.* The first *going* is a gerund: in this sentence, it performs the same function as a noun. To test this statement, try substituting something you know is a noun:

*When **the exams** get tough…*

*When **the meat** gets tough…*

But in the second part of our original sentence, *going* is the present participle of the verb *to go*, linked to the auxiliary verb *get* to make a complete, finite verb.

Here's another example to help you spot the difference:

*I admire the girl **posing** for that photograph.*	**present participle**, referring to the girl who is posing for that photograph
*I admire the girl's **posing** for that photograph.*	**gerund**, referring to the way she is posing, but not necessarily the girl herself

Note the cunning use of the apostrophe here—it carries a wealth of meaning. And guess what? There will be lots more about apostrophes later in the book (see page 168).

KIND OF FUNNY LOOKING (OR, ADJECTIVES)

Most of us were taught the simple rule: an **adjective** is a "describing word." Adjectives modify nouns or pronouns. They tell us what they are like: what they look like, how big they are, and how many of them there are. For example:

*An **ugly** bug*

*A **lovely** girl*

*A **blue** moon*

***Thirty** people*

Adjectives can be derived from proper nouns to describe such things as historical periods (*Elizabethan, Napoleonic*), literary or musical styles (*Shakespearean, Dickensian, Wagnerian*), nationality or geographical location (*French, Parisian*), or other things more loosely associated with people or places (a *Freudian* slip, *Victorian* values, a *Caesarean* section). The suffix *-ian/-ean* means "of or pertaining to (this person/place)"; *-esque* means "in the style of (the person)": so

Dantesque, Kafkaesque, or *Junoesque.* The last of these, intriguingly, is defined as either "of regal beauty" or "large, buxom, and (usually) beautiful," depending on which dictionary you read. Really, if the dictionaries can't agree, what hope is there for the rest of us?

Most of these adjectives are spelled with a capital letter, though *caesarean* has come a long way from Julius Caesar and is now often seen with a lower case *c.* Foods that are named after their place of origin—champagne, parmesan, and the like—are another vague area: strictly speaking they are based on proper nouns, but the more generically they are used, the more it becomes acceptable to drop the capital. It seems bizarre, for example, to insist on using a capital *C* for *New Zealand Cheddar,* on the basis that the cheese is named after a place in Somerset, England.

A Big Bunch of Adjectivals

A group of words can act as an adjective. If they contain a subject and verb, they are known as an **adjectival clause**. If not, they are described as an **adjectival phrase**. (No, we haven't done phrases and clauses yet, but we'll get there—see pages 295 and 299.)

My colleagues, ***who all earn more than I do,*** *never work overtime.*	**adjectival clause,** describing my colleagues
He is the one person in the department ***earning less than I do.***	**adjectival phrase,** describing the person in the department

A Fine Piece of Writing—or Not?

It is easy to go overboard with adjectives (and adverbs, too, see page 88). The author Graham Greene once wrote:

> Adjectives are to be avoided unless they are strictly necessary; adverbs too, which is even more important. When I open a book and find that so and so has "answered sharply" or "spoken tenderly," I shut it again: It's the dialogue itself which should express the sharpness or the tenderness without any need to use adverbs to underline them.

Oh dear—what would he have made of this paragraph from *Tess of the D'Urbervilles* by Thomas Hardy?

> The young girls formed, indeed, the majority of the band, and their heads of luxuriant hair reflected in the sunshine every tone of gold, and black, and brown. Some had beautiful eyes, others a beautiful nose, others a beautiful mouth and figure; few, if any, had all... A young member of the band turned her head at the exclamation. She was a fine and handsome girl—not handsomer than some others, possibly—but her mobile peony mouth and large innocent eyes added eloquence to color and shape...

Limpet Adjectives (or, Clichés)

Some adjectives are so often attached to certain nouns that they seem permanently stuck together and have become **clichés**. Please do not stick these in your writing:

absolute truth	*new innovation*
close proximity	*original source*
definite decision	*personal friend*
end result	*safe haven*
free gift	*true facts*
local resident	*unexpected surprise*
major breakthrough	*violent explosion*
necessary requisite	*work colleague*

Rule: Verbs and nouns are the bricks of a sentence. They give it structure. Adjectives and adverbs are decorative embellishments. If an adjective or adverb doesn't add anything, don't add it.

☞ **See Me after Class:** *The object is small in size, square in shape, and blue in color.*
Do not waste words on unnecessary description.
The object is small, square, and blue says it all.

257

Reverently, Discreetly, Advisedly, Soberly... (or, Adverbs)

"When it absolutely, positively has to
be there overnight."
—Federal Express slogan (1978–1983)

An **adverb** describes a verb, adjective, or adverb. Adverbs answer questions such as *how, where, when, how much, how often?*

Many but by no means all adverbs in English end in *-ly* (*almost, once, twice, never, well, hard, fast, soon,* and *there* are all adverbs), and many but by no means all the words that end in *-ly* are adverbs (*manly, beastly,* and *holy* are adjectives and *family, butterfly,* and *barfly* are nouns). But it seems that in everyday speech adverbs are steadily disappearing and the adjectival form is being used instead.

The following are all commonly heard but grammatically incorrect:

*He did the task **clever** and I was **real impressed**.*

*He always drives **careful** so he won't get any points on his license.*

*It rained **so heavy** the roof started to leak.*

*She divided them **fair** but the children still weren't happy.*

They should be:

*He did the task clever**ly** and I was real**ly** impressed.*

*He always drives careful**ly**.*

It rained so heavily.
She divided them fairly.

Note that in the first example, *cleverly* is an adverb describing the verb *he did* (How did he do the task? Cleverly), and *really* is an adverb describing the adjective *impressed* (How impressed was I? Really impressed).

Ones That Got Away

*He doesn't play **fair**.*
*I've got it **bad**.*
*They're going **steady**.*
*Go **slow**!!*

All of these are acceptable colloquialisms, but you might think twice about using them in formal writing.

And here's an oddity: *She worked **extremely hard**. Hard* is an adverb qualifying the verb *worked* (How did she work? Hard). And *extremely* is an adverb qualifying the adverb *worked* (How hard did she work? Extremely hard). Despite the fact that *hard* looks like an adjective, we know that it is an adverb because it qualifies the verb. If you invented an adverbial form for it, you would get *she worked hardly*, which just sounds odd, or *she hardly worked*, which means something altogether different. Go figure.

Correctly Placing the Adverb Correctly

Although **word order** is usually important in English (see page 281), the position of the adverb is remarkably flexible. It may go after the verb, *She answered the question **hesitantly***, or it may go before the verb: *She **hesitantly** answered the question.* In fact sometimes it can go just about anywhere in a sentence:

> ***Scarily***, *she must have been dancing too close to the cliff.*
> *She **scarily** must have been dancing too close to the cliff.*
> *She must **scarily** have been dancing too close to the cliff.*
> *She must have **scarily** been dancing too close to the cliff.*
> *She must have been **scarily** dancing too close to the cliff.*
> *She must have been dancing **scarily** too close to the cliff.*
> *She must have been dancing too close to the cliff, **scarily**.*

Time, Manner, and Place

As with adjectives (see page 84), a group of words can serve as an adverb in an **adverbial clause** or **phrase**:

*I'll go to bed **when this TV show has ended**.*	Answering the question *When will you go to bed?*
*I'll pick you up **just up the road from the movie theater**.*	Answering the question *Where?*
*Some people do this **for fun**.*	Answering the question *Why?*—or perhaps *Why, oh why?*

That's a Bit Intense

Extra adverbs, used for emphasis, are called **intensifiers**: *soon **enough**, **very** nicely, **remarkably** good, **clearly** inadequate.*

But don't overuse adverbs too much: while adverbs can be used to great effect—

> *He is **tremendously** tiresome. She is **fantastically** daring.*
> *He's **disgustingly** rich.*—

it is easy to fall into the trap of using them tautologically (unnecessary repetition of meaning). One way of assessing whether your adverb adds anything is to consider a sentence with the opposite:

*She screamed **loudly**.*	As opposed to screaming quietly, perhaps?
*He clenched his fists **tightly**.*	How else could he clench his fists?

These are the adverbial equivalents of *close proximity* and *free gift* (see page 341).

Likewise, don't fall into the trap of using words such as *fourthly*. Where possible, just keep it simple:

First, I heard a bang.

Second, I switched on the light.

Third, I grabbed a hairbrush.

There is no need for *Fourth**ly**, I checked my make-up… Ninth**ly**, I went back to bed.*

Rule: If in doubt, leave your adverb out.

DANGLING BY A THREAD (OR, MISPLACED MODIFIERS)

"80 percent of married men cheat in America…"
(The rest cheat in Europe.)

*

"Set against the murky background of gangland London
and missing children—buy yours for $14.99…"
—Radio advertisement for a book

Misplaced modifiers, **dangling modifiers**, **dangling participles**, **misrelated participles**—these are all expressions that grammarians toss into the conversation on purpose to confuse and embarrass the rest of us. So what do they mean? Well, consider a sentence such as:

Walking down Main Street, the new shoe store caught her eye.

We probably all know what is *meant*, but grammatically what this sentence *says* is that the shoe store was walking down the street. The participle is dangling (or misplaced or misrelated) because it seems to relate to the wrong part of the sentence. *As she was walking down Main Street, the new shoe store caught her eye* is correct and unambiguous. As is *Walking down Main Street, she was thrilled to notice the new shoe store.*

Rule 1: The (unexpressed) subject of the participle clause—that is, the person or thing that is *walking down Main Street*—should have the same subject as the (expressed) subject of the main clause: *she.* Careless positioning of all sorts of modifiers can cause amusement, confusion or actions for libel:

Rule 2: The modifying clause or phrase (*walking down Main Street*) should always come as near as possible to the noun or pronoun it modifies. Otherwise you'll create unclear sentences like these:

- John still attends his local church where he was married regularly.

- We will continue to sell goods to people in plastic wrapping.

- She was taken to the hospital having been bitten by a spider in a bathing suit.

- American Catholic theologians will have to wait and see the exact wording of a French document permitting the use of condoms before engaging in theological debate.

- The mother of the accused said that God would judge her son in a news conference on Friday.

- The bride was given away by her father wearing her mother's wedding dress.

- Q: Doctor, how many autopsies have you performed on dead people? A: All my autopsies are performed on dead people.

"I once shot an elephant in my pajamas. How he got into my pajamas I'll never know."
—Groucho Marx

May I Compare Thee to a Summer's Day? (or, Comparatives)

"Poets and writers who are in love with the superlative all want to do more than they can."
—Friedrich Nietzsche

Comparatives (which may be adjectives or adverbs) compare two things. We say that one thing is *larger, faster, more lovely*, and *more* *temperate **than*** another thing, or that it runs *more swiftly, more elegantly, less galumphingly **than*** another.

> *The African elephant has **larger** ears **than** the Indian elephant.*
> *In Aesop's fable, the tortoise was **steadier than** the hare.*
> *Shoplifting is **less evil than** murder.*

Comparative adjectives usually employ the suffix *-er* if the original adjective is short enough for it not to become a mouthful. If it doesn't sound right to add *-er* (*beautifuller? temperater?* Don't think so), use the modifier *more: more beautiful, more temperate.* And if we want to say that it is *less* ugly or *less* beautiful—that's how we do it, however short the original adjective is.

Does it sound right? is often a good rule (the proper term is *euphony*, but *does it sound right?* will do just fine). *More big* when we mean *bigger* sounds just as silly as *beautifuller* when we mean *more beautiful.*

Also, there is the question of ambiguity. *The African elephant has **more big ears than** the Indian elephant* sounds as if the elephants have a collection of ears in large and small sizes.

> ☛ **See Me after Class:** Each comparison needs only one comparative suffix or word: *more better* is bad, *more betterer* is even worser.

For Better, for Worse

So often, it is the really common words that have irregular forms.

> *The movie he took me to see was **good**, but this one is **better**.*
> *The movie he took me to see was **bad**, but this one is **worse**.*

> *My father has **many** mansions, but Donald Trump probably*
>   *has **more**.*
> *I have **a lot** of trouble with grammar, but some sports*
>   *commentators have **more**.*

See also **superlatives,** below.

Comparing Like with Like

Most comparatives say that something is *more* or *less* something
than the other something, if you see what we mean. But it is also
a comparative to say that something is *the same* (or *not the same*) ***as***
something else:

> *He is **as** cunning **as** a fox.*
> *This ring is not **as** expensive **as** that one. (I want that one.)*

That's Superlative

> *And the **best** and the **worst** of this is*
> *That neither is **most** to blame,*
> *If you have forgotten my kisses*
> *And I have forgotten your name.*
> —Algernon Charles Swinburne, *An Interlude*

Superlatives are beyond compare. Nothing can be better or
worse. They are simply the b**EST**.

> *The giraffe is the tall**est** living animal.*
> *The Concorde was the fast**est** plane.*
> *Churchill was the great**est** prime minister.*

Most superlatives end in -*est*, although not *most*. Nor indeed
worst. And, as with comparatives, neither do longer words. Where
a comparative has *more* or *less*, a superlative has *most* or *least*:

Lord of the Rings *is the **most overrated** book of the twentieth century.*

All's Well That Ends Well *is perhaps the **least performed** of Shakespeare's plays.*

Superlatives refer to more than two things: you can't be the *best* of two players; the best you can manage is to be the *better.*

☛ **Teacher's Corner:** The Swinburne verse above may be very pretty, but it's another example of poets being allowed to break the rules:
*neither is **more** to blame,* please, Algernon!

The Most Worstest Thing You Could Say

As with comparatives, you need only one superlative, so all of these are howlers:

*It is **most nicest**.*

*I think that's the **biggerest**.*

*She is the **most wonderfullest** cook.*

*He is the **bestest** player the Tampa Bay Rays ever signed.*

*He is the **most best** teacher we've ever had.*

AND NOW WE'LL MOVE ON (OR, CONJUNCTIONS)

Conjunctions are joining words; they are used when we want to join two words, phrases, clauses, or sentences together.

*Friend **or** foe*   *Sad **but** true*
*Old **and** wise*   *Rich **though** poor*

There are four kinds of conjunctions: **coordinating**, **subordinating**, **correlative**, and **compound**.

Coordinating conjunctions join sentences (or parts of sentences) of equal importance. They can be remembered by the mnemonic **FANBOYS**:

For

And

Nor

But

Or

Yet

So

I like cats. She likes dogs.

*I like cats **and** she likes dogs.*	I'm doing no more than stating a fact here.
*I like cats **but** she likes dogs.*	…which is perhaps a bit of a shame.
*I like cats **so** she likes dogs.*	She is doing it on purpose, just to be contrary.

When a coordinating conjunction connects two independent clauses, it is often accompanied by a comma: *Should we run through that again, **or** can it wait until tomorrow?* The comma performs no real grammatical function, it simply suggests that you pause for breath. Which is a large part of a comma's job—see page 136.

Subordinating conjunctions link a main clause and a subordinate clause:

*I feel tired **because** I couldn't sleep last night.*
*I feel tired **although** I slept well last night.*
*I hope **that** I have made enough pizza.*
*I wonder **whether** I have bought enough wine.*

> ☛ **Teacher's Corner:** *Asyndeton* is the joining together of two or more complete sentences without the use of a coordinating conjunction—*I came, I saw, I conquered*—whereas *polysyndeton* is the use of multiple conjunctions, usually where they are not strictly necessary: *His hat **and** book **and** pen **and** pencil.*

Correlative conjunctions are used in conjunction with other conjunctions:

> *She owns **not only** an apartment in town **but also** a country house.*
> *She plays **not only** hockey **but also** lacrosse.*
> *Bob will grow up to be **either** sporty **or** clever.*
> *Bob grew up to be **neither** sporty **nor** clever.*
> *Bob's brother is **both** sporty **and** clever.*
> *I like **both** beer **and** lager.*

Rule: In sentences such as these, decide the position of the conjunction by checking on what follows it. They should be the same construction, whether noun, noun phrase, adjective, clause, or whatever. Consider the difference between these sentences:

> *She owns **not only** an apartment in town **but also** a country house.*
> *She **not only** owns an apartment in town, she **also** rents a villa in Tuscany.*
> ***Not only** does she own an apartment in town, but her parents **also** have a country house.*

In each case, the words following *also* balance the words following *not only*. And if you are remotely interested, see the bit about coordination on page 270.

Compound conjunctions is a fancy term for conjunctions made up of several words, often ending with *as* or *that*:

> *I don't mind family Christmases* **as long as** *I am allowed to come home for New Year's Eve.*
>
> *We can go* **as soon as** *you decide what to wear.*
>
> *He built a shed at the bottom of the garden* **so that** *he would have somewhere to keep his ferrets.*

A Word on *While* and *Although*

Although some grammarians argue that using *while* in the same way as *although* is perfectly acceptable, there are times when this can lead to confusion, miscommunication, and other bad things that grammar rules strive to avoid.

While she was writing, her pencil broke.	No problem here: her pencil broke at the same time as she was writing.
While I like tea, I would prefer gin.	Fine, but *although* would work equally well in place of *while*.
While Cyprus is hot, you can ski.	You're unlikely to misunderstand this, but replacing *while* with *although* would remove any possibility of ambiguity.
While Sally plays the triangle, Judy sings.	Aha. Now we have genuine ambiguity. Does Sally accompany Judy's singing, or is Judy's specialty singing and Sally's playing the triangle? If the latter, use *although*.

☛ **See Me after Class:** *While Father was away, Mother seemed to have a lot of fun.* Meaning?

A Bit of Coordination

Some conjunctions have a **coordinating** role between two parts of a sentence, and positioning them correctly can be something of a minefield. Let's start with *both. Both* goes directly before the first word of the two to which it refers. So in the sentence *I was **both** unhappy with your work and your time keeping*, the word *both* suggests that there is more than one person involved—which there can't be because there is only *I*.

The correct versions of this sentence are either:

*We were **both** unhappy with your work and your time keeping.*	I and whoever else makes up the *both* were unhappy with two things: your work and your time keeping

or

*I was **both** unhappy with your work and disappointed in your time keeping.*	I experienced two emotions

or

*I was unhappy with **both** your work and your time keeping.*	I was unhappy with two things

The same rule applies in sentences offering a choice of *either/or.*

Not *They had **either** decided to make an offer for the house in the suburbs or the apartment in town;*

nor   *They had decided **either** to make an offer for the house in the suburbs **or** the apartment in town;*

but   *They had decided to make an offer for **either** the house in the suburbs **or** the apartment in town;*

or   *They had decided **either** to make an offer for the house in the suburbs **or** to pay the asking price for the apartment in town.*

IT'S BEHIND YOU! (OR, PREPOSITIONS)

The word *preposition* means "something that is placed before." **Prepositions** are usually placed before nouns or pronouns. It's their job to show where one thing is in position to another; for example, *The cat is **on** the mat, I was **in front of** you.* Expressions such as *in front of, out of* and the like, made up of more than one word, are known (to the in-crowd) as **complex prepositions**.

If you are unsure what a preposition is, you might like to employ the following sentence:

The squirrel ran ———— the tree.

All you have to do is fill in the missing word. Almost any word you choose will be a preposition. For example:

to	*down*	*under*	*near*
by	*up*	*off*	*along*
around	*past*	*in*	*through*
for	*across*	*behind*	*in front of*
through	*over*	*from*	*out of*

Even *at, with,* and *after* would fit—if this particular squirrel is suicidal or we're in some sort of dream sequence. Others, such as *of, between,* and *before,* do not fit at all here, but you get the point.

For non-native speakers prepositions can be tricky. *I get **down off** the bus* tells us exactly what the person is doing, but most native speakers would make do with *I get **off** the bus.* However, even native speakers often think that two prepositions are better than one:

*I get **off of** the bus.* ☒   What's that *of* doing there?

*Put that **back down** on the table.* ☒

*I took a day **off from** work.* ☒

Sometimes even one is too many:

*Where did he go **to**?*

*She admitted **to** her mistakes.*

*All **of** the people present at the rally protested peacefully.*

*I'm going **down** south.*

> ✍ **Smart Aleck:** The use of more words than are necessary is *pleonasm* or *prolixity*.

Let's Not Ask for the Moon

Many prepositions are firmly wedded to other words:

*I **approve of** his choice. They're **discriminating against** us.*

However, others are more loosely connected:

*When I want your opinion I'll **ask for** it*	…but I might ***ask after*** your health.
*They've **taken in** everything you said to them*	…but she's ***taken off*** everything except her feather boa.
*You are **good at** what you do*	…which is better than being ***good for*** nothing.

Some prepositions tend to ruffle our feathers a bit:

absorbed in/by

> *I was **absorbed in** my book.*
> *All of a sudden I was **absorbed by** a giant sponge.*

agree with/approve of

> *I **agree with** your ideas.*
> *But I don't **approve of** children being taught grammar.*

aim at/to/for

> ***Aim at** that target.*
> ***Aim to** arrive at work before lunchtime.*
> ***Aim for** Paris and try to fly in a straight line.*

among/between

> *I put the cat **among** the (many) pigeons with my thoughtless comment.*
> *I placed a pigeon **between** my two cats to see what would happen.*

bored of

> *Wrong. We should be bored by or bored with something or somebody.*

center around/on

> *How can something center around something else? Presumably it would need to center around another center. Something centers on something—or is based on it.*

compare with/to

> *You can't **compare** my feet **to** an elephant's: they are too dissimilar to be compared.*
> ***Compared with** an elephant's, my feet look dainty.*

different to/from

Many books claim that *different from* is preferable to *different to* without explaining why. However, Fowler's *Modern English Usage* says "that *different* can only be followed by *from* & not by *to* is a SUPERSTITION. Not only is *to* 'found in writers of all ages' (OED); the principle on which it is rejected (You do not say differ to; therefore you cannot say different to) involves a hasty & ill-defined generalization." All of which is a long-winded way of saying that you can say *different to* if you like.

made of/made from

This one is a bit persnickety, but something is made *from* something that has been transformed; it is made *of* something that is still visible or recognizable:

*This ice cream is **made from** raspberries.*	So if you don't like raspberries, have the chocolate mousse instead.
*This pavlova is **made of** raspberries, cream, and meringue.*	So if you don't like raspberries, you can pick them out, and I'll eat them.

✋ Smart Aleck:

Why does your house burn up as it burns down?
How come you have to fill in a form to fill out a form?
Why can you see stars out but not lights out?

Get Us Out from under This

"May I end this sentence with a preposition?"
—Pickup line

Rule: It is wrong to end a sentence with a preposition. This seems to be a rule for a rule's sake. In fact, ending a sentence with a preposition rarely hinders its meaning and often sounds more natural, certainly in speech. Compare:

That's the office in which I work.	*That's the office I work in.*
The choir shown on Songs of Praise *is the one with which I sing.*	*The choir shown on* Songs of Praise *is the one I sing with.*
About what the heck are you talking?	*What the heck are you talking about?*

"This is the sort of English up with
which I will not put."
—Attributed to Winston Churchill

Ha-Ha

Suffering from impotence, a man visits several doctors asking for help, all to no avail. Finally, out of desperation, he visits an herbalist. The herbalist gives him a potion that can only be used once a year and tells him to take it before he is ready to be intimate. Then, when the time is right, he should say "one, two, three" and his impotence will be cured for as long as he likes. The man asks, "How do I make the potion stop working?" "Oh, that's easy," the doctor replies, "You just say, 'one, two, three, four.'" That evening before he enters the house, the man drinks the potion. He surprises his wife by immediately leading her to the bedroom. Things are going well and the man whispers, "One, two, three." His wife gives him a funny look and asks, "What'd you say 'one, two, three' for?" And **that** is why you never end a sentence with a preposition!

HOLY MOLY!
(OR, INTERJECTIONS)

An **interjection**—often followed by an exclamation mark—is used to show emotion. It is not grammatically linked to other parts of a sentence.

> *Bah! Darn! Eek! Good Lord! God bless you! Heavens! Yikes!*
> *Hey! Ouch! Oh no! No way! Nonsense! D'oh!*

Well, that was easy, wasn't it? We're not even going to bother to say, "Don't overdo exclamation marks!" at this stage, because there'll be plenty of that when we get to punctuation (see page 145).

3
Sentence
Structure

Do I Get Time Off for Good Behavior? (or, Sentences)

"A perfectly healthy sentence, it is true, is extremely rare.
For the most part we miss the hue and fragrance
of the thought; as if we could be satisfied
with the dews of the morning without their colors,
or the heavens without their azure."
—Henry David Thoreau

According to the dictionary, a **sentence** is "a sequence of words capable of standing alone to make an assertion, ask a question or give a command." All sentences…

1. Have a subject and a predicate (see page 281)
2. Begin with a capital letter
3. End in a period, a question mark, or an exclamation mark

There are various types of sentences, depending on how complicated they are:

A **simple sentence** consists of a single main clause or statement (we'll come back to what a clause is shortly—see page 295): *I like pink roses,* or *You prefer white roses.*

A **compound sentence** consists of two or more main clauses: *I like pink roses best, but I expect you'll choose white ones.*

Complex sentences have main clauses and subordinate clauses:

The roses, when they finally arrived, were yellow.

Really complex sentences (or **compound-complex sentences**, if we're going to be technical) have clauses coming out of their ears and often get a bit carried away with themselves: *The roses, which you say you ordered several days ago, didn't arrive until this morning, and were yellow, not pink or white by the way, so the bride is not happy.*

> ✋ **Smart Aleck:** The longest sentence in English literature is spoken by Molly Bloom in James Joyce's *Ulysses*. It contains 4,391 words, which makes it far too long to be quoted here.

Fragments

Complete sentences need a subject and a verb. Without these, they are known as **fragments**.

That wretched dress.
Waiting in the mall for her prescription.
Never in agreement about anything.

Fragments need the context of other sentences in order to convey their meaning:

I had an awful time at the party. Sally again. Going on and on about having worn the same dress as that new actress. That wretched dress.

I saw Sally again this morning. Waiting in the mall for her prescription. At least, that's what she was pretending to do. I'm sure she was really watching to see if I bought anything for the weekend.

What Kind of a Sentence Is That?

Many sentences simply make statements. The formal term for this is a declarative sentence. But sentences can also ask questions, give instructions or make exclamations:

A **declarative sentence:** *I saw you copying the files.*

An **interrogative sentence:** *Did you copy the files?*

An **imperative sentence:** *Don't even think of copying the files.*

An **exclamatory sentence:** *I repeat, I did not copy the files!*

Note, by the way, that an imperative sentence doesn't need a subject. In this instance the pronoun *you* is clearly implied.

Imperatives don't have to be bossy, just gently persuasive—which is probably why advertisers love them:

> *Just do it.*
>
> *Let your fingers do the walking.*
>
> *Don't leave home without it.*

SUBJECT–VERB–OBJECT

Here's a simple sentence: *I wrote a simple sentence.* It is made up of a subject, a verb, and an object. We know about verbs, so we can probably tell that in the above sentence the verb is *wrote.* The rest of the sentence consists of a subject and an object...

Rule 1: The **subject** is the person or thing carrying out the action in a sentence. (In this case *I.* Who wrote the simple sentence? I did.) The **object** is on the receiving end of the action. It is the thing being done to. (In this case, *a simple sentence.* What did I write? A simple sentence.) To determine the subject of a sentence, first find the **verb** and then ask *who?* or *what?* is doing the action. The answer will be the subject.

Rule 2: In a straightforward English sentence the subject will come first, the verb second, and the object third. (Grammarians refer to this as SVO.)

Subject	**Verb**	**Object**
Simple Simon	*met*	*a pieman*
Mary	*had*	*a little lamb*
Little Bo Peep	*has lost*	*her sheep*

Another useful piece of terminology here is the **predicate**. This is the verb and the object (or indirect object, or anything else that isn't the subject) considered together. So, in the above examples, *met a pieman, had a little lamb* and *has lost her sheep* are all predicates. So are *sat on a wall, jumped over the moon, sat on a tuffet* and *went up the hill to fetch a pail of water.* Who would have thought that nursery rhymes could prove so useful?

"Proper words in proper places
make the true definition of a style."
—Jonathan Swift, *Letter to a Young Clergyman*

*

"I have the words already. What I am seeking is the perfect order of words in the sentence.
You can see for yourself how many different ways
they might be arranged."
—James Joyce

Breaking the Subject-Verb-Object (SVO) Rule

The SVO rule can be broken for emphasis or stylistic effect:

John I can convince	…but James would never let me get away with such nonsense.
Chicken I can live without	…though I am rather partial to duck.

It's also broken with questions, when the verb commonly precedes the subject: *Who was that lady I saw you with last night?*

Direct and Indirect Objects

So far, so good. In some sentences, however, there is more than one object—a direct one and an indirect one.

Take this sentence: *My boss paid me a bonus.*

If you have been paying attention so far, you know that *my boss* is the subject of the verb *paid*. But now you have to ask:

What *did the boss pay?*	*He paid a* **bonus**	**direct object**
To ***whom*** *did he pay it?*	*To* **me**	**indirect object**

Hang on, you may say, how about *The boss paid me?* Doesn't that make *me* the direct object? Well, no. The test here is to see if you can rework the sentence to put a preposition in front of the object. If you can, it's an indirect object. You could easily rephrase the above example to become *My boss paid a bonus to me.* Clumsy, perhaps, but it makes sense (and it would be absolutely fine if you wanted to say *My boss paid a bonus to everyone in my department*).

Don't trip up on a sentence that begins with *there* and a form of the verb *to be. There* is not the subject in this case: *there were lots of people out for a walk today.* To find the correct subject, ask *who?* or *what?* before the verb. *Who was out for a walk today?* Answer: *lots of people.*

The Exception: It Would Be, Wouldn't It?

The exception to the subject-verb-object rule concerns— guess what—the verb *to be*. It doesn't take an object, it takes a **complement**. *To be*, and verbs used in a similar way, such as *to become, to seem, to taste* are called **copulative verbs** (honestly, they are—look it up in the dictionary yourself if you don't believe us)—they express a state rather than performing an action. So in sentences such as:

> *I am a New Yorker*
> *You became an artist*
> *He seems respectable enough*
> *The chocolates tasted of arsenic*

the words after the verb are the complement, and they may be nouns, pronouns, adjectives or adverbs, or phrases serving the same purpose (in the above example, *of arsenic* is an adverbial phrase qualifying the verb *tasted*).

ON THE SUBJECT OF I AND THE OBJECT OF ME (OR, SUBJECT AND OBJECT)

Unlike Latin, English nouns don't bother much with cases (different endings to show their relationship with other words in the sentence) because we express that sort of thing with prepositions (see page 271) and word order. In Latin a noun would have a different ending depending on whether it was the **subject** or the **object** of the verb, and if you wanted to say *to the noun* or *of the noun,* the endings would be different again. Then you could put the words in pretty much any order you liked and the endings would sort the meaning out for you. But English sentences such as *the dog chased the cat* and *the cat chased the dog* have exactly the same words in them and it is the order that establishes the meaning.

Pronouns don't follow this no-change rule. They do their own thing. Or their own thing is done to them.

Rule: **I = subject**

                            me = object

I is used for the subject of a sentence—the person doing the action.

Me is used for the object of the sentence—the person the verb is acting upon.

Not *Me telephoned Jim* but *I telephoned Jim.*	Because I performed the action.
Not *Jim rang I back* but *Jim rang me back.*	Because Jim performed the action.

Similarly: he/she/it/they = subject
him/her/it/them = object

Not *I adore he* but *I adore him.*	He is the *object* of my affection.
Not *Them were responsible* but *They were responsible.*	They *subjected* us to the horror.

This rule applies, but may be less obvious, when you have a **compound subject** or a **compound object**—that is, a subject or object that consists of more than one noun or pronoun.

*John and **I*** (compound subject) *went fishing.*

He gave the bait to John (or ***him***) *and **me*** (compound object).

*My husband and **I*** (compound subject) *are both going to the wedding.*

The groom has invited my husband (or ***him***) *and **me*** (compound object) *to the wedding.*

Hint: If you are unsure whether to use *I* or *me*, or *he* or *him*, in a compound subject or object, take out the other part. If you omit your husband from the last two examples you are left with:

I am going to the wedding (OK, you've had to change the verb from *are* to *am* because there's only one person involved now, but that's not the point here).

The groom has invited me to the wedding.

What's Wrong with Songwriters?

Beach Boys: *"My buddies and me are gettin' real well known…"*

The Beatles: *"Take a good look, you're bound to see that you and me were meant to be for each other…"*

Rule: The rules don't apply to songwriters. But surely they can't get no satisfaction from their writing.

Who Goes There? I or Me?

*It is **I** or It is **me**?*

*It wasn't **I** who said it or It wasn't **me** who said it?*

*It is **I** who am at fault or It is **me** who is at fault?*

> "'Somebody's sharp.' 'Who is?' asked the gentleman, laughing. I looked up quickly, being curious to know. 'Only Brooks of Sheffield,' said Mr. Murdstone. I was relieved to find that it was only Brooks of Sheffield; for, at first, I really thought it was I."
> —Charles Dickens, *David Copperfield*

Traditionally, *It is I* is correct, because Latin rules state that subject forms are found after the verb *to be*. However, modern thinking is that this sounds rather pretentious and old-fashioned. Most people will not bat an eyelid if you say *It was me*.

If that isn't good enough for you, try avoiding the issue by rephrasing:

He can't run as fast as me (or *I*) becomes

*He can't run as fast as **I can**.*

He's earning more than her (or *she*) becomes

*He's earning more than she **is**.*

Or, if you aren't happy with that, just decide which way you are going to go and stick to it. This sentence—heard on a radio news bulletin recently—fails on every count: *It was he who fired the gun and it was him who was killed.*

"Heedless of grammar, they all cried, 'That's him!'"
—Rev. R. H. Barham, *A Lay of Saint Gengulphus*

Between You and I

Here's the **I-me error** creeping in again. Lots of people are anxious about using *me*. But—between you and me—it is wrong to say *between you and I*.

Rule: Always use an object pronoun (*me*) after a preposition (*between*). (See page 101 for a list of prepositions.)

They can't take that away from me…

I've been to paradise but I've never been to me…

It's good night from me, and it's good night from him.

> "Between you and me and the grand piano, I'm afraid my
> father was rather a bad hat."
> —*The Uninvited* (film), 1944

My Grammar and I (or should that be "me"?)

Few of us will have cause to ask (or answer, or give a darn about) this question in real life. However, this book does ask it, so it seems only courteous to try to answer it:

> *This book is **about** (preposition) my grammar and **me** (object pronoun).*

> ***My grammar** (subject) and **I** (subject pronoun) are not on good terms.*

In a book title, we think it is safe to assume that *Grammar and I* form a compound subject (see page 286).

Remember Your Manners

If you are talking about yourself and another person, it is polite to mention the other person first.

> *Wishing you both great happiness from me and Gary.* ☒
> *Wishing you both great happiness from Gary and me.* ☑

> *I and my wife would like to thank everyone for coming.* ☒
> *My wife and I would like to thank everyone for coming.* ☑

But there's no need to be too humble:

> *With lots of love from the children, the dog and me...*

Nor too full of oneself:

> *James and **myself** went fishing.*
> *James and **I** went fishing* will do very well.

On the Subject of Who and the Object of Whom

"What is fame? The advantage of being known by
people of whom you yourself know nothing,
and for whom you care as little."
—Lord Byron

*

"As far as I'm concerned,
whom is a word that was invented
to make everyone sound like a butler."
—Calvin Trillin

Rule 1:   **who = subject**
whom = object

*This is the woman **who** swallowed a fly.*	The woman swallowed the fly. The woman is the subject of the verb.
*This is the woman **whom** the fly choked.*	The fly choked the woman. She is now the object of the verb.

Rule 2: As with other pronouns, the object form is used after a preposition (see page 271):

*The people **to whom** I spoke didn't seem to know anything about it.*

*That boy **above whom** we all towered when we were at school is taller than any of us now.*

*Send not to ask **for whom** the bell tolls.*

DON'T YOU AGREE?
(OR, AGREEMENT)

Rule: Parts of a sentence must agree with each other. A singular subject takes a singular verb, while a plural subject takes a plural verb.

> *I **was born** in a caravan.*
>
> ***She is** only a bird in a gilded cage.*
>
> *What **were we** talking about?*
>
> *They **don't** make them like that any more.*

Straightforward enough? Less obvious, perhaps, are:

*He is one of those **men who sing** in the shower.*	*Those men*, plural, are the subject of the verb *sing*.
*A **person knows** when **he/she is** being rude.*	Many people nowadays would say, *A person **knows** when they are being rude.* Perhaps better to avoid the issue by saying, *People **know** when **they are** being rude* instead.

And what about:

> *My brother **and** his girlfriend (two people) **have** taken the spare room.*
>
> *It sounds as if my brother **or** his girlfriend (one or the other but not both) **has** used all the hot water.*

Rule: Use a plural verb with two or more subjects when they are connected by *and*. Two singular subjects connected by *or* or *nor* take the singular form of the verb.

And another rule: *Either* and *neither* are both singular. ***Neither of them has*** *thought about my needing to wash.* ***Either he*** *or* ***she is*** *bathing last tomorrow, if I have any say in the matter.*

Along Came a Distraction

Sometimes an expression may creep between a subject and its verb. Don't let this lead you astray.

> ***The nanny***, *along with the cook and the housekeeper,* ***has*** *caught chicken pox from the children.*
>
> ***Poisoning***, *as well as the shock of the bite,* ***was*** *the cause of death.*
>
> ***My husband***, *with our neighbor and his dog,* ***is*** *walking the coastal path.*

We'll have a closer look at those parenthetical commas in the next chapter, but for the moment just note that they are precisely that—a parenthesis or bracket—and everything between them could be lifted out of the sentence without altering the grammatical relationship between the subject and the verb.

☛ **See Me after Class:**
Each *of the boys* ***were*** *good at grammar.*
Were he indeed?
Every *cat* ***have their*** *own bowl.*
No: ***every*** *cat* ***has its*** *own bowl.*
Just as ***every*** *cat* ***has*** *a tail.*

Useful mnemonic: think of these words as *each one* and *every one*, and you'll remember to use a singular verb and a singular pronoun.

Rule: The following words are singular and require singular verbs:

anybody	*every*	*one*
anyone	*everybody*	*somebody*
each	*everyone*	*someone*

However, *any, all, most,* and *some* can be either singular or plural. It depends whether they are being applied to countable or non-countable nouns (see page 217).

*All of the petty cash **has** been stolen.*

*All of the suspects **have** gone to the pub together.*

*Some of their discarded kebabs **have** been discovered.*

*Some of the money **has** been found.*

*Most of it **is** still missing.*

*Most of the culprits **are** nursing hangovers.*

Rule: *Many, both, a few,* and *several* are always followed by a plural verb.

I've Got Your Number

Numerical expressions can be rather tricky, but just remember that the expression *the number* is singular, which means it should be followed by a singular verb:

*The number **is** 6.*

*The number in question **is** 666.*

*The number of people unaccounted for **is** 6,000.*

*The number of people who died **was** 60,000.*

Exception: *A number of* is used with plural nouns and takes a plural verb:

*A number of people **were** in shock after the incident.*

Numerical expressions, however, take either the singular or plural form of the verb, according to whether they are being referred to as a single entity or as individuals within a group.

*A million dollars **is** a lot of money.*

*A million homes **are** reported to be without power today.*

***Two** years **is** a long time to wait.*

*The **two** years since I saw you **have** dragged by.*

***Half** the people at the party **have** food poisoning.*

*The **remainder** of the guests **are** still enjoying the party.*

And Then There Was None…

You're likely to come across conflicting views on this one. Many people believe that *none* is a contraction of *not one*, and therefore should always take the singular verb. *None* may also mean *not any*, however, in which case it takes a plural verb.

Rule: *None* is singular only when it means *no amount*. If you mean *not one* you could always say *not one*, particularly if you want to add emphasis.

*None of the wine **was** left in the bottle.*

*None of the drinks **are** paid for.*

*None of the food **is** fresh.*

*None of the people **are** well.*

How Many Objects Exactly?

Another common area of confusion between singular and plural comes in sentences such as:

Many men cheat on their wife/wives?

The boys put their hands on their head/s?

Are we talking about bigamists as well as adulterers here? Or a number of men sharing a single wife? Many-headed boys? Or boys sharing a single head?

Rule: The two elements should agree. ***Men***, plural, even monogamous ones, *have **wives***, plural. ***Boys***, even non-freaky ones, *have **heads***.

Or you can write the sentences differently and duck the issue:

Many a man cheats on his wife.

Each boy put his hands on his head.

FROM MAJOR TO MINOR (OR, CLAUSES)

A **clause** is a sentencelike construction with a subject and predicate, including a finite verb (see pages 242 and 293 for an explanation of those things). Some clauses, but by no means all, stand alone as sentences. A clause that can stand alone as a sentence is known as the **main clause**; anything else is a **subordinate clause**.

I can't play the piano as well as my sister, even though I practice more than she does.

I can't play the piano as well as my sister is a perfectly good sentence on its own. It has a subject (*I*) and a finite verb (*play*) and makes a complete statement. *Even though I practice more than she does* is not. It has a subject (*I*) and a finite verb (*practice*), but it depends on the first clause (*I can't play the piano as well as my sister*) to become a complete statement.

But it's perfectly possible for a sentence to have two main clauses, in which case they are called **coordinating clauses** and are usually linked by *and, but,* or *or*:

*I'm going to play the piece by Mozart, **and** she will play the piece by Chopin.*

*I wanted to play the Chopin, **but** she had first choice.*|
*I might play in the concert, **or** I might decide to go to a bar
    instead.*

In all these examples either of the two clauses can stand alone.

As its name suggests, a **subordinate clause** carries information that is of secondary importance to that contained in the main clause.

A subordinate clause often begins with a subordinate conjunction such as *after, although, as, because, though, if, in order to, rather than, since, so that, unless,* and so on.

*Unfortunately I won't be playing, **because I've broken my
    finger.***
*She won the role, **although nobody thought she had a
    chance.***

Or it may begin a relative pronoun (*that, which, whichever, who, whoever, whom, whose, whosoever, whomever*), in which case it is called a **relative clause**.

*I used to know the spy **who came in from the cold.***
*I used to know the spy **whom the Russians codenamed
    Smirnoff.***
*I will claim to have known **whichever of the spies you bring
    into the conversation.***

Which Is That?

Restrictive clauses (also sometimes called **defining clauses**) define or classify a noun or pronoun in the main clause. **Non-restrictive** or **non-defining clauses** offer further description. A non-restrictive clause is usually preceded by a pause in speech or a comma in writing, whereas a restrictive clause is not. A non-restrictive clause is also usually *followed* by a pause or a comma, if it does not end the sentence.

Rule: Non-restrictive clauses are dispensable. Their role is merely to give additional information.

Sorry, have we lost you? Let's look at some examples. Although the following sentences make grammatical sense without their subordinate clauses, they do not convey much information—the restrictive clause is essential.

*The man **that died on the trip** was once my history teacher.*
*The car **that broke down** is now in the garage.*
*You look like the cat **that got the canary**.*

Take out that clause and you are left with:

The man was once my history teacher.	Which man? Why are you telling me this? Why should I care?
The car is now in the garage.	Again, which car? So what?
You look like the cat.	Duh? I think you'll find I don't have whiskers or a tail.

On the other hand,

*The history teacher, **who had a trusty aim with the eraser**, ensured that we never forgot important dates.*
*The car, **which broke down halfway through France**, had to be towed back to England.*
*My new cat, **which somehow jumped on the counter and ate the hot dogs last night**, came home with someone's trout today.*

You don't feel obliged to ask *Which history teacher?*, *Which car?*, *Which cat?* at the end of these sentences. The information given in the subordinate clause is a bonus.

Now consider the difference between these:

The dogs that barked at night did not recognize the thief.	**Restrictive:** Some of the dogs *did* recognize the thief and therefore did not bark.
The dogs, which barked in the nighttime, did not recognize the thief.	**Non-restrictive:** None of the dogs recognized the thief and all of them barked.

Or

I cut down all the trees that were evergreen.	**Restrictive:** Some of them were deciduous and I left them alone.
I cut down all the trees, which were evergreen.	**Non-restrictive:** I've destroyed the entire forest and, by the way, all the trees were evergreen.

In both cases illustrated above, restrictive clauses are introduced by that. Non-restrictive clauses are introduced by the relative pronouns *who*, *whom*, *whose*, and *which*, but never by *that*.

It boils down to this: if you can tell what is being discussed without the *which* or *that* clause, use *which*; if you can't, use *that*. Or, as a rule of thumb, if the phrase needs a comma, you probably should use *which*.

Is It Which or That?

Grammarians are divided over whether *which* or *that* should be used in restrictive clauses. While researching this book, we came across all of the following in apparently respectable sources:

> "Many grammarians insist on a distinction without any historical justification."

> "*Which* and *that* are equally acceptable in restrictive relative clauses; *that* is perhaps the less formal of the two."

> "Don't mix *which* clauses with *that* clauses."

It boils down to this: if you can tell what is being discussed without the *which* or *that* clause, use *which*; if you can't, use *that*. Or, as a rule of thumb, if the phrase needs a comma, you probably mean *which*.

A paradoxical mnemonic: use *that* to tell which, and *which* to tell that.

HOW DO YOU PHRASE THAT? (OR, PHRASES)

A **phrase** is a group of words that has either no subject or no predicate, meaning it cannot form a complete sentence on its own. You can have verb phrases (*may sink in gradually*), noun phrases (*grammatical rules*), and adjectival phrases (*even the most complicated*) but until you put them all together (*even the most complicated grammatical rules may sink in gradually*), you don't have a sentence.

Actually there are lots of other kinds of phrases, too:

Participial phrases: *Having to get up in the morning is the worst part of my day.*

Infinitive phrases: *My ambition is **to retire by the time I am fifty**.*

Adverbial phrases: *I work a long way away, so I need to leave home **before my wife**.*

Prepositional phrases: *I would love to be able to stay **in bed**.*
But you don't really have to worry about these technical terms—as long as you remember *to set the alarm.*

4
Punctuation

PUNCTUATION:
THE VIRTUE OF THE BORED?

Author Evelyn Waugh once said that *punctuality* was the virtue of the bored, but he doesn't seem to have said anything witty about punctuation, so we thought we'd just paraphrase him in the title above.

Punctuation can be defined as "the act, practice, or system of using certain standardized marks and signs in writing and printing," and punctuation marks are symbols that are used in sentences and phrases to make their meaning clearer. Those most commonly used in English are the period (.), comma (,), question mark (?), exclamation point (!), semi-colon (;), colon (:), apostrophe ('), and quotation marks (" ").

Cecil Hartley's poem from *Principles of Punctuation* or *The Art of Pointing* (1818) reveals the old-fashioned way that people were advised on how to interpret punctuation when reading sentences out loud.

> The stops point out, with truth, the time of pause
> A sentence doth require at ev'ry clause.
> At ev'ry comma, stop while *one* you count;
> A semicolon, *two* is the amount;
> A colon doth require the time of *three;*
> The period *four,* as learned men agree.

Though it's not a verse that most grammarians would encourage these days, it does give you an idea of the difference between the most common punctuation marks.

> ☛ **Teacher's Corner:** Punctuation existed in Greek texts from at least the fourth century B.C., although Greek and Latin scribes rarely used more than two marks, the equivalent of the period and the comma.

STOP! (OR, PERIODS)

The **period** is the strongest mark of punctuation. It shows its muscle by telling us we need to make a definite pause at the end of a sentence, giving us time to gather our breath or our thoughts, before moving on to the next sentence. Ignore the pause and sentences run together: meaning becomes confused. Periods are also used in (some) abbreviations (see below). They are not used:

- when we end a sentence with another punctuation mark, a question mark or an exclamation point, for example. *Understand? Of course you do!*

- if a sentence ends with an abbreviation. In this case, the period indicating the abbreviation does the job of two: *I have to go out at 9:00 P.M.*

From the Long to the Short of It

An **abbreviation** (from Latin *brevis,* meaning *short*) is a shortened form of a word or phrase that for whatever reason we do not choose to write out in full. Strictly speaking, an abbreviation is a word or words with the end(s) left off (*Prof.*, *vol.*, *CD*, *VP*), whereas one where something is left out of the middle (*Mr.*, *Dr.*) is a **contraction**, but most people use *abbreviation* indiscriminately to cover both. If an abbreviation of several words forms something that is pronounced as a word in itself (*UNESCO*, *radar*, *scuba*, *AIDS*), this is an **acronym**.

Unlike British English, American English uses the period after contractions such as *Mr.*, *Mrs.*, and *Dr.* Both, however, still use the period for *No.*, *A.M.*, and *P.M.*

A number of common words such as *cello*, *flu*, and *phone* are actually abbreviations or clipped forms (of *violoncello*, *influenza*, and *telephone*) and would once have been written with an apostrophe (or two): *'cello*, *'flu'*, *'phone*. Some people still do this, but most would say it was old-fashioned. Some shortenings have become so accepted that to use the long form of the word would sound pompous:

> *Jane will not be at work today because she thinks she might have **influenza**.*

> *Tim works out at the **gymnasium** every day and then catches the **omnibus** home.*

On the other hand, *stache* instead of *moustache*, *doc* instead of *doctor*, or *gator* instead of *alligator* may be too casual for formal writing.

> ☝ **Smart Aleck:** How come the word *abbreviation* is so long?

TAKE A DEEP BREATH (OR, COMMAS)

"For want of merely a comma, it often occurs
that an axiom appears a paradox."
—Edgar Allan Poe, *"Marginalia"* (1848)

Historically, the **comma** marks a short pause, a place where you might pause for breath after reading a fragment of text aloud. In grammar, the comma is used to facilitate meaning by separating the different elements of a sentence. Some people are comma-happy; they put commas anywhere and everywhere:

Dear Professor Purvis, [comma, pause for breath]

Please may I have an extra, short, extension on my very late, and, at this point in time, largely unfinished, English dissertation?

Other people prefer to leave them out altogether:

Dear Professor Purvis

Please may I have an extra short extension on my very late and at this point in time largely unfinished English dissertation?

In the first example, there are so many pauses that it takes forever to get to the point. In the second, with no pauses at all, we risk losing the plot. How should we interpret *an extra short extension*? Is it *an extra, short extension* (that is, a short extension in addition to the longer extension already granted) or *an extra-short extension* (an extremely short one, much shorter than the sort of extension that would usually be requested)? Just a smattering of punctuation would have helped here.

Ha-Ha

My apologies for using this terribly old joke, but it illustrates the point.

A college professor wrote on his blackboard: *a woman without her man is nothing.* He then asked his students to punctuate the sentence. All of the males in the class wrote: *a woman, without her man, is nothing.* All of the females in the class wrote: *a woman: without her, man is nothing.*

So Where Does a Comma Go?

We spent most of our time sitting on the back porch
watching the cows playing Scrabble and reading.

A comma can go in lots of places. Here are seventeen examples:

1. At a place in a sentence where you wish your readers to pause:

    Take a breather, will you?

2. After introductory words or phrases that come before the main clause:

    In the autumn of 1066, the English lost the Battle of Hastings.
    Once upon a time, there lived a boy called Jack.
    Of course, .../However, .../Finally, .../Yes, ...

3. Between separate clauses within a sentence:

   In the beginning, when God created the universe, the earth was formless and desolate.

4. Before direct speech:

   He asked, "Can you tell me why I should pay attention to these rules?"'

5. In addresses and place names where one part of the place name gives further information about the other:

   The White House, 1600 Pennsylvania Ave., Washington, D.C.
   The President was assassinated by a gunman in Dallas, Texas (as opposed to any other Dallas).

6. On either side of parenthetical phrases or clauses (those non-restrictive parts that contain extraneous information; see page 309). These are known as paired or parenthetical commas, so there must always be two of them:

   She backed up into the traffic barrier, which she could have sworn was not there an hour before, causing considerable damage to her car.
   One day in the near future, if we can believe what scientists tell us, this planet will run out of oxygen.

7. After items in a list:

   My favorite Victorian novelists are the Brontë sisters, Wilkie Collins, Charles Dickens, and Thomas Hardy.

8. In large numbers. In numbers of more than three digits, use a comma after every third digit (reading

from right to left):

I make that 6,000 people.

20,000 leagues under the sea.

The population of Argentina is 34,663,000.

But note that in scientific texts and particularly in tables of figures the comma is sometimes replaced by a space: *6 000, 20 000, 34 663 000.*

9. Around a non-restrictive clause. Be careful with commas here. They change what you mean to say:

I pulled up all the flowers that looked like weeds.	**Restrictive:** I pulled up only the flowers that looked like weeds.
I pulled up all the flowers, which looked like weeds.	**Non-restrictive:** I heartlessly tore all the flowers out of the ground; they also looked like weeds.

10. Before and after an appositive (that's a word or phrase that defines or modifies a noun or pronoun that comes before it):

I, Jane Jones, declare that I was at home on the evening of September 25.

Chérie Blair, wife of former Prime Minister Tony Blair, was accused of not liking cats.

And again, note the difference between:

My upstairs neighbor Bill plays loud music.	There could also be an upstairs neighbor called Ben, for all we know.
My upstairs neighbor, Bill, plays loud music.	Bill is the only upstairs neighbor.

11. Between a dependent clause and an independent clause, where the dependent clause comes first:

    After lunch, my stomach was upset.

    The comma here is optional, but it does indicate (the possibility of) a pause for breath. However, you wouldn't pause for breath in the sentence *My stomach was upset after lunch*, so no comma is necessary.

12. After consecutive adjectives that are equally important in describing a noun:

    In the dreary light of the morning, the rows of gray, pebble-dashed houses, with their unkempt, litter-strewn gardens, failed to inspire tender thoughts of home.

13. In front of conjunctions such as *like, although, but, or, so, and* and *yet* when they are used to link two independent clauses:

    The show was over, but the crowd refused to leave.
    It's going to be a long night, so let's get those coffees in.

14. In place of a word that has been deliberately omitted:

    The room was cold, the bed hard.

15. Before the word *too* when it means *also*:

    Two pairs of ballet shoes and two tutus, too.

    Parenthetical commas can also add emphasis to the word *too* if it appears in the middle of a sentence:

    He'd never really thought about where to put commas in a sentence, but then, too, he'd never thought much about punctuation at all.

16. To emphasize an adverb:

I wrote it down, quickly, which is why I went to the wrong address.

17. After greetings and before closings in letters:

Dear Sir,

Sincerely,

This used to be a hard-and-fast rule, but it is beginning to fall out of favor. Now the hard-and-fast rule is *be consistent:* if you use a comma after *Dear Sir,* use one after *Sincerely,* too.

☞ **See Me after Class:** *I find writing English essays really difficult, I'm sure everyone finds that inspiration does not always come instantly, I think you'll find that is so.*

These could be treated as three distinct sentences, separated by periods; or they could be clauses, separated by semicolons. Or, in informal writing, if you wanted to make them sound a bit breathless, you could use dashes. But, sorry, the commas here are just wrong wrong wrong.

Are you feeling tired? Bored? Confused? Let's move on to something more straightforward.

The Serial Comma

The Oxford, Harvard, or serial comma is placed before the final *and,* *or,* or *nor* in a list of more than two elements. (The names are derived from the Oxford University Press and Harvard University Press, both advocates of this usage.) In British English, it is mostly used to avoid ambiguity, but it is more often used in American English.

He introduced me to Mr. Brown, his teacher and his friend. (He introduced me to one person, Mr. Brown, who happened to be both his teacher and his friend.)

He introduced me to Mr. Brown, his teacher, and his friend. (He introduced me to two people: his unnamed friend and a teacher, whose name was Mr. Brown. Or indeed, if the speaker is particularly grammatically unaware, to three people: Mr. Brown, plus the teacher of either Mr. Brown or the speaker, plus a friend of the teacher, Mr. Brown or the speaker.)

Serial commas are particularly useful if one of the items in a list already contains the word *and,* or in sentences such as this one, where the items of the list are a complicated collection of phrases or clauses. Dick King-Smith's novel *Poppet* contains this perfect example: "He asked beetles and grubs and worms and caterpillars and little lizards and small frogs, and some replied jokily and some replied angrily and some didn't answer."

WHAT IS THIS, THE SPANISH INQUISITION? (OR, QUESTION MARKS)

'To whom, then, must I dedicate my wonderful, surprising and interesting adventures? to whom dare I reveal my private opinion of my nearest relations? the secret thoughts of my dearest friends? my own hopes, fears, reflections and dislikes? Nobody!'
—Frances Burney

Question: When do you use a **question mark**?

Answer: At the end of a direct question.

Well, we'd probably better go into just a little more detail.

Direct questions are things such as:

Where were you when I needed you?

When did you last see your father?

Who's the best team this year?

Indirect questions are things such as:

I wonder who's kissing her now.

I didn't hear what he said.

I know where you are coming from.

These sentences aren't questions, they are statements: *I wonder, I didn't hear, I know,* so they don't need a question mark.

Rule: A direct question needs a ?; an indirect question does not.

Hint: To spot an indirect question, look out for the words *ask* or *wonder,* often followed by *if.*

A question in the form of a statement, known as an **embedded question**, also doesn't require a question mark: *The question whether children learn enough grammar remains to be answered.*

Hint: Look out for the words *whether* or *if*—they often indicate embedded questions.

But *The question is, "Do today's children learn enough grammar?"* The opening words plus the comma have set the scene for direct speech, and the direct speech takes the form of a direct question. So—yes, you've guessed, go to the head of the class—it needs a question mark.

Note: One *asks* a question.
"How much does it cost?" he said. ☒
"How much?" he asked/inquired/questioned. ☑

Rhetorical questions—questions to which we do not expect an answer—are still questions and deserve to end with a question mark: *How much longer must our people endure this injustice?*

Question upon Question

Sometimes a question will be followed with a series of brief questions. When that happens, especially when the brief questions are more or less follow-up questions to the main one, the little questions can begin with a lower-case letter and end with a question mark. Both of the following are correct:

Who is responsible for this? The boy who cheated? The girl who told? Or the teacher who left the answers on her desk?

Who is responsible for this? the boy? Sarah? or Mrs. Dean, who was out smoking a cigarette in the middle of the exam?

But, as so often when there are alternative ways of doing things, you should decide which style you are going to use and use it consistently.

Rule: Do not put a period after a sentence that ends with a question mark. But when a question ends with an abbreviation, end the abbreviation with a period and then add the question mark. *Do you mean 3:00 P.M. or 3:00 A.M.?*

Are You Questioning My Orders?

When a question is really an instruction, use a period instead of a question mark.

Would you take these books back to the library for me?	A polite request. Is it convenient for you to do this?
Would you take back the books as I asked you to do yesterday.	An order. You'd better or else.

SOMETHING TO SHOUT ABOUT (OR, EXCLAMATION MARKS)

"Cut out all these exclamation points.
An exclamation point is like laughing at
your own joke."
—F. Scott Fitzgerald, quoted in *Beloved Infidel* (1958)

The **exclamation point** may be used at the end of a sentence in the place of a period, in order to express strong emotion, such as excitement, delight, fear, anger, or surprise.

Hey!	*Watch out!*
Boo!	*Stop!*
Woohoo!	*Run!*
Wow!	*Fire!*
Ouch!	*Detention! Now!*

They may also be used to catch the reader's attention. Compare:

Slow workmen in road.

Slow! Workmen in road.

Elephants please stay in your car.

Elephants! Please stay in your car.

But beware of overkill. Too many exclamation points make writing overheated. There are no real rules about using them, except *Please restrain yourself.* If you overdo it—

I'd love to! Thank you so much for asking! I'll be there in plenty of time! Oh, I'm so excited!

I'll kill you!!!!!!

Get out!!!!!

It tastes disgusting!!!!!

—you lose the impact that a single, well-placed exclamation point might have. A well-written sentence should be able to pack its own punch. Besides which, exclamation points are visually distracting and can get really annoying!!!!

Rule: An exclamation point ends a sentence in place of a period and should be followed by a capital letter.

➤ **See Me after Class:**
"You won't give me detention, will you?!"
"What is the meaning of this '?!'"

(**Answer: An interrobang**. In formal writing, don't use a question mark in combination with other marks.)

TWO DOTS
(OR, COLONS)

Rule: A **colon** informs the reader that what follows sums up or explains what has come before.

For example, it may be used to link two main clauses, where the second clause explains the first.

> *She was delighted to have the offer accepted: It was the third time she had bid on the house.*

Or to introduce a list of items (or, indeed, an example):

> *The cake contained ingredients found lying in the back of the kitchen cupboard: flour, baking soda, dried orange peel, sultanas, raisins, brown sugar, nutmeg, cinnamon, and mixed spices. To this, we just added some milk and an egg from the fridge.*

> *You will need: strong footwear, waterproof clothing, a change of clothes, high-energy snacks, a small first-aid kit, a good map, and a flashlight.*

SUPERCOMMA TO THE RESCUE (OR, SEMICOLONS)

"There were pears and apples, clustered high in blooming pyramids; there were bunches of grapes, made, in the shopkeepers' benevolence, to dangle from conspicuous hooks, that people's mouths might water gratis as they passed; there were piles of filberts, mossy and brown, recalling, in their fragrance, ancient walks among the woods, and pleasant shufflings ankle deep through withered leaves; there were Norfolk Biffins, squat and swarthy, setting off the yellow of the oranges and lemons, and, in the great compactness of their juicy persons, urgently entreating and beseeching to be carried home in paper bags and eaten after dinner."
—Charles Dickens, *A Christmas Carol*

Now fighting a losing battle against the less elegant dash (see page 150), the **semicolon** connects two or more independent clauses that don't *quite* justify being sentences in their own right. It often replaces *and* or *but*. It may be helpful to think of it as a "supercomma."

I have tickets for the U.S. Open tomorrow. I bet it rains.	These two short sentences read a bit jerkily.
I have tickets for the U.S. Open tomorrow but I bet it rains.	A little clumsy.
I have tickets for the U.S. Open tomorrow; I bet it rains.	Much better!

Rule 1: You must have a finite clause sentence (see page 295) on both sides of the semicolon.

Rule 2: Semicolons are followed by a lower-case letter, unless the word in question is a proper noun. A semicolon is also used instead of a comma to break up items in a long and complicated list, particularly when the list has plenty of commas in it already, as in the Dickens quote above.

DASH AWAY ALL (OR, DASHES)

A **dash** (—) is a horizontal line that may be used alone, or as a pair in place of brackets. It introduces an aside, an interruption, or an additional piece of information, indicates a sudden change of emotion or thought, or shows that words have been omitted at the end of a sentence that has been broken off.

> *He had said that he would marry her when he got his next promotion—and she, poor girl, believed him.*
> *She—poor girl—believed him.*
> *After hours of careful preparation the experiment actually worked—eureka!*
> *They want that contract—which means they get that contract—by the end of today.*
> *He is an excellent employee, but—*

A dash can also indicate that we are carrying on where we left off: *—as I was telling you, I wouldn't be seen dead in a ditch with her.*

Nowadays, dashes are riding roughshod over the poor old semi-colon (*I have tickets for the U.S. Open tomorrow—I bet it rains*), and this is becoming more acceptable, especially in informal writing.

Americans use the longer em-dash (—) and no spaces, while British English usually uses an en-dash (–) with a space on either side of it.

A dash also sometimes takes the place of letters in order to "disguise" curse words (does this really fool anybody?). In this case, the closed-up em-dash, or something longer, is usual on both sides of the Atlantic:

That man who hit me was a real b———d.
Oh, s———.

> ✋ **Smart Aleck:** An en-dash is named for the width of a typesetter's *n* key. The longer em-dash is the width of a typesetter's *m* key.

JOINED-UP WRITING (OR, HYPHENS)

"A knave, a rascal, an eater of broken meats, a base proud, shallow, beggarly, three-suited, hundred-pound, filthy-worsted-stocking knave; a lily-livered, action-taking, whoreson glass-gazing super serviceable finical rogue, one-trunk-inheriting slave."
—William Shakespeare, *King Lear*

A **hyphen** looks like a short dash but isn't used in the same way. Its function is to join two or more words to show that they belong to each other, and also to separate syllables when necessary—for example, when a word is split in half at the end of a line of type. Hyphens are rather going out of fashion these days, particularly in American English, but they are often useful (and sometimes essential) in clarifying meaning, as the examples below illustrate.

Hang glider pilots in training today.

He wore a new dress shirt and jacket to the dinner.

Fox hunting supporters.

It was a long overdue visit.

They were speaking a nonnative language.

Thirteen year-old boys take placement exams here tomorrow.

She went through it with a fine tooth-comb.

In the above examples, common sense tells us where a hyphen would have been useful. (*Fine-toothed comb*, please!)

Some hyphen rules:

- Be careful with compound adjectives. Hyphenating these incorrectly, or not hyphenating them at all, can cause confusion because we don't know which words go together: *Thirteen-year-old* boys take placement exams; *thirteen year-old boys* would be far too young, and are an unlucky number anyway.

- A hyphen is unnecessary if other punctuation makes the meaning clear without it:

  The old English teacher droned on and on.

  The Old English teacher droned on and on.

  The fact that the word old is capitalized in the second sentence makes all the difference: in the first sentence we know that the teacher is old; in the second, it is the English that is old.

The usefulness of the hyphen in forming compounds that serve as adjectives before nouns is demonstrated in the entries ill- ajd well-.

Example: *She wore a well-tailored suit.*

But the hyphen is omitted when the words follow the noun they modify: The suit was well tailored.

"Quotation Marks"

"'You are old, Father William,' the young man said,
'And your hair has become very white;
And yet you incessantly stand on your head—
Do you think, at your age, it is right?'"
—Lewis Carroll, *You Are Old, Father William*

Rule: In direct speech (when we write the actual words that are spoken) we need quotation marks. These may be single or double. Both are correct, in some instances although if you quote within speech, use single within double: *"I find the government's 'nanny state' attitude really irritating," he said.*

Another rule: Punctuation goes inside the closing quotation mark:

"Punctuation goes inside the closing quotation mark," I said.

"Where did you say the punctuation should go?" he asked for the umpteenth time.

"Inside the inverted comma!" I snapped.

If the spoken words end the sentence, there is no need for extra punctuation:

He asked, "Is this the end?"
They replied, "This is the end."
She screamed, "Help!"

Note that in such a sentence as *"Can anybody hear me?" she yelled.* there is no capital letter after the question mark, because it is all the same sentence despite all that punctuation.

Something to Report?

Rule: Do not use quotation marks for **indirect** (or **reported**) **speech**.

They say that you can't have too much of a good thing.
He asked me how to use a comma.

WHAT'S ALL THE FUSS? (OR, APOSTROPHES)

The **apostrophe** (') is probably the most misunderstood piece of punctuation we have. At its simplest, it is used to show possession (*his master's voice*) or omission (*you wouldn't dare*). But, of course, it isn't as simple as that.

Thoughts on *Ain't*

"A*in't* ain't a word, so you ain't going to find it in no dictionary."

*

"Ignorant people think it is the noise which fighting cats make that is so aggravating, but it ain't so; it is the sickening grammar that they use."

—Mark Twain

Leave It Out, Will You?

Rule: When you omit a letter or letters in a word, you should replace it/them with an apostrophe.

If you choose to write *can't* instead of *cannot, we've been here before* rather than *we have been...,* *'or 80s* instead of *1980s,,* you need to replace the missing letters with an apostrophe. Note that the apostrophe in *'80s* tells us that something is missing from the *front* of the word, but it is still an apostrophe. Do not reverse the apostrophe and write *'80s*. And if you write *rock 'n' roll rather* than *rock and roll,* you need apostrophes before and after the *n*.

> ☞ **Teacher's Corner:** The ancient Greeks invented the rhetorical device *apostrephein* (meaning "to turn away"). This had nothing to do with grammar. It described the moment when a speaker turned away from the audience to address a usually absent person or a thing personified—" O Liberty, what things are done in thy name!" This is still known as *apostrophe* today. However, over time, the word's meaning has widened to include "something missing," such as letters and sounds.

Common contractions requiring an apostrophe include:

aren't	*hadn't*	*they're*
can't	*hasn't*	*they've*
couldn't	*isn't*	*weren't*
didn't	*it's**	*won't*
don't	*shouldn't*	*wouldn't*

Such contractions aren't normally used in formal writing, unless someone's speaking, but in a friendly book such as this one they're OK. But remember—the apostrophe is replacing a missing letter, so please put it in the right place.

> "There ain't nothing more to write about, and I am
> rotten glad of it, because if I'd a' knowed what a trouble
> it was to make a book I wouldn't a' tackled it,
> and I ain't agoing to no more."
> —Mark Twain, *The Adventures of Huckleberry Finn*

WHAT'S NOT IN A NAME?
(OR, POSSESSIVE APOSTROPHES)

At one time in the history of the English language, a common way of indicating that something belonged to someone was to add the suffix *-es*.

---

*But only when it's short for *it is*. See page 237.

Singular	Possessive singular
mann	*mannes*
James	*Jameses*

At some point, however, people omitted to pronounce and write the *es*. So instead of an *e* we gained an apostrophe.

The man's hand.

James's book.

This use of apostrophes to indicate possession caught on. In fact, people started adding them to any old word, whether they carried the suffix *-es* or not.

Rule: The apostrophe is placed at the end of a noun to indicate that something belongs to someone or something. It replaces the word *of* in a sentence. If the noun is singular, add *'s*. If the noun is plural, just add the apostrophe.

The boss's chair is for the boss only.	The chair **of the boss**
The animals' feed is insufficient to last the winter.	The feed **of the animals**

Another rule: In the singular the apostrophe is always on the left of its *s*; in the plural it is usually on the right.

The school's rules (one school)

The schools' rules (two or more schools)

The princess's slippers (one princess)

The princesses' slippers (more than one princess)

What the Heck Do I Do with That Apostrophe?

There are—of course—**exceptions** to the apostrophe rules. These are they:

1. When the plural doesn't end in *s*, add an apostrophe followed by an *s*:

   *The **children's** party*

   *The **mice's** lack of eyesight*

2. Names ending in an *s* should be followed by *'s* if singular and *-es'* if plural:

   ***Charles's** last name was Dickens.*

   *Charles **Dickens's** novels are well loved.*

   *The **Joneses'** standards weren't worth keeping up with.*

   Our old friend euphony (see page 94) also crops up here: the moment the word becomes a mouthful, you stop adding an *s*. So:

   *St. **Agnes's** Church*

   ***Jesus's** sandals*

   but ***Barabbas'** criminal record*

3. If the last syllable is pronounced *-iz* or *-eeze*, stick to *s'*, don't add the extra *s*—***Sophocles'** plays*—although, with longer words, it's often easier to paraphrase:

   The inventions of Archimedes rather than Archimedes' (or *Archimedes's*) *inventions.*

   The odyssey of Odysseus rather than Odysseus' (or *Odysseus's*) *odyssey.*

   It also sounds better—and makes you less likely to spit at the person you are speaking to.

4. Then there are organizations that have simply decided that they are above having to employ correct grammar:

   Diners Club International and Walgreens, for instance.

There appears to be no logic to this, but presumably an organization has the right to choose how to spell its own name. That said, ten out of ten for *Macy's, McDonald's,* and *Bloomingdales.*

But Who Really Care's?

The problem is that, in the course of the last few decades, lots of people have become confused about this and—rather than, as they fear, looking ignorant by leaving the apostrophes out—they have started putting apostrophes in places they shouldn't. This is often called the **greengrocer's apostrophe**.

> *APPLE'S HERE! FREE BANANA'S! FAIR DEAL'S! NO DOG'S!*
>
> *Free Margarita's before 7:00 P.M.*

But free Margarita's what? You could write *Free Margarita's lover before 7:00 P.M.,* if you wanted him to get out of the office in time to go to the movies. However, assuming that Margarita is an alcoholic drink, there is no need for a possessive apostrophe in either of these examples.

Similarly *VPs, GIs, and the 1970s* don't need apostrophes, unless they are followed by a possessive or attribute. *An* (individual) *VP's expenses,* (all) *GIs' uniform requirements. A 1970s' trend* would belong to the whole decade; *1970's music* is specifically music from the year 1970.

Conclusion: Using an apostrophe in a plural that is not a possessive form is to be frowned on. No if's, and's, or but's.

To avoid confusion, it is permissible—but not necessarily necessary—to include an apostrophe in:

do's and don'ts
the three R's
There are two s's in that word
dotting one's i's
Minding your p's and q's

But in all of these cases, it is a matter of personal taste, and the apostrophe is included only for ease of reading.

The Typo Hunt

Jeff Deck of Somerville, Massachusetts, and his friend Benjamin Herson of Virginia Beach, Virginia, decided they had seen one too many signs with misspelled words.

Armed with chalk and adhesive letters, the duo, who called themselves the Typo Eradication Advancement League, set out in 2008 on a nationwide search to stamp out grammatical errors. After correcting a misplaced comma and apostrophe on a sign in Grand Canyon National Park, they were arrested and charged with conspiracy to vandalize a historic marker. They were ordered to pay restitution and were banned for one year from national parks.

Yours, Mine, and Ours

Rule: The personal pronouns *yours, theirs, its, his, hers* and *ours* never need an apostrophe.

> The **boys'** burgers, but the burgers are **theirs**.
> The **girl's** cakes but the cakes are **hers**.

The only possessive personal pronoun that needs an apostrophe is *one's*. However, be careful when using it. *One's well* could mean either *one is well* or *the well that one owns*—though with a bit of luck, the context will help you work out which!

> ✋ **Smart Aleck:** We also use an apostrophe in possessive indefinite pronouns: *Is that someone's idea of a joke? That's anyone's guess.*

What Happens When Two People Own Something?

Rule: An apostrophe is placed after the second name when the possession belongs to two people who are mentioned in the same sentence: *Jane and Peter's dog*, not *Jane's and Peter's dog*.

That one is easy because you only have to add *'s*. If, however, you—yes, you—co-owned Jane's dog, you would have to say *Jane's and my dog*, because you can't say *Jane and my's* nor, God forbid, *Jane and I's*.

> ✋ **Smart Aleck:** Achilles heel is the Achilles heel here. Neither Achilles heel nor Achilles tendon has an apostophe.

And Finally...

Useful mnemonics for remembering the difference between a plural form and a singular form in need of a possessive apostrophe.

Rose's are red
Violet's are blue
Which color underwear
Belongs to these two?

Got that? Oh good. Because we're exhausted.

5
Odds and Ends
(or, Elements of Style)

Being a Bit Fancy

There's more to grammar than knowing the difference between a dangling conjunction, a subordinate object, and a non-restrictive apostrophe. So this chapter rounds up a few other points that sometimes cause bafflement.

A Big No-No
(or, Double Negatives)

> "…nor your name is not Master Cesario;
> nor this is not my nose neither."
> —Shakespeare, *Twelfth Night*

Double negatives may not have mattered to Shakespeare, but they do matter in standard modern English.

Rule: Two negatives equal a positive and therefore negate each other. If you want to be negative, use only one.

Sometimes a double negative is obvious—

*I did**n't** do **nothing** right*

*I did**n't** **never** do well in that*

– while others are more elusive:

*His essay **scarcely** needs **no** correction*

*There is**n't** **nowhere** I'd rather be than here with you.*

They are all equally wrong.

> ☛ **See Me after Class:** *I ain't never heard of no one by no name like that.*
>
> On the other hand, when Al Jolson said, "Wait a minute, you ain't heard nothin' yet." in *The Jazz Singer* in 1927, he made movie history.

Yes-Yes to No-Nos

Double negatives are permissible—indeed, useful—when they convey cunning nuances of meaning:

*It was a **not unusual** reaction for someone who has been given bad news.*	Sounds more sympathetic than *It was a usual reaction.*
*I **wouldn't** say I **don't** like your new house.*	I am too polite to admit that I hate it.

And they are allowed for emphasis when they belong to different phrases or clauses:

*I will **not** give up, **not** now, **not** ever.*

*You **don't** ask for much, **no** more than the rest of them, anyhow.*

Positive or Negative?

Interpretation of a **deliberate double negative** may depend on context and intonation.

*She's **not un**attractive.*	This may mean that she is not ugly, but neither is she beautiful—she's not **un**attractive. On the other hand, we may be leaping to the lady's defense—she's **not** unattractive!
*Your visits are **not in**frequent.*	You could visit more often—or you visit regularly enough.
*I can't **not** come if you're singing.*	I don't want to come but I'm obliged to if you are singing—or I wouldn't miss your singing for the world.
*That's **not bad**.*	That's good—or it could be better.

Sometimes double negatives contradict themselves to make positive statements:

I'm not not doing my job!	I *am* doing my job!
There isn't a day when I don't think about him.	I think about him every day.
*He **cannot** just do **nothing**.*	He doesn't understand the concept of idleness.

Ha-Ha

A linguistics professor was lecturing to his class.

"In English," he said, "a double negative forms a positive. In some languages, such as Russian, a double negative is still a negative. However, there is no language wherein a double positive can form a negative."

"Yeah, right," said a voice in the back of the room.

PLEONASM, PROLIXITY, AND TAUTOLOGY (OR, WORDINESS)

Wordiness—also known as long-windedness, pleonasm, prolixity, redundancy, verboseness, verbosity, windiness, wordage, verbiage, garrulousness, redundancy, tautology, or logorrhoea—is to be avoided at all costs.

"Vigorous writing is concise. A sentence should contain no unnecessary words, a paragraph no unnecessary sentences, for the same reason that a drawing should have no unnecessary lines and a machine no unnecessary parts. This requires not that the writer make all his sentences short, or that he avoid all detail and treat his subjects only in outline, but that every word tell."

—William Strunk Jr., *The Elements of Style*

Imagine what Mr. Strunk would have had to say about either of these examples:

> *As the firemen climbed up the steps of the ladder to reach the people trapped in the building that was on fire (people with no escape!), the piercing sound of a shrill cry could be audibly heard from up high on the rooftop. Above the loud roar of the burning flames, we heard a woman screaming out at the top of her voice to the rescuing fireman. We sighed a sigh of relief when they finally reached her and she was brought down.*

> *This quarter, we are presently focusing with determination on an all-new, innovative integrated methodology and framework for rapid expansion of customer-oriented external programs designed and developed to bring the company's consumer-first paradigm shift into the marketplace as quickly as possible.*

Rule: Be clear; be concise; be simple.

Some Thoughts on Pomposity

"We must have a better word than 'prefabricated.'
Why not 'ready-made?'"
—Winston Churchill

❋

"His speeches left the impression of an army of
pompous phrases moving over the landscape
in search of an idea."
—U.S. politician William McAdoo
about President Warren Harding

❋

"Speak properly, and in as few words as you can,
but always plainly; for the end of speech
is not ostentation, but to be understood."
—William Penn

❋

"Clutter is the disease of American writing.
We are a society strangling in unnecessary words,
circular constructions, pompous frills,
and meaningless jargon."
—William Zinsser

A Waste of Space

Try not to punctuate your speech (and certainly don't litter your writing) with **verbal apologies** such as *and that sort of thing, as it were, do you know what I mean?, to all intents and purposes, needless to say*. Nine times out of ten, they will add nothing. Mark Twain had it right when he said, "Substitute 'damn' every time you're inclined to write 'very'; your editor will delete it and the writing will be just as it should be." The same applies to these empty phrases.

Many of us also diminish powerful words by using them in a trivial way. What we mean is, don't use *awfully, fearfully, terribly,* or *horribly* when you mean *very*. In formal writing, keep these words for when they are needed: *He was horribly scarred by the accident.*

Er, Um, Room for Improvement

Recent research concludes that English speakers use a meaningless word about every nine seconds and that 10 percent of English speech consists of **filler words**. And, um, you know, if you don't mind our saying so, it's sort of boring to listen to.

Rule: If it is possible to cut out a word, do so.

It's Déjà-Vu All Over Again...

Tautological phrases or synonyms (words that mean the same) simply repeat a meaning with different words. Making free with these weakens your writing and suggests that you don't know what the words mean. Our pet peeves are *safe haven* (what other kind of haven is there?) and *PIN number* (what do people think the *N* stands for?) but we seem to be fighting a losing battle on these two. However, there are lots of other nonsenses against which we can still fight:

absolute certainty	*factual information*	*honest truth*
accidental mistake	*fall down*	*new innovation*
added bonus	*fictional story*	*stupid idiot*
awful tragedy	*final conclusion*	*sum total*
climb up	*free gift*	*terrible disaster*
close scrutiny	*grab hold*	*true fact*
complete opposite	*end result*	*unconfirmed rumor*
8:00 P.M. in the evening	*HIV virus*	*variety of different*

☝ **Smart Aleck:** How come *needless to say* is always followed by something being said?

Note: One particularly common misuse is of the word *unique*. *Unique*, from the Latin for *one*, means "being the only one of a kind; without parallel." So it is (just about) possible for something to be *almost unique* (that is, there might be two of them, whatever they are) but not for it to be *quite unique* or *very unique*.

"It was a sudden and unexpected surprise."
—BBC correspondent
✳
"Every Superbowl is totally unique—and
this one is just the same."
—Young football athlete

Let Me Repeat Myself

Not all **repetition** is bad. The repetition of key words, phrases and sentence patterns is obviously important in poetry.

It was many and many a year ago,
In a kingdom by the sea,
That a maiden there lived whom you may know
By the name of ANNABEL LEE;
And this maiden she lived with no other thought
Than to love and be loved by me.
I was a child and she was a child,
In this kingdom by the sea;

> But we loved with a love that was more than love—
> I and my Annabel Lee;
> With a love that the winged seraphs of heaven
> Coveted her and me.
> —Edgar Allan Poe, *Annabel Lee*

And it can be effective in prose too:

> "She turned towards me immediately.
> The easy elegance of every movement of
> her limbs and body as soon as she
> began to advance from the
> far end of the room, set me in a flutter
> of expectation to see her face clearly.
> She left the window—and I said to myself,
> *The lady is dark.* She moved forward
> a few steps—and I said to myself, *The lady is young.*
> She approached nearer—and I said
> to myself (with a sense of surprise which
> words fail me to express), *The lady is ugly!*"
> —Wilkie Collins, *The Woman in White*

Of course, as with all good things in life, this can be taken to extremes:

> *If one doctor doctors another doctor does the doctor who doctors the doctor doctor the doctor the way the doctor he is doctoring doctors? Or does the doctor doctor the way the doctor who doctors doctors?*

Say That Again

A word that has two meanings that are the opposite of each other is called an **antagonym** or **contranym**.

> *That horse will **bolt** unless you **bolt** the stable door.*
>
> *The soldier was **bound** for home, when they caught him and **bound** him.*
>
> *Having **clipped** off his baby hair, she **clipped** the pieces in his baby book.*
>
> *We escaped from the mudflats as **fast** as we could, before we were stuck **fast**.*

These examples are all grammatically correct, every word is used accurately, but they still manage to sound silly. It's best to avoid them.

✋ **Smart Aleck:** What's another word for *thesaurus?*

Choose Your Words Carefully

As we said earlier, English is full of easily confused, similar-sounding words, with plenty of opportunity for deliberate puns and inadvertent verbal gaffes.

Visiting relatives can be boring.	Are they visiting you or are you visiting them?
I had been driving for forty years when I fell asleep at the wheel and had an accident.	No wonder, I expect you were rather tired.
Q: *What gear were you in at the moment of the impact?*	A: Gucci sweats and Reeboks.

Yogi Berra was a master of this form of miscommunication—"He hits from both sides of the plate. He's amphibious."—but while not many of us would aspire to his heights, he is an object lesson in what can happen if you don't watch what you say. On the other hand, you can have a lot of fun with words if you don't mind what you say. See what we mean?

The Third Degree • The Fo

Sheets to the Wind • Take the

nth Heaven • Cloud Nine •

Dressed to the Nines Dixie

Niners • 86 • 411 • 007 • 8 1/

Dozen • Ocean's 11 • The T

Hawaii Five-O • Fahrenheit

ins • Social Security Num

even Wonders of the Ancien

Catch-22 • Four Horsemen

Roman Numerals • Prime

Fahrenheit 451 • The Binary S

Easy as Pi

π

The Countless Ways We
Use Numbers Every Day

JAMIE BUCHAN

INTRODUCTION

As you read this, the world may still be in the grip of a severe economic crisis. Chances are you were woken up this morning by an alarm so you could get to work at or before a specific time. Your cell phone is assigned its own specific number and, like all electronic devices, its functioning is based on manipulating numbers. The timing and placement of traffic lights on your way to work would have been mathematically designed to maximize efficiency, despite appearances to the contrary. Every man-made object will have been designed with numbers in mind, and many (including this one) are given unique numeric identifiers.

As Pythagoras once said, numbers rule the universe. From the bizarre complexity of economics and statistics to the words and expressions we use every day, numbers are an inescapable influence on the world—even for the least mathematically inclined. It's with this in mind that I have written this book—as a wide-ranging look at the pervasive influence of numbers.

For many people, math remains a confusing and inaccessible field of study, and although this isn't a math textbook, I have tried to make any mathematical details fairly straightforward. A short glossary of mathematical terms is included, which I'm hoping will make the math stuff somewhat simpler (and perhaps refresh memories of having learned it in school).

I should also make an important disclaimer: I am not a mathematician, nor any other kind of relevant professional. I've researched the subjects here as an interested amateur, and I've done everything possible to make it accurate and, I hope, interesting and amusing.

Despite all my efforts, though, we can only scratch the surface of how numbers—whether culturally, linguistically or scientifically—affect our lives. The world of numbers stretches on before us, forever growing as science and mathematics continue to make new strides. So here we go, from zero to infinity via Amazonian tribes, drug culture, and nuclear paranoia.

NUMBERS
IN
LANGUAGE

DO A NUMBER

To seriously damage something or someone. The origins of this phrase are very murky, but it seems to be derived from the world of boxing, where a fighter might be instructed to "do a number" on his opponent's face; that is, hit it a number of times—hard.

THREE SHEETS TO THE WIND

A nautical expression, meaning "extremely drunk." Surprisingly, the origin of the term seems not to be sails (which, after all, are sheetlike and should as a matter of course to be "to the wind"), but ropes, which have a number of names, depending on their function. "Sheet" ropes control the horizontal movement of sails; therefore, having three of them loose and flapping around in the wind would be a serious problem. Sailors appear to have used a system of ratings this way, going from one sheet to the wind (slightly tipsy) to four (unconscious).

THE THIRD DEGREE

Originally, this referred to American police interrogations, which used intensive methods, sometimes including physical violence, to get an answer or confession from the suspect. Now the phrase is often used to describe any needlessly intense or intrusive behavior, where someone might complain of being given "the third degree" about a past misdeed. It may derive from the membership rituals of Freemasonry, where members are graded by degrees. Admission to the third degree and the rank of Master Mason requires the member to submit to an exacting interrogation ceremony.

THE FOURTH ESTATE

Derived from the 1789 Estates-General, an assembly of French citizens from three social ranks. The First Estate were clergy, the Second the nobles, and the Third the wealthiest bourgeoisie. In this highly unrepresentative system, a fourth group—newspapers and reporters—were extremely influential on ordinary French people. In Britain philosopher and Member of Parliament Edmund Burke pointed to the House of Commons press gallery and remarked: "Yonder sits the Fourth Estate, and they are more important than them all."

FOURTH WALL

Originally defined by the writer Denis Diderot as the "wall" separating a theatrical performance from the audience (with the set forming the other three walls and the stage being the floor), the term is now often applied to films and TV, particularly where a character "breaks" the fourth wall and addresses the audience directly. The opening scenes of *Ferris Bueller's Day Off* are a particularly good example, if not precisely what Diderot had in mind.

FIVE BY FIVE

Originally a term from NATO radio-speak (see also Police Radio Codes, page 360), part of a system of rating radio signals. Signal strength and clarity are each rated on a scale of one to five, so five by five refers to the strongest, clearest signal possible. As such, the phrase (and sometimes its contracted form "five by") is frequently used outside its original setting, usually to mean something has been understood (similar to "crystal clear") or just to report that something is proceeding as planned.

FIFTH COLUMNIST

This phrase was, apparently, coined in 1936 during the Spanish Civil War when, in a radio address, Nationalist General Emilio Mola proclaimed his intention to take over Madrid with only four columns of troops, plus a "fifth column" of Nationalist sympathizers inside the city who would sabotage the Republican defense. Mola's plan was unsuccessful, but the term gained popularity during the World War II to describe possible enemy sympathizers in the Allied ranks, such as Japanese-Americans and German expatriates.

TAKE THE FIFTH

In an everyday setting, the term has increasingly been used to refer to refusing to answer a question where the truth would embarrass you. The Fifth Amendment to the U.S. Constitution guarantees, among other things, the right to remain silent when arrested and during trial, making it illegal to force people to incriminate themselves:

No person shall be held to answer for a capital, or otherwise infamous crime, unless on a presentment or indictment of a Grand Jury, except in cases arising in the land or naval forces, or in the Militia, when in actual service in time of War or public danger; nor shall any person be subject for the same offense to be twice put in jeopardy of life or limb; nor shall be compelled in any criminal case to be a witness against himself, nor be deprived of life, liberty, or property, without due process of law; nor shall private property be taken for public use, without just compensation.

DEEP-SIX

Whereas one might "86" (see page 368) an unneeded internal memo, one would "deep-six" an incriminating one—that is, get rid of it in a secretive way. The term is supposedly derived from navigation in earlier centuries, where anything more than 6 fathoms (36 feet/11 m) deep under water was unlikely to be recovered. This may also be related to burial at sea, as some sources suggest that 6 fathoms was the legal minimum depth for the body to be immersed.

AT SIXES AND SEVENS

An expression that refers to a person in a state of confusion or chaos. According to Michael Quinion's World Wide Words (www.worldwidewords.org), the phrase, which has been in use in some form since Chaucer, probably derives from the dice game, *hazard*, an old and rather complex French precursor of craps, in which players placed bets on numbers they then hoped to roll. Five and six were considered the riskiest (although in probability terms they'd be no less likely than any other two numbers), and the phrase was used to describe someone considered foolish or confused enough to bet on them. As the Middle French words for five and six (*cinque* and *sice*) entered the English language, they were apparently mistranslated to six and seven, despite the obvious absence of a number seven on the standard die. (It probably helps that 6+7 equals unlucky 13 [see page 440].)

SEVENTH HEAVEN

To be in seventh heaven is to be at the very height of ecstasy, similar to "on cloud nine" (see opposite). The phrase seems to come from religious ideas (in Judaism and Islam, as well as sometimes in Christianity) of heaven as being subdivided into seven levels (sometimes shown as concentric circles surrounding the world), with the seventh (known as *Abja'* in Islam and *Arabot* in Judaism) being the highest one, where God has his throne.

ONE OVER THE EIGHT

This expression, which refers to one who's just over the threshold of drunkenness, seems to come from British military slang in the early twentieth century, where 8 pints of beer was apparently considered the amount a man could drink before being drunk. Given that beer was weaker then, and that soldiers may have had high alcohol tolerances anyway, literally drinking "one over the eight" now would be inadvisable. Appropriately, though, binge drinking is now officially defined in the U.K. as any drinking session in which more than eight units of alcohol are consumed (for men—it's six for women; in the United States and Canada, it's five and four).

CLOUD NINE

To be on cloud nine is to be elated or extremely happy—usually as a result of love, substance abuse, or some combination of the two. The term seems to derive from the U.S. National Weather Service's system for classifying cloud formations, where nine was the highest—towers of cumulonimbus clouds reaching up to 40,000 feet (12,200 m). (The fact that cumulonimbus tends to produce severe storms seems rather apt.)

THE WHOLE NINE YARDS

If you are giving something your best effort or using all your resources, you might be going "the whole nine yards." It's very difficult to be certain about the origins of this expression, and many (mostly incorrect) claims have been made about it. One of the more credible theories is that American bombers during the World War II were issued 9-yard (27-foot/8-meter) belts of machine-gun ammunition (around 900 bullets) and might have to fire them all during a particularly difficult mission. This seems slightly unlikely, however, given that "the whole nine yards" didn't become widespread until the 1960s. Perhaps a more likely possibility is that the phrase derives from the average capacity of cement-mixing trucks—about 9 cubic yards … or from a rather rude story about a Scotsman's kilt.

DRESSED TO THE NINES

Like "the whole nine yards" (see page 359), the origins of this phrase, referring to someone dressed in fancy clothing, are murky. One of the more popular theories is that it alludes to the elegantly dressed 99th Lanarkshire Regiment of the British Army, but that regiment was raised well after Robert Burns's use of the phrase in the 1790s. As with "the whole nine yards," it has also been suggested that the phrase derives from 9 yards of cloth being required to make a man's three-piece suit. If this is true, however, anyone truly "dressed to the nines" would also be morbidly obese! (It usually takes 5 to 7 yards.) It may simply be that nine is chosen because it's the highest single-digit number.

POLICE RADIO CODES

In any emergency situation, communications failures can be fatal, and managing police radio traffic across an entire city is exceptionally difficult and confusing. The situation was far worse, however, when the idea of police radio was a new one, in the 1920s and 1930s. Operators, often not comprehensively trained, had difficulty understanding what was said and handling large amounts of traffic. Charles L. Hopper, a radio officer in Illinois, recognized the need for a more efficient method of communication and invented a system to simplify it with numeric codes.

Hopper proposed the 10-code—comprising the number 10 followed by another number—as an efficient method of relaying information that was harder to mishear. The "10–" part is used so that it doesn't matter if the first syllable isn't heard, allowing time for radio adjustment, and the "10–" is often dropped in speech (for example "I need a 29 on a Marge Gunderson"). The number 10 may have been chosen because Hopper was working for District 10 of the Illinois State Police. In 1940 the Association of Police Communications Officers (APCO) rolled out the system of numeric codes, which have remained similar ever since.

Aside from simplifying the process of communication, the 10-codes have another major advantage—they make it comparatively difficult for criminals or intrusive reporters to figure out what's being said. At least, they used to—the proliferation of lists like this one, especially on the Internet, have robbed the 10-code of some of its tactical edge.

British police have no real equivalent to the 10-code, opting instead for a charmingly obscene range of abbreviations which unfortunately we cannot discuss here. But American police slang has become entrenched in our popular culture through movies and TV, and in some cases (particularly the term "10-4") through the adoption of 10-codes by Citizens Band (CB) radio users.

Some of the More Interesting "10-codes"

10-00: Officer down, immediate response needed

10-0: Danger

10-4: Message acknowledged

10-10: Fight in progress

10-14: Suspicious person or prowler

10-16: Domestic disturbance

10-20: Location is … (One might ask, "what's your 20?")

10-24: Emergency backup needed

10-26: Detaining suspect now

10-29: Check past arrests and outstanding warrants

10-31: Crime in progress

10-32: Person with gun

10-35: Major crime alert

10-39: Unit is to use lights and siren (also referred to as Code 3; page 363)

10-40: Unit is to move silently (to avoid alerting suspects)

10-57: Hit and run

10-80: Pursuit in progress

10-105: Dead on Arrival (DOA)

10-109: Suicide

Police responses are also graded numerically:

Code 1: Respond at earliest convenience
Code 2: Respond quickly (whether lights and/or siren
      are used depends on the police force)
Code 3: Urgent response—lights and siren

Please note that the codes given above are the definitions used by APCO. They've come to vary significantly across police forces and states, and it is for this reason that the 10-code is now being retired. Operations involving multiple forces, particularly in responding to the 9/11 attacks (September 11, 2001) and Hurricane Katrina, highlighted the confusion of different police forces trying to communicate with this "standard" set of codes. As a result, the Federal Emergency Management Agency (FEMA) now prohibits the use of 10-codes where complex emergencies involve more than one police force.

Radio technology has advanced significantly since 1940, both in signal quality (see Five by Five, page 16) and traffic handling, and it's not nearly as hard to hear spoken phrases as it was when the 10-codes were first introduced. Nonetheless, many officers mourn the loss of what has become an essential part of police culture, finding it difficult to return to ordinary English. (See also: 419 Scams [page 402], 187 [page 369].)

DIXIE

A popular term for the American Deep South—the states of Virginia, North and South Carolina, Florida, Alabama, Georgia, Mississippi, Tennessee, Arkansas, Texas and Louisiana. These slave-owning states seceded from the Union after the election of President Abraham Lincoln, forming the short-lived Confederate States of America and sparking the American Civil War (1861–65). In many ways, the war was concerned less with the moral implications of slavery than with major differences that had developed in the economies and societies of the two halves, and Southerners often viewed the "War of Northern Aggression" as an attempt by the ethnically more diverse, industrial and rapidly urbanizing northern states to destroy their more traditional society.

For many Southerners even today, songs like "Dixie" ("I wish I was in Dixie") recall nostalgic memories of the old Southern way of life. The fact that the song in question depicts a racist caricature of a freed slave who wants to go back to slavery on a plantation has led to considerable controversy surrounding its continued performance in the South, much like the flying of the Confederate flag.

The term may simply be derived from the Mason-Dixon line, which divided free and slave states, but it could also refer to the number 10. In the days before centralized banking and minting, it was fairly common for even relatively minor banks to print their own currency. One bank in Louisiana, which was named by the French for King Louis XIV and retains a strong francophone tradition today, printed their own ten-dollar bills with the word *dix* (the French word for ten) on one side. These rare bilingual bills were particularly sought-after, and the area (and therefore, the South as a whole) became known as Dixieland, or simply Dixie.

NINETEEN TO THE DOZEN

This term (also sometimes ten or twenty to the dozen) refers to very energetic activity, usually talking extremely fast. Etymological facts are especially thin regarding this—no one seems to have an explanation for why this term is used.

23, SKIDOO!

This slang expression from the past is still occasionally found now, referring to taking the opportunity to leave quickly, or being socially or physically compelled to do so. Although it started off well before then, the phrase took the United States by storm in the 1920s, and even then its origin was disputed. The "skidoo" is almost certainly a corruption of "skedaddle," but the source of "23" is less clear.

Perhaps the most amusing theory is that it refers to 23rd Street in New York City, where the iconic Flatiron Building was constructed in 1902. At a time when skyscrapers were only in their infancy, the building's odd angular shape led to

complex wind-tunneling down 23rd Street, which tended to wreak havoc with women's skirts, making them billow in an unseemly manner. This being 1902, the possibility of catching a glimpse of ankle attracted a number of voyeurs, who were moved along by policemen giving them the "23, skidoo."

However, most sources put the use of 23 (with no "skidoo") as a slang term a few years before, with reports of annoyed New Yorkers yelling the number at beggars. Some have claimed "23" is telegrapher's Morse code for "away with you," much as -30- (originally meaning "end of transmission") is still sometimes used by journalists to signal the end of a story. Although this explanation is rather uncertain, the use of numeric codes by telegraphers certainly helped popularize the use of numbers as slang expressions in this period (see 86, page 30).

A third popular explanation is that "23, skidoo" derives from a highly-regarded 1899 theater production of Charles Dickens's *A Tale of Two Cities*. The climactic final scene, in which the hero Sydney Carton is guillotined, has an old woman counting the victims, and shouting "twenty-three!" as Carton dies. This melodramatic scene was parodied by comedians of the time, and it almost certainly popularized the expression, even if it isn't the origin.

FORTY-NINERS

With the discovery of gold in the Sierra Nevada in 1848, the California Gold Rush drew hundreds of thousands of forty-niners (as in 1849-ers) to the area, and this went on until about 1855. Although most forty-niners did not find the massive wealth they expected, they generally made some profit, and their presence created extremely fast economic growth in the area. A local government and infrastructure had to be established quickly, and California became a state in 1850. Even now, California is perhaps America's most prosperous, populous and glamorous state.

77

This otherwise unremarkable number took on enormous importance for Sweden during World War II. Seventy-seven, written *sjuttiosju* in Swedish, is extremely difficult to pronounce in that language, and it was the pronunciation—or mispronunciation—of it that helped guards at the border of neutral Sweden to distinguish between native Swedes and others from Germany or occupied Norway.

86

This expression, dating back to jazz-age America, and meaning to dismiss or get rid of, has its roots in American restaurants and diners and originally referred either to being out of stock of an item on the menu or to ejecting a troublesome client. As with "23, skidoo" (see page 365), numerous mostly unsupported theories have been offered. Supposedly, section 86 of the New York State liquor code defined the circumstances under which a patron could be ejected—that is, "86ed"—but this seems unlikely, given the origins of the expression. It could also be rhyming slang for "nix," but if so it would be an unusual instance of American rhyming slang.

187

This number refers to section 187 of the California Penal Code, which defines the criminal act of homicide, and "187" has become an American slang term for murder, particularly in major cities. The term appears to have spread to gangs across America, as well as to more general usage, through West Coast "gangsta rap" in the 1990s, with a number of songs making reference to 187s. A 1997 film, *One Eight Seven*, about gang violence in an L.A. high school, further popularized the term. The term "419 scam" (see page 402) originated in a similar way.

411

The telephone number used for directory assistance in most parts of the U.S. and Canada, "411" is American slang for essential information. It's pronounced—like 911—as three separate digits and always used as a noun, similar to "the lowdown"—one would get the "411" on someone or something.

420

Because marijuana use is illegal but comparatively mainstream, the number "420" is sometimes used, mainly in the United States as a code for marijuana use in everyday situations. For example, particularly liberal-minded students might advertise shared apartments as being "420 friendly."

Like "187" (page 369), "420" is a three-digit code for illicit activity, which might lead one to think it refers to a penal code or that it's related to 419 scams in some way, because it's the very next number (see page 402). In fact, though, the origins of this widely used term are surprisingly esoteric. In the early 1970s, a group of legendarily stoned students at San Rafael High School in California held regular meetings to smoke at 4:20 p.m., and the phrase "four-twenty" became a usefully innocuous-sounding reminder of a planned meeting, eventually passing into heavy usage from there. Rather aptly, California State Senate Bill 420, passed in 2003, clarifies the politically liberal state's law on medical use of the drug.

NUMBERS IN FICTION

00000

The mysterious number at the heart of *Gravity's Rainbow*, a fascinating but exceptionally confusing novel by Thomas Pynchon, published in 1973. The book touches on religion, math, quantum physics, conspiracy theories, and obscure 1940s pop culture as it follows a bewildering cast of characters in a multistranded epic storyline centering on an elusive V2 rocket (numbered 00000), in the closing years of the World War II.

π: FAITH IN CHAOS

Darren Aronofsky's inventive 1998 debut film stars Sean Gullette as Max Cohen, a reclusive mathematical genius with a pervasively numeric worldview, as he tries to uncover mathematical patterns in the world around him. Cohen is fascinated by the digits of π (see page 469), but the film also touches on the Golden Spiral (see page 387) and Kabbalistic gematria (see page 419). It's one of my favorite films, and Cohen's tendency to see numbers in everything partly inspired this book.

THE PRISONER

A highly popular 1960s British TV series starring Patrick McGoohan, *The Prisoner* followed on from the spy series *Danger Man*. The titular incarceree is a former secret agent who resigns but is confined by his former masters to a surreal village until he gives them the information they want. The prisoner is frustrated at being known simply as Number Six, prompting his famous cry "I am not a number. I am a free man!"

SE7EN

David Fincher's grim, gory neo-noir 1995 film stars Morgan Freeman and Brad Pitt as detectives on the trail of a fanatically religious serial killer (Kevin Spacey) who, in various unpleasantly apt ways, kills those he judges to be committing the Seven Deadly Sins (see page 410), starting with an obese man killed by extreme force-feeding.

THE SEVEN SAMURAI

A seminal Japanese film about…seven samurai (technically *ronin*, see page 380), who are brought together to defend a village against marauding bandits. The 1954 film's treatment of the effects of violence was extremely influential across the world and across genres, while the plot device of several very different heroes brought together to fight a common enemy was particularly innovative—as well as appearing in the film's Western remake *The Magnificent Seven*, it's the basis for *Ocean's 11*, *The Dirty Dozen*, and countless others.

007

The number assigned, of course, to James Bond, the British secret agent created by Ian Fleming who has since appeared in innumerable books and films. However, the character (who, for a spy, is remarkably eager to introduce himself to his enemies) owes far more to fantasy than reality. Matt Damon's description of Bond as an "imperialist, misogynist sociopath" doesn't always seem far off the mark, either. The "00" indicates that Bond is one of few agents with a license to kill; the "7" appears to have been chosen simply for its mystical and lucky connotations (see page 410).

8 MILE

A 2002 film starring American rap star Eminem (and apparently partly based on his life), which is about a young white, working-class rapper in Detroit who tries to become successful in this predominantly black subculture, and who is confronted by various racial and class divisions as he does so.

The film is named for the 8 Mile Road, one of a number of major roads that make up a grid (with a mile between each road) in the area around Detroit. The road has long been known as a socio-economic dividing line between the rich suburbs to the north and the deprived inner city to the south, and therefore serves as a relevant setting for the film.

8½

This 1963 autobiographical film by the Italian director Federico Fellini (1920–93) follows a struggling director who suffers from a creative block in the middle of making a film and retreats into his memories and dreams. With great simplicity, the title comes from the number of films Fellini had directed before this one—six full-length films and two short films (which he added together to make one full one), plus a film he codirected (which he counted as half a film). The total is 7½ , making *8½* his 8½th film.

UP TO 11

A classic line in the seminal film *This Is Spinal Tap* (1985), in a scene where guitarist Nigel Tufnel (Christopher Guest) is showing off his guitars and amplifiers. Tufnel demonstrates a special Marshall amplifier with an extra volume setting, in case he needs to go "one louder." The phrase "up to eleven" has come to refer simply to taking things to slightly absurd extremes, and real amplifiers with volume dials going "up to 11" have been produced.

12 MONKEYS

A superbly innovative science-fiction/mystery film, directed by former Monty Python member, Terry Gilliam in 1995, *12 Monkeys* stars Bruce Willis as an inmate of a dystopian prison in a post-apocalyptic future, who is sent back in time (with the aid of an unusually imperfect time-travel process) to stop the disaster. Back in the 1990s, he meets a mental patient (Brad Pitt), whose involvement with the environmentalist extremist group the Army of the Twelve Monkeys seems to be the answer. The film is filled with symbolism and uncertainty, but Gilliam's reason for choosing 12 is unclear.

21 GRAMS

A 2003 film directed by Alejandro González Iñárritu and starring Benicio del Toro, Naomi Watts, and Sean Penn. The film, which follows interweaving plot lines around a fatal car accident, is named for the supposed weight of the human soul (about 0.75 oz.), a figure that has more weight as a religious and cultural idea than it does as any sort of scientific data.

The number is derived from a series of experiments performed by Dr. Duncan MacDougall in Massachusetts in 1907, which aimed to measure a loss of weight at the moment of death, and thus "prove" that the soul existed and had physical mass. Unsurprisingly, MacDougall's experiments were deeply unscientific in their methods and ultimately inconclusive. Not only did he record a fairly wide range of weights, some of which increased over time, but his sample size (see page 485) only included six patients. Some subjects in other experiments *gained* a tiny amount of weight at death. Furthermore, such small losses of weight at death can easily be accounted for by the lungs emptying, by the evaporation of fluids, and by simple experimental error.

CATCH-22

Coined in the novel of the same name by Joseph Heller, the term "Catch-22" has come to mean a no-win situation created by circular logic. The book is a vicious, hilarious, dark satire of bureaucracy, the military, and society in general, set among the U.S. Air Force pilots of the Fighting 256th Squadron (often jokingly referred to as "Two to the Fighting Eighth Power") on an island in the Mediterranean, where they're confronted by bizarre military bureaucracy as well as the horrors of war. Among the pilots, Catch-22 applies to those attempting to avoid flying missions on the grounds of insanity. Catch-22 stipulates that anyone who would fly missions at all must be insane, but that a pilot attempting to claim insanity (and thus avoid flying) is demonstrating self-preservation and hence sanity, and can therefore be sent out on missions.

The choice of 22 is, aptly, a rather complex and convoluted story. In the early stages, Heller had intended to call it Catch-18 (a number significant to Heller's Jewish heritage, and Jewish themes which were prominent in the early drafts—see page 421 for why), but the number had to be changed as the lengthy writing process finally came to an end, in order to avoid confusion with a contemporaneous war novel, *Mila 18*, by Leon Uris. The repeated digit in Catch-11 seemed appropriate to the repetition that occurs throughout the book, but was considered too close to the film *Ocean's Eleven* (the 1960 Rat Pack version, of course). Catch-17 and Catch-14 were also rejected, for being respectively too similar to the war film *Stalag 17* and not "funny" enough, before "22" was the final choice.

THE 25ᵀᴴ HOUR

David Benioff's novel, filmed in 2002 by Spike Lee, follows a convicted drug dealer on his last day of freedom before going to prison.

THE THIRTY-NINE STEPS

The classic spy novel by John Buchan about a conspiracy to plunge Europe into war and steal British military secrets. "The thirty-nine steps" in question refer to a meeting point, but the phrase is also used by the enemy spies in the book as a mysterious sign. The book has been filmed four times, most famously (and with substantial alterations to the plot) by Alfred Hitchcock in 1935.

The novel was written in 1915 while Buchan was staying at Broadstairs, Kent, for health reasons. His daughter, then about age six and still learning to count, went down a set of stairs leading to the beach, and on returning to her father, proudly announced that there were 39 steps.

42

The meaning of Life, the Universe, and Everything, in the *Hitchhiker's Guide to the Galaxy* series by Douglas Adams. The enormous supercomputer Deep Thought produces this cryptic answer, requiring the construction of an even larger machine (I won't spoil the surprise) to work out the corresponding question. Adams is believed to have chosen the number entirely at random, and not with an actual hidden meaning in mind, though many have tried to find one.

THE 47 RONIN

Probably Japan's best-known folk tale—and apparently one with a fairly solid basis in fact—is that of 47 samurai whose master, Asano, assaulted an official, Kira Yoshinaka, and was compelled to commit honor suicide (*seppuku*, similar to *hara-kiri*). Without a master, the samurai became *ronin*—wandering outcasts who acted a little like mercenaries.

The 47 were compelled by the samurai code of honor (*bushido*) to avenge Asano and constructed an elaborate plan to do so. In order to put Kira off his guard, they would deliberately give the impression of being dishonorable— drinking and debauching themselves, and never showing interest in avenging Asano. After two years of this charade, they were able to enter Kira's house easily, and killed him.

The *ronin* had known from the beginning that this course

of action would end in their deaths. They turned themselves in to the authorities (except one, who had departed to carry back the news of Kira's death, and seems to have been spared), and they were sentenced to death for murdering Kira. Because they had acted according to the precepts of *bushido*, however, they were allowed to commit *seppuku*, a more honorable death than that of an ordinary murderer.

HAWAII FIVE-O

A long-running American cop show, much loved around the world, set in, and named for, the fiftieth state of the Union.

ROOM 101

The room where dissenters are tortured with their greatest fears in George Orwell's *1984*. Orwell worked for the BBC for some time, and is thought to have numbered the room after a hated conference room on the first floor of BBC Broadcasting House. The cultural influence of the Room 101 from the novel, is so well-known that the chief of East Germany's Stasi, Erich Mielke, had the rooms in his building renumbered so that his office would be Room 101 and, in a wonderfully circular development, the BBC now has a popular television series called *Room 101*, in which celebrities discuss their pet peeves.

LES 400 COUPS

Named after a French expression similar to "the third degree" (see page 353), *Les 400 Coups*—literally, the 400 blows—is the first in a series of heavily autobiographical films by French New Wave pioneer François Truffaut. The film follows the adventures of a young French boy—Antoine Doinel—as his mischievous ways are harshly judged by society.

FAHRENHEIT 451

Ray Bradbury's bleak novel, about an anti-intellectual dystopian future in which all books are burned, is named for the temperature at which paper burns (about 233°C/451°F).

24601

Jean Valjean's prisoner number in *Les Misérables*, and since used for many fictional prisoners. Supposedly, Victor Hugo used the number because it was the date of his conception—24 June 1801.

NUMBERS
IN
CULTURE

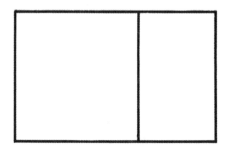

1.618—THE GOLDEN NUMBER

Although not commonly known today, the Golden Number or Golden Ratio (1.6180339887…, also known simply as φ [phi]) has been credited with great importance in art and design for over two thousand years, as well as being of mathematical interest.

A perfect rectangle?

The Golden Number's main contribution to aesthetics comes in the form of the Golden Rectangle—a rectangle where one side is φ times longer than the other, meaning the Golden Rectangle can always be divided into a square and another Golden Rectangle (see illustration above).

The symbol φ may have originated in Ancient Egypt, appearing in the proportions of the pyramids at Giza and in admittedly vague references to a "sacred ratio." It was certainly important to the Greeks—the Greek sculptor, painter, and architect Phidias used it in his design of the statues in the Parthenon, and it is designated φ after him (the first letter of his name in Greek).

Plato and Euclid later studied the Number, although the term Golden Number emerged later, during the Renaissance. The

supposed significance of the Golden Number in Greek art and architecture (particularly the claim that it formed the basis for temple front designs) appears to have been exaggerated, but the renewal of interest in classical disciplines during the Renaissance brought enormous interest in the Golden Number and the Rectangle, among other theories of anatomical and aesthetic proportion. In particular, Leonardo da Vinci's illustrations for Luca Pacioli's *De Divina Proportione* applied the Golden Ratio to human faces, and many claim that his paintings, including the Mona Lisa, employ the Golden Ratio very heavily in their composition.

More recently, the twentieth-century painter Piet Mondrian used the number to compose his abstract geometric works, and the pioneering Modernist architect Le Corbusier used the Rectangle to develop his Modulor system of architectural scaling, designed to mimic human proportions.

A degree of skepticism is needed, however, when considering the rectangle's importance in aesthetics and proportion. In particular, it's important to bear in mind that body and facial proportions vary widely between individuals, not always coming especially close to any Golden form. As in nature, many of the sightings of the Golden Rectangle in art and design have been disputed.

One Point Six One Eight Zero Three Three Nine Eight Eight Seven ...

Like π (see page 469), φ is an irrational number (see page 461)—a decimal whose digits never end and never repeat. Mathematically, the Golden Number is defined by the ratio of two different positive constants, *a* and *b*, with *a* being the larger of the two. If a + b is the same proportionally to *a* as *a* is to *b*, *a* will be φ times larger than *b* (and a+b will be φ times larger than *b*); that is,

$$\frac{(a+b)}{a} = \frac{a}{b} = \varphi$$

φ is also equal to $(1+\sqrt{5})/2$.

Phi bears a close mathematical relationship to the Fibonacci sequence (see page 480). Look what happens if each term of the sequence is divided by the previous one:

$$
\begin{aligned}
1 \div 1 &= 1, \\
2 \div 1 &= 2, \\
3 \div 2 &= 1.5, \\
5 \div 3 &= 1.666666..., \\
8 \div 5 &= 1.6, \\
13 \div 8 &= 1.625, \\
21 \div 13 &= 1.61538462, \\
34 \div 21 &= 1.61904762, \\
55 \div 34 &= 1.61764706, \\
89 \div 55 &= 1.61818181....
\end{aligned}
$$

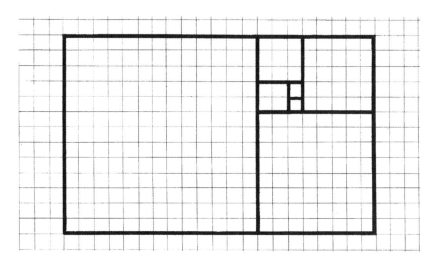

The relationship extends to geometry as well. If the Fibonacci sequence is represented as a series of squares (1×1, 1×1, 2×2, 3×3, 5×5, and so on....), they rapidly start looking like a Golden Rectangle (see illustration above).

The corners of the Golden Rectangle can be joined to form a Golden Spiral, which gets 1.6180339887 times wider with each 90-degree turn:

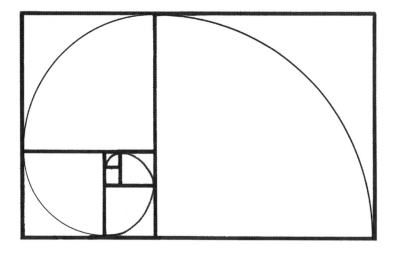

Although logarithmic spirals* of this type occur frequently in nature—from the swirls of milk in coffee to the spirals of galaxies—any claims about the Golden Spiral in particular having some sort of cosmic significance need to be treated with skepticism.

The Fibonacci rectangle can also be turned into a spiral, which—because the terms of the sequence relate to each other by factors approaching φ—looks a lot like a Golden Spiral. The Fibonacci spiral does occur frequently in nature, particularly in plant growth, where seeds and fruitlets follow a Fibonacci-type pattern.

078-05-1120

In 1936 America was still recovering from the Great Depression, and Franklin D. Roosevelt's wide-ranging New Deal program of social spending was being put in place. It included, among many other things, the introduction of Social Security, with every American over the age of fourteen being assigned a unique Social Security Number (SSN), printed on a Social Security card.

The system was still not fully understood by most Americans two years later, and it was perhaps with this problem in mind that a wallet manufacturer, the E. H. Ferree company of Lockport, New York, decided to produce sample SSN cards to show how their product would accommodate

---

* Logarithmic spirals are those that get wider by a fixed factor with each quarter turn; that is, the gap between lines is x times wider at a given point than it is 90° before that point.

the new cards. The example card closely resembled a real one, despite the word SPECIMEN stamped on it, and the SSN used, 078-05-1120, was a valid one taken from Mrs. Hilda Whitcher, a secretary at the company.

When the wallets were distributed to shops nationwide, thousands of confused buyers decided that SSNs must be issued through wallet purchases. In the peak year 1943, nearly six thousand people claimed the number as their own (the unfortunate Mrs. Whitcher, by this point, was not among them, because she was issued a new one).

Similar problems have occurred with duplication of SSNs, but the abuse of 078-05-1120 was by far the worst. Even as recently as 1977, twelve people were still using the number. To prevent this kind of thing from happening again, the Social Security Administration assigned a block of invalid SSNs (987-65-4320 to 987-65-4329) solely for use in advertising (similar to the 555 area code, see page 396).

THE INDIANA PI BILL

In 1897 came one of the strangest incidents in mathematical history—the Indiana Pi Bill. It was proposed by Dr. Edwin J. Goodwin, an amateur mathematician who was obsessed with squaring the circle—an ancient mathematical problem that had troubled mathematicians for centuries, until ultimately proven impossible—and almost got his crank theories through the state's senate.

He persisted in claiming that it was possible to find a circle's area by using a straightedge and a set of compasses to construct a square of the same area as the circle, and by finding the area of the square, one could also find the area of the original circle. The problem was that this relied on π (see page 469) not being a transcendental number, but in 1882 Ferdinand von Lindemann had proved that it was, and hence that squaring the circle was impossible. Goodwin kept claiming he had done so, however, listing it alongside other impossible accomplishments in the text of the bill:

> ...his solutions of the trisection of the angle, duplication of the cube, and quadrature of the circle having been already accepted as contributions to science by the *American Mathematical Monthly*, the leading exponent of mathematical thought in this country. And be it remembered that these noted problems had been long since given up by scientific bodies as insolvable mysteries and above man's ability to comprehend.

Pi in the face

Dr. Goodwin's bill proposed, seemingly without irony, a "new and correct" value for π—3.2. Crammed with impenetrable language and convoluted, self-contradictory math, which many senators were unable to understand, he generously allowed the Indiana school system to use his profoundly wrong thesis free of copyright. In fact, the bill would probably have passed were it not for the timely intervention of C. A. Waldo, a mathematics professor at nearby Purdue University. It was Waldo who explained the problem with Goodwin's math to the senators, who postponed the bill indefinitely, and Goodwin was laughed out of the senate house.

NUMBERS GAMES

Numbers games are illegal lotteries that were extremely popular among America's urban poor from around the mid-1850s to the 1950s, after which they were largely superseded by state lotteries. Typically, players would choose three or four numbers between 0 and 999, although the range of available numbers, and hence the odds of winning, varied significantly. Later on, the operators chose independent numbers such as the

U. S. Treasury balances that were published daily in American newspapers.) Attractive because of their cheap tickets and promises of enormous wealth, numbers that were especially likely to be picked—lucky 7, for instance, (see page 410)— were often eliminated from the draw. These games were also often fairly convenient, as number runners went from door to door to record players' bets.

Numbers games were also sometimes known as "policy," a euphemistic suggestion that regular betting on them was an insurance policy against the future, because you were supposedly bound to win someday. I hardly need to add that this was not the case—many numbers games were rigged, and the organizers took massive cuts. Police officers who took an interest were often paid off, so very few arrests were made.

4-11-44

Although not invented by black Americans, numbers games were especially popular in black communities and in Harlem, where they attracted many middle-class players. In the north-eastern United States, illegal gambling was viewed as being essentially a "black problem," and the popular 4-11-44 bet became a byword for black poverty, frequently used in racist songs that portrayed black Americans as superstitious and irresponsible. The 4-11-44 bet also appears in many blues songs of the time, but its origins are still uncertain.

Numbers games acquired a particular popularity in these communities in the 1920s, and the results were not entirely harmful. The racist mockery of the 1900s and 1910s had given way to a backlash—the Harlem Renaissance—in which black Americans rediscovered their cultural identity, fostered a sense of pride and developed the doctrine of "buying black"— encouraging black residents to choose local black businesses (and boycott racist ones) and thus reinvest black dollars in their community. Policy bankers in Harlem got rich from the proceeds of illegal gambling, but they were also among the first to lend money to Harlem's poorest residents.

Although the Great Depression saw an enormous surge in interest in numbers games as desperate people clung to a chance of financial salvation, it also saw a change in the balance of power among numbers operators. The Mob, which had been content to keep out of numbers games, lost a great deal of money to falling sales in other illicit sectors and decided to compensate by taking over Harlem's numbers games with intimidation and violence. The end of Prohibition in 1933 and a mass crackdown on corruption in law enforcement saw a reduction in the kind of large-scale numbers rackets that occurred in Harlem and other poor communities.

Illegal gambling, however, is still very much alive.

WHY BUSES COME IN THREES

The extremely irritating tendency of buses to lag behind scheduled timetables, before arriving in a seething glut half an hour too late, is a well-documented phenomenon of mass transit known as bunching. Bus companies have invested a lot of money and effort in attempts to alleviate it, and advances in communications technology mean that the worst bunching can now be more easily spotted.

The problem, though, is essentially mathematical in nature, and difficult to eradicate completely. Furthermore, unlike on railways and subways, where all trains are monitored and can be held in stations to even out the gaps between them, buses have to work within a much larger organic system of traffic, where they may be forced to keep moving.

Let me explain

On a given bus route in a major city, the buses leave the depot at fixed intervals a few minutes apart. As the buses start at 8:15 in the morning, a significant number of morning commuters have shown up at most or all of the stops on the route. The first bus stops at all of them, picking up a large number of morning commuters, which causes it to spend a fairly long time at each stop.

The next bus, departing at 8:25, also stops at every bus stop, but this time only picks up the smaller number of commuters who've come in the last 10 minutes, thereby spending less time at each stop, while the first bus, only a few stops ahead, is still picking up lots of people. This second bus begins to catch up with the first one. The third bus gets even closer as the number of commuters waiting on the route decreases more, and so the process continues. After rush hour, it tends to even out a little, though, as there are far fewer people, and buses can be spaced out without making people late.

But because the regularity of buses is not matched by the comparatively unpredictable patterns of passengers showing up at the stops, bunching can be brought on by an unusually large group of people arriving at a single bus stop at any given time, and thus forcing one bus to stop for quite a while as others close the distance to it.

As the bunching process is repeated over the whole day, especially when combined with traffic lights and other road delays that stop the buses in front and allow the ones behind to catch up, buses get bunched up on their route, and by the end of the route large gaps may appear in the bus service, coming between groups of several buses arriving all at once.

555

The problem with phone numbers as plot elements in TV and film is that they tend to exist in reality, usually resulting in thousands of nuisance calls by those with too much free time. American rock band Tommy Tutone's 1982 hit *867-5309/ Jenny*—about a girl's phone number written on a restroom wall—is still remembered for a spate of prank calls to the number. Some businesses, including a plumbing company in Rhode Island, have chosen to use that number because it's so widely known. In fact, this number's marketability has actually caused bidding wars and even a lawsuit as companies have vied for the privilege of using it.

American films and television have traditionally avoided such issues by agreeing with telephone companies on an area code reserved exclusively for fictional purposes. The practice appears to have begun in the 1950s and 1960s, with an early example in the film *A Patch of Blue* (1965), which also established a fake phone number—555-2368—since used in *Ghostbusters*, *Close Encounters of the Third Kind*, and *Memento*, among others.

It seems likely that *555* was chosen, and gained currency, partly because of its memorability as a repeated digit, but also because (in the days of named telephone exchanges) there were no major English place names that combined the letters J, K, and L (the letters assigned to the number 5 on the dial). The *555* number was sometimes given a fictional exchange name as well, such as Klondike-5 (KL5), which features in phone numbers in *The Simpsons.* The suffix 2368 was probably chosen for its use in 1940s telephone advertising, which referred to Exchange 2368 as a CENTral exchange (look at the letters on your phone's keypad again).

With growing pressure on the telephone system, the administrators of the North American Numbering Plan have opened up the 555 exchange code, and now only a certain range (555-0100 to 555-0199) are reserved for fictional use.

There is no true British equivalent to the 555 number, and the exchange code is used in this country like any other. However, Britain's Ofcom has reserved, for fictional purposes, the 01632 area code, blocks of numbers in most major British cities (usually in the 496-0000 to 496-0999 range), and all cell phone numbers beginning with 07700 900.

Ringing the almighty

Recently, some films and TV series have bucked this trend. *Bruce Almighty* (2003), for example, featured a personal number for God. This turned out to belong to a church in Sanford, North Carolina, who received hundreds of calls asking for help and forgiveness. And a few asking for smiting, I would imagine. (That church's pastor happened to be named Bruce!) The number also worked in several other area codes in the United States, as well as in one area in England. The number was changed to a 555- number in the DVD and TV versions to avoid such troubles. The television series *24* and *Scrubs,* among others, have been shrewder, incorporating real phone numbers as promotional devices—the number for *24*'s CTU (Counter Terrorist Unit) actually belongs to the *24* production staff, while Scrubs's Dr. Chris Turk is assigned the number 1-916-225-5887—1-916-CALL-TUR(k)—which connects to an answering machine and a message from cast members.

17, 2, 456, 76, 35, 237, 81, 9 ... with fried rice.

NUMBERS STATIONS

These cryptic radio transmissions are broadcast all over the world, usually on shortwave bands, and consist mainly of long spoken lists of numbers. The very strangeness of numbers stations has attracted a subculture of enthusiastic listeners.

Most people agree that numbers stations are linked to espionage, and this was all but officially confirmed in 1998 by a British DTI spokesman (Dept. of Trade and Industry, comparable to the FCC), who added that "they are not for, shall we say, public consumption." It seems likely that the broadcasts can be decoded only by an agent with the correct "one-time pad"—a list of randomly generated numbers that is used to encode and decode a single message, before being destroyed—as anything else would be rather unsafe.

Although it's fairly easy to trace the origin of radio broadcasts, numbers stations usually broadcast from many hundreds of miles away, and are usually located on territory friendly to their agents. It's difficult to trace radio listeners and almost impossible to tell what's being listened to, and numbers stations have survived for decades as a safe method of communication. Phones and Internet connections can be (and often are) automatically monitored for suspicious phrases, but tracing one spy amid the millions of ordinary radio listeners in any city would be absurdly impractical and probably not worth the expense. The broadcasts usually follow a regular schedule, which might be broken in exceptional circumstances (such as a Moscow broadcast during the 1991 Soviet coup, which consisted of constant repetitions of the number five). Each broadcast is usually introduced by a short, distinctive audio clip, presumably to make it easier for agents to tune in— Britain's MI6 used two bars of "The Lincolnshire Poacher" for many years. After this comes a list of numbers read by an automated voice, usually repeated once to avoid errors.

There has only been one criminal case involving a numbers station—a Cuban broadcast known as *¡Atención!*— in the mid-1990s. Infamously badly run and plagued with technical problems, ¡Atención! had conclusively revealed its origin by accidentally rebroadcasting Radio Havana on its frequency. ¡Atención! was broadcasting to the Wasp Network, a group of five Cuban agents in Florida who used a computer program to decipher the numbers. When FBI agents broke into the Cubans' apartment and copied the decryption program, they discovered a plan to infiltrate anti-Castro groups, which led to the "Cuban Five" being sentenced to long prison terms. Their case remains controversial, as the group they were infiltrating is considered a terrorist group in Cuba and the information they sent back was not classified. Many politicans and human rights groups have petitioned the United States government to release them.

THE 23 ENIGMA

This numerological theory claims that the number 23 recurs in many different and surprising places. Supposedly, 23 can be connected to any significant event or phenomenon, good or bad. For instance, people have 23 pairs of chromosomes, Aleister Crowley (who started studying magic at the age of 23) defined 23 as "the number of life," and the Earth's axis is tilted at an angle of 23.5 degrees. The 23 Enigma (which, by the way, is unrelated to the old slang expression "23, skidoo!") has inspired two films, 23 (discussed below) and *The Number 23*, a widely panned Jim Carrey effort about a man who becomes obsessed with the 23 Enigma. Carrey even named his production company JC23, not that that did the film much good.

The idea that 23 could somehow have mystic power because it can be linked coincidentally to certain events is, of course, deeply irrational and entirely unconvincing. In this case, however, that's pretty much the point. The 23 Enigma originates not in any ancient text, but in a series of novels published in 1975 called the *Illuminatus!* trilogy, by Robert Shea and Robert Anton Wilson. The trilogy is a complex satirical conspiracy story, and numerology, including the significance of the number 23, is one of its major themes.

Wilson appears to have been inspired by a story he heard from the author William S. Burroughs. While in Tangier in 1960, Burroughs made the acquaintance of a sailor, Captain Clark, who boasted to Burroughs that he had run his ferry service for 23 years with not a single accident. That same day, the ship sank, killing Clark and all the passengers. Burroughs was ruminating on this news that evening when he heard a report on the radio of a plane crash in Florida. The plane was Flight 23, piloted by a Captain Clark.

It's not funny...

Wilson and the *Illuminatus!* trilogy are strongly linked to Discordianism, a postmodern "joke" religion, that celebrates confusion and chaos and claims to worship Eris, the ancient Greek goddess of discord.* The 23 Enigma seems intended as

---

* The postmodernity of the joke here is apparently derived from blurred boundaries between what's meant to be serious and what isn't. The "holy book," *Principia Discordia*, ends with the words, "If you think the *Principia* is just a ha-ha, then go read it again." As Moe says in *The Simpsons*: "It's PoMo... Postmodern? Yeah, all right, weird for the sake of weird."

a joke about the self-fulfilling nature of numerology and the ease with which human pattern recognition can be fooled. The numbers 17 and 5 are similarly revered by Discordians, and can be said to be related to 23 because the digits of 17 add up to 8, or 2^3, and of course $2 + 3 = 5$.

It wasn't so funny, however, for a German hacker named Karl Koch. Koch and his associates hacked into a number of American military systems from Hanover and Berlin and sold the data to the Soviet KGB. Koch was obsessed with the *Illuminatus!* trilogy, using the name of the book's protagonist, Hagbard Celine, as a pseudonym for his activities. He was also severely paranoid and addicted to cocaine, and became convinced that he, like his fictional namesake, was fighting against a vast Illuminati conspiracy. Koch was captured, along with those he was working with, in March 1989, provoking an international spy scandal. He eventually killed himself on May 23, 1989—at the age of 23. The 1998 film *23* is based on his life.

419 SCAMS

You've probably received the occasional email from 419 scammers. Typically from Nigeria or elsewhere in Africa, these missives appeal, in broken English, to naïvete and greed. You know the story: there's an enormous sum of money stuck in a far-flung bank account that'll be forfeited if it's not removed from the country soon, and YOU, as a foreigner, have been selected to help. You're promised a sizeable cut of the stricken money in exchange for your help, but you do need to pay a handling fee first, for which they'll just need your bank details.

Several further techniques are used to add an air of authenticity or relatability. In many cases, the money has been left behind after the death of a major public figure and the emailer is a grief-stricken friend or relative, earning the sympathy of the victim. Particularly religious recipients can be swayed by frequent reference to Jesus. Elements of truth—an air crash death that actually occurred, for example—can be used to give a shred of credibility to the story.

This form of advance fee fraud is known as a 419 scam, after Section 419 of the Nigerian penal code, which concerns cons of this type (in much the same way as 187s; see page 369). In recent years the bad grammar and obvious lies in the emails have made them a source of humor, and Nigerian email scams are now so widespread that many legitimate emails from Nigerian businesses are filtered out by overzealous software.

Known as "yahoo boys" in Nigeria, 419 scammers are young men who spend hours in Internet cafés, trawling for Western email addresses and paying off any police who might take an interest. In a country still gripped by political violence, corruption and economic uncertainty, there are many worse ways to make a living. Many people are able to live the high life on the proceeds of Internet crime, but the "yahoo millionaire" lifestyle is increasingly condemned as dishonest, superficial and foolish (hence the name, unrelated to the search engine Yahoo!, or, as far as I know, to Swift's *Gulliver's Travels*), and many Nigerians are angry at the tarnishing of the country's image abroad.

Yahoo boys are not usually acting out of desperation, nor are they simply trying to get lucky with email addresses. Many are affiliated with dangerous organized crime gangs in Nigeria and elsewhere, and the consequences of falling for 419 scams can occasionally be disastrous. The arrangement often involves the victim traveling to Nigeria—a crime in itself if done without a visa, which can then be used by the fraudsters to blackmail their victim. If a victim then tries to get their money back, the gangsters may threaten physical violence, and several people have been kidnapped and even killed when attempting to escape 419 scams.

THE PIRAHÃ TRIBE

For one small Amazonian tribe, few of the numbers discussed here will have even the slightest meaning or relevance. (Otherwise, they'd obviously be rushing down to the local Amazon bookstore for a copy.)

The Pirahã people (the name is pronounced with the stress on the last syllable) live on the banks of the Maici river in northwestern Brazil, and currently number only a few hundred. They have had almost no contact with the wider world since they were found by Brazilian explorers in the eighteenth century. Their culture as a whole is basic and rooted in the immediate present, with no written history, and little preparation for the future. Studies of it have been controversial in academic circles, particularly in the world of linguistics.

The Pirahã language is extremely simple, and this extends to numbers, which for the Pirahã are only three—one, two and many. Even these are fairly inexact—translating more like "one or two," "a few," "a lot." While this in itself is not unheard-of among remote tribes, the issue here seems to be a deep-rooted cultural one. Most remote tribes with one-two-many counting systems can be taught to count more precisely, but the Pirahã seem incapable of grasping the idea. Daniel Everett, a linguist, former missionary, and leading expert on the tribe, conducted tests in which he placed a number of objects in front of Pirahã members, and asked them to take the same number from a can and place them in front of him. For numbers below three, the Pirahã did well in the tests, but usually failed when higher numbers were introduced.

In order to preserve their unique culture, the Pirahã tribe's land is now a reservation; but they are under constant threat, their population having declined massively since they were first discovered.

THE 10 PERCENT MYTH

"What's holding you back? Just one fact—one scientific fact. That is all. Because, as Science says, you are using only one-tenth of your real brain-power!"
—Advertisement for the Pelman Institute

"Thank God, nurse! The bullet passed through the 90 percent he didn't use!"
—Something no one has *ever* said

You've almost certainly heard this one trotted out at some point—we only use 10 percent (or another small fraction) of our brains and presumably would gain amazing intellectual powers if we could only unlock the other 90 percent. The idea is untrue, and scientifically invalid: It would make no sense for humans to evolve large brains over millions of years only to leave them mostly inactive.

It does, however, seem to have its origins in mainstream science, particularly phrenology, a Victorian pseudoscience (then mainstream) that held that brain structure, and hence personality, could be determined by measuring the shape of the skull. The central idea of phrenology—that the brain can be divided up into discrete sections with various responsibilities—has been discredited by modern brain scans. Before these scans, scientists relied on using electrodes to stimulate areas of the brain to see what happened. Areas that produced no obvious physical reaction (like twitching limbs) when stimulated were considered inactive.

Another possible origin is misinterpretation of glial cells (which "glue" neurons together, outnumbering them about 10 to 1). Additionally, a 1930s experiment by K. S. Lashley on rats found that they could lose most of their brains and still be able to run around.

Possibly the earliest, and probably the best-known, appearance of the 10 percent myth was in a 1944 advertisement for the Pelman Institute, a self-help correspondence course with rather optimistic claims. "Pelmanism" was one of the most popular miracle self-help courses in an era full of them, and millions grew up "knowing" they only used 10 percent of their brains.

The false statistic continued to appear in ads for many years, especially those promoting self-improvement and self-help, reaching something of a peak during the self-help boom of the 1990s. With the adherence to scientific method that has long distinguished them, the psychic lobby, including "paranormalist" Uri Geller, leapt on the claim as evidence of psychic powers, the idea being that these powers could be discovered if only the unused portion were unlocked.

This idea is a classic example of the argument from ignorance (because science doesn't know everything about the brain, it can't disprove psychic powers, therefore they must exist), but there's a grain of truth in it. Most people do underuse their brains, and the 10 percent myth plays on ubiquitous insecurity about intelligence and mental powers which drives the sales of so many modern-day Pelmanist quick fixes.

NUMBERS IN MYTHOLOGY AND RELIGION

SEVEN

The number seven crops up everywhere, particularly when religious or mystical elements are involved. According to Genesis (and some increasingly vocal fringe religious types), the world was created in seven days (OK, six days' work and a day of rest).

The Catholic Church features Seven Sacraments, beginning with three sacraments of initiation into the Church: Baptism (as a child or an adult), Confirmation, and the Eucharist (including Mass and Communion). There are also two Sacraments of Healing—Reconciliation or Penance (including confession), and the Anointing of the Sick by a priest; and two mutually exclusive Sacraments of Vocation: Marriage and Holy Orders. A number of these sacraments make up the Last Rites administered to dying

Deadly Sins	Heavenly Virtues
Gluttony	Temperance
Envy	Kindness
Greed	Charity
Pride	Humility
Lust	Chastity
Sloth	Zeal
Wrath	Meekness

Catholics—a final Penance (depending on whether the person can still speak), Anointment, and a last Eucharist. In deathbed conversions, hasty Baptism and Confirmation is also necessary.

Christianity also features seven Deadly Sins, which are sometimes shown counterbalanced by seven Heavenly Virtues. Multiples of seven also appear in this way—there are fourteen Stations of the Cross (observed mainly in the Catholic Church), fourteen Holy Helpers (saints venerated in less scientific times as effective against various illnesses), and events in the Bible are often described as happening on the fourteenth day of a given month.

Unsurprisingly, given the common origin of the Abrahamic religions, a similar concept of seven divine traits exists in Judaism, represented in the seven branches of the menorah. The Star of David has seven parts (six points and the center), and there are seven holidays in the Jewish year. In Islam, there are seven verses in the first chapter (sura) of the Qur'an.

The divinity of the number seven may also be the reason for the number six being traditionally unlucky in religion: If seven represents Godly perfection, six represents the imperfections and flaws of man.

Seven's everywhere

The exact reason for seven's significance is not very clear. It could have to do with the seven "heavenly bodies" visible to the naked eye in the time before astronomy—the sun, the moon, Mercury, Venus, Mars, Saturn, and Jupiter. This is probably the origin of the Jewish and Muslim (and to some degree Christian) idea of seven heavens (see page 358). It certainly helps that seven is relatively small and a prime number, though.

This theory does at least explain the fact that seven is significant well outside the context of the Abrahamic religions. In Japanese mythology, for instance, there are seven gods of good fortune (*shichi fukujin*), people are reincarnated seven times in Japanese Buddhism, and there are seven principles in the *bushido* samurai code.

We also generally refer to seven colors in a rainbow, even though we rarely see more than four and they don't generally have distinct boundaries. Isaac Newton, who discovered through experiments with prisms that white light was made up of colored components, added the colors orange and indigo so as to conform to his theory that the colors of the spectrum corresponded to the seven major notes of a musical scale.

The choice of a seven-day week is probably mainly because of convenient subdivision of time. The Babylonians, who laid the foundations of our current measurement of time 5,000 years ago, were the first to divide the year into months based on the lunar cycle*. The lunar cycle is a rather awkward 29 days long, though, so for the sake of convenience the year was divided up into months of 28 days, which could then be subdivided neatly into four seven-day weeks.

Seven is also often used for more worldly collections of things, seemingly to exploit its mythological resonance. "Seven Seas" referred to a number of different collections of bodies of water, and is still sometimes used today to refer to the Antarctic, Arctic, North and South Atlantic, North and South Pacific, and Indian oceans. It seems likely that it was simply a poetic turn of phrase meaning all the oceans, and there is some evidence for the number seven being synonymous, for a time, with "several."

---

* Before the adoption of the Julian calendar in England, the country used a lunar calendar, with 13 months of 28 days. A quick check with a calculator will show that this leaves us one day short of a full year. The old tradition of "a year and a day" as a standard time period for legal purposes, and in neopagan religions and secret societies, probably originated here, with the extra day being to bring the 13 months up to a full solar year.

THE SEVEN WONDERS
OF THE ANCIENT WORLD

* The Great Pyramid of Khufu *
Completed 2560 B.C. at Giza, Egypt.
It is the only Wonder still standing.

* The Hanging Gardens of Babylon *
Completed early 6th century B.C. on the Euphrates,
near modern Baghdad.
Destroyed by earthquake in the first century A.D.

* The Temple of Artemis *
Completed c. 550 B.C. at Ephesus,
near modern Izmir, Turkey.
Destroyed and rebuilt repeatedly—finally torn
down by a mob in A.D. 401

* The Statue of Zeus *
Completed c. 450 B.C. at Olympia, Greece.
Probably destroyed by fire in A.D. 462

* The Mausoleum (tomb of King Mausollos,
hence the name) *
Completed 350 B.C. at Halicarnassus
(now Bodrum), Turkey.
Destroyed by earthquake and subsequent Crusader
disassembly in late 15th century A.D.

* The Colossus (statue of Helios) *
Completed 282 B.C. at Rhodes, Greece.
Destroyed by earthquake in 226 B.C.

* The Lighthouse of Alexandria *
Completed c. 280 B.C. in Alexandria, Egypt.
Destroyed by successive earthquakes in
the 14th century A.D.

THE NUMBER OF THE BEAST?

Here is wisdom. Let him that hath understanding count
the number of the beast: for it is the number of a man;
and his number is six hundred threescore and six.

—REVELATIONS 13: 18

The number sequence 666 has long been considered
unlucky in Christian traditions because of this passage from
Revelations, which associates the number with the Devil. Like
thirteen (see page 440), there is a widespread superstition
about 666, so widespread that it's catchily known as
hexakosioihexekontahexaphobia. It is interesting to note
that 2006 brought concern from pregnant women expecting
children on June 6 of that year—not helped by the heavily
publicized release of a remake of the film *The Omen* on that date.

Highway 666 in the western United States was renumbered to 491 after suggestions that the high rate of accidents was due to Satanic influence, although its safety record probably had more to do with the removal of all the road signs by thieves who sold them on eBay. The town of Reeves, Louisiana, successfully petitioned to change its area code from 666 to 749. One wonders whether New York or Los Angeles residents would have been quite as concerned. In China, however, 666 is prominently displayed in shop windows (see Chinese Lucky (and Unlucky) Numbers on page 428).

There are various theories about why 666 was chosen. Many revolve around the mystic practice of "gematria," with 666 possibly representing Nero, who was known for his persecution of Christians. See the entry on gematria (page 419) for details on how the numbers are assigned here.

Gematria interpretation

If the Greek phrase Νερων Καισαρ (Neron Kaisar = Emperor Nero) is transliterated into Hebrew, we are left with:

N	R	W	N	Q	S	R
נ	ר	ו	ן	ק	ס	ר
50 +	200 +	6 +	50 +	100 +	60 +	200 = 666

(Note: Hebrew is actually written right-to-left, but is shown the other way round here for clarity's sake.)

Although this can be done with a number of Roman emperors, Nero is perhaps more likely than most to be the Beast, as he also satisfies some of the Greek manuscripts that give the Number of the Beast as 616, if his Latin name, Nero Caesar, is transliterated into Hebrew:

N	R	W	Q	S	R
נ	ר	ו	ק	ס	ר
50 +	200 +	6 +	100 +	60 +	200 = 616

Nero is the only one to satisfy both theories in this way, but numerology, even more than most pseudosciences, is full of vague definitions, suspect methods, and absurd gaps in logic. Many cranks over the centuries have tried to apply the Number of the Beast to political or ideological opponents, including Martin Luther, the Pope, Napoleon Bonaparte, and most recently President Barack Obama.

A more mundane explanation for the origin of 666 is that it's simply used as a general large number. In Roman numerals (see page 477), 666 is DCLXVI—all the Roman numerals below M used once, possibly suggesting simply that the Beast is a large or powerful force. It's also possible that, given the holiness of 7 in the Bible, 6 is intended to represent the imperfection of man (described as being created on the 6th day), and 666—"the number of a man"—is simply a numerical representation of the Beast as the imperfections of humanity. It's much easier to blame Satan than oneself, of course, and that's been a favorite activity of religious extremists for hundreds of years.

GEMATRIA AND THE BIBLE CODE

"Gematria" is a term encompassing various long-running traditions of numerology that involve assigning numeric values to letters of an alphabet in order to find some hidden meaning in them. There are a vast number of systems for doing this in the Greek, Hebrew, and Arabic alphabets among others, and it's also used in modern numerology (see page 422). The traditional Jewish system of gematria assigns letters in the Hebrew alphabet to numbers according to this scheme:

Hebrew letter	Rough English equivalent (modern Hebrew)	Numeric value
א (aleph)	glottal stop/no pronunciation	1
ב (bet)	B or V	2
ג (gimel)	G	3
ד (dalet)	D	4
ה (hei)	H	5
ו (vav)	V or O or U	6
ז (zayin)	Z	7
ח (cheit)	Ch (as in 'loch')	8
ט (tet)	T	9
י (yod)	Y	10
ך or כ (kaf)	K or Kh	20
ל (lamed)	L	30
ם or מ (mem)	M	40
ן or נ (nun)	N	50
ס (samekh)	S	60
ע (ayin)	glottal stop/silent	70
ף or פ (pei)	P or F	80
ץ or צ (tsadei)	Ts	90
ק (qof)	Q	100
ר (resh)	R	200
ש (shin)	S or Sh	300
ת (tav)	T	400

The reason for this wide-ranging distribution of numbers is that Hebrew letters were used as numbers, in a similar way to Roman numerals (see page 477), for many centuries, although modern Hebrew, like most languages, uses Western-style decimal numbers for pretty much everything. Back then, though, the assignment of letters to numbers had to jump into tens and then hundreds, since otherwise such a number system could go up to only 22. Some systems then go on to add numeric values to final Hebrew letters (those at the ends of words, which are sometimes written differently).

Anyway, once the numbers have been assigned, it's time to look at how they fit into words and their meaning. Sometimes this happens in rather an interesting way. Here's an example I stole from the film π (see page 372), though to be fair I did check it:

The Hebrew word for "father" is "ab", spelled אָב.
(Hebrew is written right-to-left, like Arabic).
The gematria value for this, according to the table
on page 79 is 1 + 2 = 3.

The Hebrew word for "mother" is "em", spelled אֵם.
Looking at the table on page 79, we get the
gematria value 1 + 40 = 41.

If we then look at the Hebrew word for "child"—
"yaelaed", spelled יֶלֶד and take that gematria value we
get 10 + 30 + 4 = 44. This is the sum of the values
for "mother" and "father," just as a mother and father
combine to create a child.

The writing's on the wall

Another well-known example of gematria has to do with the Hebrew word for live—"chai," spelled חי with a gematria value of 18. A common expression for charity among devout Jews is "to give twice chai"—an idea of a charitable life as a double life, living for others as much as yourself. This tradition is often honored at weddings, bar mitzvahs, and other celebrations, where money is traditionally given in multiples of 36—twice 18 and hence "twice chai."

The first person to use gematria was not Jewish (the idea of gematria predates its adaptation in Jewish mysticism, although this is where it's now most popular) but Mesopotamian—Sargon II, ruler of Mesopotamia in the eighth century B.C., built the perimeter wall of his palace 16,283 cubits long, to correspond to the gematria value of his name in his language. The ancient Greeks also used a form of gematria (the word is etymologically linked to the word "geometry"), but we don't really have space to look at every kind of gematria.

However, if gematria were really some sort of mystic divination system, it should hold true for pretty much everything, whereas in fact there are hundreds of words with identical numbers that are semantically unrelated. Some people, however, place great faith in this sort of thing, although gematria is generally viewed as an interesting numeric game, rather than something to live by.

Some have made some rather wild predictions with numbers in religion, however. By looking at the letters of the Bible (and the Torah), using numeric sequences to choose the relevant letters from a grid of the original Hebrew, a number of people have claimed to find hidden codes in these holy books which predict the future. Although some have been sort of successful (a period of geopolitical instability from about 2002 onward, for instance*), the prediction of nuclear apocalypse in 2006 is now significantly overdue. The Number of the Beast (see page 416) may derive from gematria, and a form of gematria is often used to link it back to some perceived evil of the current time.

MODERN NUMEROLOGY

Unlike some of the scientific ideas mentioned elsewhere, numerology occupies the most irrational end of the spectrum of ideas and theories about numbers. The practice of numerology has been going on in some form for many thousands of years—the system of lucky and unlucky numbers still used in China, for instance, goes back many centuries (see page 428). Modern numerology in the West, however, began in the late twentieth century, drawing on various historical traditions, including

---

* On the other hand, when has the world ever really been stable?

that of the Greek mathematician Pythagoras and Kabbalistic gematria (see page 419).

Modern numerology assigns fairly vague significance to various digits, usually only the digits 0–9. The meanings shown here are common ones from several different schools of thought, and hence may appear self-contradictory as well as sometimes rather obvious:

0—everything, existence, beyondness, universality

1—solitude, unity, independence, initiative

2—duality, division, cooperation

3—movement, synthesis, divinity
(in Christian tradition—see page 443)

4—solidity, resistance, materiality

5—life, love, growth, regeneration

6—union, perfection, wholeness, imperfection of man
(in Christian tradition—see page 418)

7—magic, mysticism, wisdom, divinity
(see Seven, page 410)

8—good luck (especially in China), practicality,
justice, power

9—major change, finality, achievement

There's also a numerological theory revolving around the number 23 (see page 429).

It all adds up

The actual practice of numerology generally involves analyzing numbers as they appear in the subject's life, particularly where they recur. A form of gematria (see page 429) is particularly popular, often involving adding up the letters in people's names. In this example, I'm using a popular system where the letters are numbered only up to 9, after which the numbering repeats again (so 1 could be A, or J, or S, etc.), but there are as many methods of assigning numbers to letters as there are interpretations of the numbers:

J	A	M	I	E		B	U	C	H	A	N
1	1	4	9	5		2	3	3	8	1	5

The numbers are added together in a process known as digit summing. This can be done as many times as necessary to produce a single digit, since single digits are used frequently in everyday life and hence provide more convenient coincidences. I mean, single digits are more magical.

$1 + 1 + 4 + 9 + 5 + 2 + 3 + 3 + 8 + 1 + 5 = 42$ (I quite like the *Hitchhiker's Guide to the Galaxy* associations, anyway)

$4 + 2 = 6$

So, rather confusingly, I'm either perfect or deeply imperfect. Or related in some way to notions of union. Or something.

Ultimately, numerology is concerned with nothing more than finding absurdly vague meaning in numeric coincidence. The faculty of pattern recognition is often too easily fooled by coincidence.

Numbers rule the universe

Numerologists sometimes cite Pythagoras's axiom that numbers "rule the universe" as the origin of their discipline, but this seems almost a perversion of mathematical values. Pythagoras was a mathematician as well as a mystic and is certainly more famous today for the Pythagorean Theorem than for his mysticism.* To me, the vague meanings and coincidences of numerology seem to be no match for the fascination of rational mathematical concepts like the Fibonacci sequence, which demonstrate in scientific terms how numbers really rule the universe.

One might argue that humans have believed in some form of nonsense for generations, and if they want to believe it,

---

* The postmodernity of the joke here is apparently derived from blurred boundaries between what's meant to be serious and what isn't. The "holy book," *Principia Discordia*, ends with the words, 'If you think the *Principia* is just a ha-ha, then go read it again.' As Moe says in *The Simpsons*: "It's PoMo ... Postmodern? Yeah, all right, weird for the sake of weird."

where's the harm? But when people believe such irrational things, there's always the danger that they'll act on them, and such was the case in a murder trial in Washington, D.C., in 2006. According to the *Washington Post* report of the story, the trial had already taken two strange turns—a prosecution witness testifying while under the influence of marijuana and, more sinister, a juror being tracked down by a major figure in the case—when the jury reported that one of their number was using numerology rather than evidence to determine her position. The juror was eventually removed, and two men were found guilty of the murder.

Bent as a Nine-Kyat Note

An even more bizarre story of faith in numerology comes from 1980s Myanmar (Burma). The country has been ruled by a military junta since 1962, and between 1974 and 1988 was effectively ruled (but not ruled effectively) by General Ne Win, who suppressed political dissent with autocratic laws and military force. Ne Win's economic policy was especially disastrous, characterized by extreme isolationism. Not only that, but he was also corrupt—as crooked as a nine dollar bill.

The general was a keen numerology enthusiast, and when his personal astrologer and numerologist advised him that his lucky number was 9, and that he'd live to be 90 if he placed the number all around him, he announced one day that he was reissuing the kyat (Burma's currency) in notes which were multiples of 9, and that, by the way, everyone's decimal-system life savings were now entirely worthless. In a rather pleasing numeric twist, this conversion was one of the major catalysts for the "8888 Uprising," which began on August 8, 1988. Ne Win, however, got his wish—he died in 2002, at the age of 91.

CHINESE LUCKY (AND UNLUCKY) NUMBERS

The nature of Chinese languages, with many very similar-sounding words, leads to most digits being considered lucky or unlucky usually because of homophony (words sounding similar to other words when spoken) in the same way as text-messaging uses 2 for "to," 4 for "for," etc. This is a non-exhaustive list of them (which vary significantly across China's 1.3 billion inhabitants and numerous dialects).

1

Much as in the West, the number 1 can be interpreted as representing either unity or loneliness.

2

The number 2 sounds like the word "easy" in the Cantonese language spoken in much of China, but the idea of a pair has wide-ranging importance. Doubling— "double happiness" or "double prosperity"—is a common way of intensifying good wishes.

3

A homophone of the word "life," the number 3 is a
rather auspicious number, especially when combined
with other lucky numbers.

4

An unlucky number across the Far East, in much the
same way as 13 is in Western cultures (see page 440).
Four, and by extension all numbers containing the
digit, is associated with death because the two words
sound similar in most dialects. Many Chinese-made
products, including Nokia phones and Canon cameras,
skip from 3 to 5 in model numbers. In some areas,
however, it sounds closer to the word "task" and is
considered lucky for this reason.

5

The number 5 is associated with the five elements
(fire, earth, air, water, and the ether) and also, in
Mandarin, with the word meaning "I" or "me." In
Cantonese, however, 5 sounds closer to the word "not."

6

While 666 is still the subject of Satanic superstition in
the West (see The Number of the Beast?, page 416),
it's routinely displayed in Chinese shop windows. The
number 6 sounds like the word for "smooth" or "easy,"
and repeating it three times maximizes the effect.

7

Although the number 7 is associated with death and tragedy, it does not carry the same dread as 4. It also has associations with togetherness, expressed in the folk tale of the Cowherd and the Weaver Girl, two lovers forced apart by the gods and permitted to meet only once a year, on the seventh day of the seventh lunar month. In China, this day is celebrated as *Qi Xi*—similar to Valentine's Day, with an element of supernatural tragedy—and similar celebrations occur elsewhere in Eastern Asia.

The seventh month of the Chinese calendar (generally around August) is "The Month of the Hungry Ghosts," when the spirits of the dead wander among the living. It isn't a wholly inauspicious time— many families pay homage to dead ancestors, but it's considered wise to try not to annoy them. Many people leave gifts for the ghosts and avoid disturbing them by traveling or moving to a new house.

8

The start time of the Beijing Olympics—around 8:08 p.m. on August 8, 2008—reflects China's relationship with the number 8. It's something of a national obsession—license plates and telephone numbers containing eights can command thousands of dollars. The root of this phenomenon is partly in homophony, with the word "eight" sounding similar to "wealth" or "prosper," but there's also a deeper philosophical meaning. The number 8 resonates with the Buddhist Eightfold Path, which defines eight morally correct courses of action for Buddhists, who make up about half of the Chinese population.

The other major Chinese philosophies, Confucianism and Taoism, also have eight at their root. The Bagua is a fundamental philosophical concept that breaks the universe into eight elements whose numerous manifestations include weather, natural formations, family members, compass points and moods. As such, eight is not simply a number of wealth, but one that touches the very root of China's spiritual life.

9

Like 6 and 8, the number 9 is considered lucky. Through homophony, it's associated with stability and lasting happiness, and hence is much in evidence at weddings and similar major life events. In Cantonese, it's roughly homophonous to "sufficient," which is similarly auspicious. As the highest single-digit number, it's also associated with greatness and particularly the Emperors of China.

These numbers are especially lucky (or unlucky) when combined with each other. Repeated lucky digits are preferable to single ones, as this intensifies their effect, and combining numbers can create especially lucky phrases. For instance, 168 can be taken to mean "smoothly prosperous together"—a good omen for any business deal—while even 4 can be redeemed in this way—54 in Cantonese suggests immortality ("no death")—but is especially unlucky when combined with 1 into 14, suggesting one's own death, or dying alone. Many high-rise buildings in China skip the fourteenth floor (and sometimes all floor numbers with 4 in them), as well as increasingly adopting the Western custom of skipping the thirteenth. There are marketing advantages here as well, of course—a shrewd Chinese developer can sell a fiftieth-floor apartment in a thirty-six-story building.

ZODIACS

Western zodiac

The traditional Western zodiac consists of twelve symbols, each corresponding to a period of roughly a month, based on the position of the sun relative to certain constellations in the sky, which changes across the year. People born at certain times are assigned "star signs" based on their date of birth, which are associated with vaguely defined personality traits:

Aries (Ram)—March 21 to April 20—Energetic, enthusiastic, and confident, but may also be quick to anger, impatient, and impulsive.

Taurus (Bull)—April 21 to May 21—Reliable, placid, and loyal but possibly possessive and stubborn.

Gemini (Twins [Castor and Pollux])—May 22 to June 21—Versatile, eloquent, and witty but, on the other hand, may be nervous and scheming.

Cancer (Crab)—June 22 to July 23—Loving, protective, and intuitive but prone to be over emotional and clingy.

Leo (Lion)—July 24 to August 23—Enthusiastic, generous and creative but also associated with pompousness, interference, and bossiness.

Virgo (Virgin)—August 24 to September 23—Modest, reliable, and intelligent but with a fussy, conservative side.

Libra (Scales)—September 24 to October 23—Diplomatic, sociable, and idealistic but sometimes indecisive and easily influenced.

Scorpio (Scorpion)—October 24 to November 22—Determined and passionate but might be jealous, obsessive, and deceitful.

Sagittarius (Archer)—November 23 to December 21—Optimistic, honest, and philosophical, with the potential for carelessness and irresponsibility.

Capricorn (Goat)—December 22 to January 20—Prudent, careful, and reserved but perhaps also pessimistic and grudging.

Aquarius (Water Bearer)—January 21 to February 19—Friendly, intelligent, loyal, and inventive but contrary and prone to detachment.

Pisces (Two Fish)—February 20 to March 20—Sensitive, unworldly, and sympathetic but might be escapist, vague, and weak-willed.

There's also a thirteenth sign—"Ophiuchus" the serpent-bearer—which is not recognized by most astrologers, perhaps to avoid the unlucky association of 13 signs, or to keep it down to a conveniently composite 12.

The zodiac is subdivided in a number of ways to make use of 12's divisibility—into two genders (rather oddly, Aries, the ram, is masculine while Taurus, the bull, is feminine), three "qualities" (cardinal signs at the start of a season, changeable at the end and fixed in the middle of a season), and according to the four classical elements (supposedly, people of certain element signs are especially compatible with those of the same element). As unscientific as astrology is, it was a genuine and respectable discipline in less enlightened times—the movement of constellations across the sky seemed a confirmation of Earth's place not at the center of the universe, but as part of a wider celestial system. It was only after the Renaissance that a distinction between superstition and the science of astronomy began to be drawn.

Signs	Elements	Qualities	Gender
Aries	Fire	Cardinal	Male
Taurus	Earth	Fixed	Female
Gemini	Air	Mutable	Male
Cancer	Water	Cardinal	Female
Leo	Fire	Fixed	Male
Virgo	Earth	Mutable	Female
Libra	Air	Cardinal	Male
Scorpio	Water	Fixed	Female
Sagittarius	Fire	Mutable	Male
Capricorn	Earth	Cardinal	Female
Aquarius	Air	Fixed	Male
Pisces	Water	Mutable	Female

Supposedly, your star sign says a great deal about your personality, but the scientifically verifiable link between the movements of planets and stars and human affairs on Earth is non-existent. It hardly needs to be said again, but much like numerology (see page 422), astrology is manifestly nonsense, which relies on harnessing credulity in vague predictions (invariably positive) for financial gain. Regrettably, this doesn't stop it being a major industry that makes millions for its practitioners.

The Chinese zodiac

Equally unscientific but perhaps more interesting by virtue of its novelty to Westerners is the Chinese zodiac, which assigns one of twelve animals to your birth year (although it does, of course, go by the Chinese year, which usually begins in late January or early February). Which animal are you?

Rat	1900, 1912, 1924, 1936, 1948, 1960, 1972, 1984, 1996, 2008
Ox	1901, 1913, 1925, 1937, 1949, 1961, 1973, 1985, 1997, 2009
Tiger	1902, 1914, 1926, 1938, 1950, 1962, 1974, 1986, 1998, 2010
Rabbit	1903, 1915, 1927, 1939, 1951, 1963, 1975, 1987, 1999, 2011
Dragon	1904, 1916, 1928, 1940, 1952, 1964, 1976, 1988, 2000, 2012
Snake	1905, 1917, 1929, 1941, 1953, 1965, 1977, 1989, 2001, 2013
Horse	1906, 1918, 1930, 1942, 1954, 1966, 1978, 1990, 2002, 2014
Ram	1907, 1919, 1931, 1943, 1955, 1967, 1979, 1991, 2003, 2015
Monkey	1908, 1920, 1932, 1944, 1956, 1968, 1980, 1992, 2004, 2016
Rooster	1909, 1921, 1933, 1945, 1957, 1969, 1981, 1993, 2005, 2017
Dog	1910, 1922, 1934, 1946, 1958, 1970, 1982, 1994, 2006, 2018
Pig	1911, 1923, 1935, 1947, 1959, 1971, 1983, 1995, 2007, 2019

TWELVE

Perhaps the best-known example of the religious significance of the number 12 is the Twelve Apostles of Jesus. (Judas Iscariot's presence as the thirteenth person at the Last Supper may also be the origin of the superstition surrounding the number 13 [see page 440].) The holy books of Judaism and Christianity refer to the Twelve Tribes of Israel, descended from the twelve sons of Jacob. This may well have influenced the Twelve Days of Christmas, the period lasting from Christmas to the eve of Epiphany (Twelfth Night).

Islam was split into two major branches—Sunni and Shia—by a conflict over the rightful succession to the Prophet Muhammad. The vast majority of Shi'ite Muslims believe the succession runs through twelve Imams, the last of whom was born in A.D. 868 and is, impressively, still alive, but hidden to the world. It should be stressed that the Imams are not prophets, but simply carry out the Prophet's message. This subgroup of Shi'ites are known colloquially as Twelvers, and make up most of the population of Iran and Iraq, as well as being numerous in most other Muslim countries.

Part of this ubiquity must have resulted from 12 being a

highly composite number—one with many factors that can be divided up in many different ways. Twelve is the smallest number with six factors—1, 2, 3, 4, 6, and 12. The Duodecimal Society (now known as the Dozenal Society), founded in 1944 in New York, tried to promote the adoption of a duodecimal (base-12) number system to take advantage of this quality. Unsurprisingly, they were entirely unsuccessful.

The number of factors in the number 12 has made it convenient for measuring time for thousands of years. The calendar has 12 months, although the actual number of lunar cycles in a year is closer to 13. The lunar cycle is too irregular to use for time measurement, though, so 12 months are used to fit it in with solar years. Much of this derives from the Babylonian time system, which used 360 days of the year (which is also the origin of our circle being divided into 360 degrees). Twelve months are conveniently divisible into four seasons of roughly three months each. Each day is then divided into 24 hours (a practice that originated with the Sumerians splitting day and night into 12 parts each), and each hour and minute are divided into 60 parts—a multiple of 12.

Western and Eastern zodiacs (see page 433) make use of 12 signs, which again tend to be divided into categories to make use of 12 being composite. Twelve is also traditionally the number of people on a jury, although there seems to be no particular reason for choosing that number other than convenience, and possibly because 12, being even, allows for a jury opinion to be split exactly in half—although modern jury trials generally require either most or all of the jury to agree on a verdict.

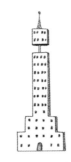

THIRTEEN

From Biblical times to the present, 13 is the West's unluckiest number. This superstition supposedly derives from the number present at the Last Supper—a Biblically resonant 12, plus a treacherous thirteenth—Judas Iscariot—who was supposedly the last to sit. A similar Norse myth involves 12 gods sitting at a table in Valhalla, only for the treacherous Loki to turn up and kill one—Baldur, the heroic god of beauty.

Thirteen may also be unlucky in Christian traditions simply because it is holy to some pagan religions, whose calendars contain 13 lunar months. At a more abstract level, it may be that the real reason has to do with 13's mathematical awkwardness—while 12 is recognized in many cultures for having many factors, 13 right after it is awkwardly prime (see page 462). It seems likely that more than one of these theories is at least partly correct, given that the superstition about 13 doesn't really make an appearance until the Middle Ages, well after the ill-fated meals of Biblical and Norse stories.

The fear that Friday the 13th, specifically, will bring bad luck, seems to be more recent, but it's linked to a long tradition of superstition surrounding Fridays generally, including Good Friday and the British tradition of public hangings on Fridays. Some historians suggest that the day and the number were only brought together in 1907, by Thomas W. Lawson's little-known novel *Friday, the Thirteenth* (which is apparently about turn-of-the-century Wall Street and not a hockey-masked serial killer). Another theory, recently given some popularity by *The da Vinci Code*, is that it derives from Friday October 13, 1307, when King Philip IV issued a death warrant for the Knights Templar.

Although there's obviously no verified causal link between Friday the 13th and bad luck, the date might lead indirectly to cause for concern. A number of studies have found higher rates of accidents, including car crashes, on Friday the 13th. These could, however, be due to Friday the 13th nerves distracting drivers, as well as a degree of confirmation bias—those who believe Friday the 13th is unlucky are more likely to attribute even slight bad luck to the date.

Despite the comparative lack of superstition in modern society, triskaidekaphobia (fear of the number 13) remains prevalent. At dinner parties and wedding receptions, the hosts will go to great lengths to avoid seating 13 guests at a single table, since, so the superstition goes, one of the guests would die within a year. Tenants in many skyscrapers will notice that the floors skip from the 12th to the 14th (or the 13th floor has been called 12A), and airlines frequently do the same with their seating rows. In China, tetraphobia (fear of the number four) is even more pervasive—see page 90 for more on China's lucky and unlucky numbers.

Sensing the absurdity of this superstitious fear in a supposedly rational society, Captain William Fowler, an American Civil War veteran, set up the Thirteen Club in New York City in 1880. Captain Fowler's life featured an improbable recurrence of the number 13 (including his early education at Public School No. 13, his construction of 13 public buildings as an architect, and his experience of 13 Civil War battles), and he came to view it as lucky rather than cursed.

The highly exclusive Thirteen Club's dinner parties always had 13 people at each table, and its members included future President Theodore Roosevelt and former President Chester Arthur. A later imitator, the London Thirteen Club, was similarly well appointed, counting a number of Members of Parliament among its members. Other superstitions were also ridiculed—members might enter the room by passing under a ladder, before deliberately spilling salt during dinner and breaking mirrors afterward.

THREE

In the West, the Holy Trinity of the Father, the Son, and the Holy Ghost is probably the best example of a number possessing religious significance. The superstitious fear of walking under a ladder seems to have its origin here—a ladder propped against a wall forms the longest side of a triangle, with the ground and the wall forming the other two sides, and a person passing under the ladder is symbolically breaking the Trinity and bringing themselves bad luck. The Holy Trinity is by no means unique in assigning significance to the number three, though. The Bible describes Jesus receiving three gifts from three wise men, preaching for three years and rising three days after his death. Celestial realms are often divided into three levels—Heaven, Hell, and Purgatory.

Islam, the third of the three Abrahamic religions, has three holy cities—Mecca, Medina, and Jerusalem. The fairly numerous gods of the Hindu religion are headed by a trinity (*trimurti*) of Brahma (creator of the universe), Shiva (destroyer and recreator), and Vishnu (wise protector). Ancient Greek mythology featured three Furies, three Muses (which later increased to nine), and three Gorgons (most famously the snake-haired Medusa), among other trinities. In the neo-pagan Wiccan religion, the Rule of Three dictates that a person's actions, good or bad, will be visited threefold upon them, much like the concept of karma in Hinduism and Buddhism.

The mystic significance of the number three may be linked to ideas of completeness and harmony—if two suggests a duality in conflict, three might suggest a more stable balance, particularly since the triangle is the simplest, and thus the most structurally efficient and geometrically common, two-dimensional shape.

Public speakers and mottoes frequently list three things in a technique known as tricolon—"life, liberty and the pursuit of happiness," "liberty, equality, fraternity," "education, education, education."* In the visual arts, a triptych is an arrangement of three panels, traditionally part of an altarpiece but also adopted by secular artists for its striking effect. Francis Bacon's *Three Studies for Figures at the Base of a Crucifixion*, painted in 1944, is an excellent and very influential example.

Three is a good number for stories as well, where the third

* A tricolon of tricolons.

person can act as a balancing element between two conflicting parties, or as someone who upsets the balance, such as in a "love triangle" scenario. Traditionally, stories are said to consist of three parts—an introductory beginning, a middle that further develops the story, and an end that concludes it, and trilogies of books and films often work in much the same way. In children's stories, the number three (little pigs, bears, etc.) allows the beginnings of a pattern to be set with the first two before the pattern is overturned with the third (the house is still standing, Goldilocks is discovered). Jokes, particularly those at the expense of certain nationalities or hair colors, often use a similar format.

FOUR

Although not really possessed of the same mystique as three (see page 443), four nonetheless holds an interesting place in the world's culture of numbers, probably at least partly because it's an even number and the smallest perfect square (see page 463) above one, and also perhaps because humans have four limbs and four fingers (not counting the thumb) on each hand.

Four humors

The number four appeared in Ancient Greece as the four classical elements—earth, water, air, and fire. Similar systems of several different elements were used in other cultures, such as Hinduism and Chinese Taoism, which had five—fire, wood, water, metal, and earth.

The classical elements were believed to form all earthly matter when combined together, but there was also a fifth special element, generally known as the "idea" or the "ether." All heavenly bodies were made from aether, and it was the medium in which the gods lived. The word "quintessence," meaning a completely pure quality or archetype, is derived from the fifth element in this theory. The idea of the four (or five) elements continued to influence science for centuries, lasting through the Middle Ages.

Even after the classical elements had been dropped, scientists continued to believe up until the twentieth century that the universe was filled with a substance called ether. Although we now know that the universe is mostly empty and that light can travel through a vacuum, these discoveries came as an enormous surprise to the scientists who made them, who assumed that light, like sound, could travel only through some sort of medium.

The four elements mapped neatly onto the four "humors" of ancient medicine, a theory based on bodily fluids. Ancient Greek and Roman doctors reasoned that having too much of one of four fluids (blood, phlegm, yellow bile, and black bile) would cause ill health, and associated each imbalance with a personality type or "temperament." Despite the complete refutation of this theory, it continues to influence English adjectives for personalities.

Blood (associated with air)—Sanguine personalities are considered outgoing, friendly, and confident but with the potential to become arrogant and impulsive, finding it difficult to concentrate on one thing.

Phlegm (water)—Phlegmatic people are calm and rational and able to keep a cool head, but they're often dispassionate and unenthusiastic to the point of laziness.

Yellow bile (fire)—"Choleric" tends to denote practical-minded, passionate, dynamic types whose greatest fault is generally their suspicion and quickness to anger. Cholera, a dangerous disease contracted from infected water supplies, was once thought to be caused by bile.

Black bile (earth)—Melancholic personalities are, obviously, those overly preoccupied by sadness and tragedy. Melancholic people were considered the most creative and poetically minded, though. Basically, they were goths.

This theory continued to affect medicine right up to the nineteenth century, and is the origin of bloodletting—bleeding a patient who has been diagnosed as excessively sanguine.

Although the four humors theory of medicine is long dead to all but the craziest quacks, a similar concept of four temperaments has been applied in modern psychoanalysis. Carl Jung (1875–1961), a pioneering psychoanalyst who broke away from Freudian tradition to embrace some occasionally rather odd ideas, viewed the idea of "fourfoldness" as one of humanity's most important and profound cultural building blocks. Jung's views of people as being divided into introverts and extroverts influenced the development of various personality classifications over the following decades. In some ways, the four temperaments are very much alive.

Four horsemen

The Four Horsemen of the Apocalypse are described in the Book of Revelation, the last book of the Bible—which also gave us the Number of the Beast (see page 416)—as the harbingers of the end of the world. Only Death, riding a pale horse, is named in the text, but from the description the others are generally considered to include War, on a red horse and carrying a sword, Conquest, a regal figure on a white horse, and another horseman bearing scales and measuring out food, who is generally considered to represent Famine. In many interpretations, Pestilence replaces Conquest, who has a rather large overlap with War anyway.

More recently, the term "Four Horsemen" has been used, usually humorously, to refer to the four leading authors of the "New Atheist" movement: Richard Dawkins, Daniel Dennett, Sam Harris, and Christopher Hitchens. It hasn't yet been suggested which author is meant to be which horseman.

Other instances of the number four in religion are the four official Gospels (the books of Matthew, Mark, Luke, and John, which kick off the New Testament with an account of Jesus' life) and the four rivers that flowed through Eden in the Old Testament (the Pishon, the Gihon, the Tigris, and the Euphrates).

FIVE

As with several other numbers already mentioned, the number five is important to various religious faiths. In Islam, there are five sacred duties for all Muslims, known as the Five Pillars of Islam:

Shahaadah— a declaration of faith in God alone, and in Muhammad as his prophet

Salah— prayers five times daily

Zakat— giving to charity

Sawm— fasting from dawn to dusk during Ramadan

Hajj— a pilgrimage to Mecca, which should be made at least once in a Muslim's lifetime

Some branches of Islam prescribe more than five duties, adding a sixth or seventh pillar.

Five is also important in Judaism, where the Torah is composed of five books—the "Pentateuch" of Genesis, Exodus, Leviticus, Numbers, and Deuteronomy. In Sikhism, Sikhs have to wear the symbolic "five Ks"—*kesh* (long hair), *kara* (steel bracelet), *kanga* (comb), *kachha* (cotton pants) and *kirpan* (a ceremonial sword or dagger). Sikhism has five Virtues and five Evils, similar to the Seven Deadly Sins and Heavenly Virtues (see page 410):

Virtues	**Evils**
Sat—truth	*Kaam*—lust
Santokh—contentment	*Krodh*—anger and hatred
Daya—compassion	*Lobh*—greed and covetousness
Nimrata—humility	*Moh*—attachment to worldly things
Pyare—love (including love of God)	*Ahankar*—pride and egotism

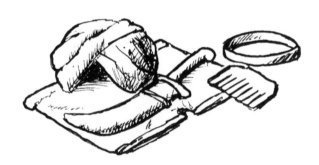

The pentagram

No discussion of five's religious significance would be complete without a look at one of the world's oldest, most controversial, and most versatile symbols—the pentagram.

At least 6,000 years old, the pentagram may have originated in ancient Sumer as a pictogram for the heavens, and subsequently been adopted by the Babylonians. The Pythagoreans (followers of the Greek mathematician, philosopher, and mystic Pythagoras of Samos [around 580–500 B.C.]) viewed the pentagram with a certain reverence: Not only could the five points be considered representative of five classical elements (earth, fire, water, air, and the ether), but the main lines of a geometrically regular pentagram are divided in the Golden Ratio (see page 384).

$1.618^2 = 2.618$

$1.618^3 = 4.236$

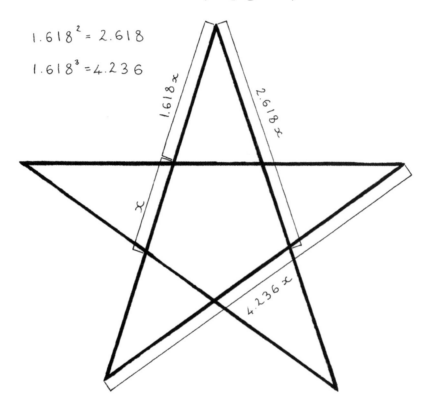

Despite the common occult and even Satanic associations of the pentagram (which is known as a pentacle when it has a circle around it), it was actually a popular Christian symbol for many centuries. It symbolized the Five Wounds of Christ (one in each hand, one in each foot, and one in the side) and was often written on doors to protect against witches, demons, and other evil spirits.

In this way, the pentagram became associated with the occult, often linking back to the Pythagorean view of it as representative of the elements. Eventually it became very important which way up the pentagram was drawn—one point upward would ward off evil, but the other way around would attract it.

In modern times, the pentagram and pentacle are used mainly by members of the neo-pagan Wicca religion, who use a pentacle, usually point-up but sometimes the other way around, to denote the five elements. Modern Satanism, as promoted by Aleister Crowley and Anton LaVey, frequently uses the upside-down variant to denote a rejection of Christianity and the embracing of earthly ideals. Satanic black masses and human sacrifice are basically confined to horror films, but the pentacle is still often associated with devil-worship, and uncertainty surrounding the use of the symbol leads to many Wiccans being confused with Satanists.

NUMBERS IN
MATH AND
SCIENCE

$\pi = 3.141592653589793238462643383279502884197...$

A MATHEMATICAL GLOSSARY

Before we go deeper into the math, it might be a good idea to review some of the mathematical terms you've probably learned at school...

Average

The average is a number—actually several different numbers—that can help to summarize the distribution of statistical data in an easily readable way. There are three main types of average (mean, mode, and median), and numerous more complex ones.

The mean—generally what's meant by "average." It's a "middle" value, which is calculated by adding together all the values and then dividing that by the number of values. (For example, $4 + 5 + 6 = 15 \div 3 = 5$.)

The mode—simply the most common value in any set of data. The modal number of legs per person is two, because most people have two legs. (The mean is a little below two, as it accounts for people with fewer than two legs.)

The median—the middle value in a set of data: the point that separates the lower half from the higher half. It's calculated by ranking the data in ascending or descending order and then choosing the middle value, or, where there's an even number of values (and hence no middle one) the mean of the two middle values. (For example, 7, 8, 9, 15, and 200 is 9.)

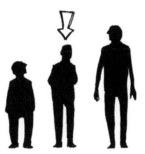

Base

In number systems that use positional notation (like ours), the base is the number defining the relationship between the positions. "Positional notation" refers here to the fact that our numbers make use of a small number of symbols (the digits 0–9), but these are then interpreted according to their position in a number. So we know 900 is bigger than 9 because the digit 9 occupies the hundreds column in 900 but the ones column in 9.

Although this system has been drummed into us all since elementary school, positional notation wasn't always the norm. The best-known example of non-positional numbering is the Roman numeral system (see page 477). Anyway, the "base" is the number that links the "positions" of positional notation—in a base X system, a number written 10 is X times bigger than 1, and each step to the left moves one up the powers (see below) of X.

Our decimal system uses base 10 ("decimal" comes from the Latin for "ten"), so children learn to think of complex numbers as "hundreds, tens, and ones (or units)." A more grown-up approach would be to see it as groups of 10^2, 10^1, 10^0 (the last column in any positional notation system is multiples of one, as anything to the power of 0 is 1).

Several other positional systems have been used in the past: The Babylonians used a sexagesimal one (base 60*), which isn't

---

* In our decimal (base-10) system, the digits are related by powers of ten. Similarly, a base-60 system is based around powers of 60, with the rightmost digit representing multiples of one (any number to the power of zero is one), the next multiples of 60 (60^1), the next multiples of 3600 (60^2), and so on. Such a large base is complex enough by itself, but added to this was the Babylonian method of writing the numbers 0–59, which was sort of decimal—a single symbol signifying 10 could be repeated and combined with other digits in a similar way to Roman numerals, within the sexagesimal system.

to be confused with hexadecimal—a base-16 number system used by some computer applications, with the digits 0–9 being extended with the letters A–F. Because 16 is a power of 2, the hexadecimal system can be used easily to represent numbers from the base-2 binary system (see page 490).

Incidentally, the word "hexadecimal," like "television," has a mixture of Greek and Latin roots—so, why not call it sexadecimal, and be consistent with "sexagesimal"? From what I understand, the IBM managers of the 1950s considered the word "sexadecimal" too rude!

Cube number (or perfect cube)

A number equal to the cube of an integer (see page 461)—the integer times itself twice (for example: $3 \times 3 \times 3 = 3^3 = 27$, the third cube).

The first 10 cubes are:

1, 8, 27, 64, 125, 216, 343, 512, 729, 1000

Degree

The most common way of measuring the angle between two lines, represented by this symbol: °. There are 360 degrees in a circle, which might seem a rather odd number to use. The reason for this is partly that 360 is a highly composite number (with 24 factors that divide into it). It is also because—the 360° circle appears to have been popularized by the Greeks—the ancient Babylonians who divided the circle into degrees used a 360-day year and a number system with base 60 (60 being one-sixth of 360). For the most precise measurements of angle (such as measuring exact latitude and longitude, or the accuracy of a rifle), the degree is subdivided into 60 minutes of arc, which are each made up of 60 seconds of arc.

The number of factors in 360 allows the circle to be easily divided into various parts, such as the right angle of 90 degrees, which is exactly a quarter of the full circle, or 60 degrees, which is the angle found in equilateral triangles. By contrast, the radian, the second most common measurement of angle, is not nearly as intuitive, being defined as $1/(2\pi)$ of a circle, or roughly 57.3 degrees. This is all just fine for calculus but a bit awkward for ordinary geometry.

Factor

A number that divides into another number. Some numbers have many factors, and hence are said to be highly composite, while prime numbers have no factors except 1 and themselves.

Twelve, for instance, is a highly composite number, while 13, a prime, is not.

Factors of 12: 1, 2, 3, 4, 6, 12
Factors of 13: 1, 13

Integer

This is simply another word for a whole number; that is, one that doesn't have to be expressed as a fraction.

Irrational number

A number which, unlike rational numbers, cannot be expressed as a fraction. Irrational numbers are non-repeating decimals with infinite decimal places. Square roots of integers that aren't perfect squares, such as

$$\sqrt{47} = 6.85565460040104412493587144490848\ldots$$

are irrational. However, this number could be approximated to a rational number if we rounded it to a finite number of decimal places.

$$6.85565 = 685{,}565/100{,}000.$$

Prominent examples of irrational numbers include φ (see page 386) and π (see page 469).

Natural number

A positive whole number of the type that occurs in nature. You can have one stone or two stones or three, but not half a stone or -7 stones. You can also have 0 stones, of course, but it remains undecided in the mathematical world whether 0 can be considered a natural number.

Powers

A number multiplied by itself a certain number of times, that second number being known as the power or the exponent, and written in superscript, $^{\text{like this}}$. Squared and cubed numbers are respectively second and third powers of the original number. Positional number systems are based around powers—in our decimal system the digit positions refer to powers of 10—thousands, hundreds, tens etc. Any number to the power of 0 equals 1, and of course any number to the power of 1 is the number itself.

Prime number

A number that is divisible only by itself and 1 (1 is not a prime number, however). Prime numbers are useful in cryptography, because large prime numbers can be multiplied together into much larger numbers, and it's then very complicated to figure out what the original prime numbers were. Because of this application of prime numbers, figuring out patterns in their distribution remains a major mathematical project. The first ten prime numbers are:

2, 3, 5, 7, 11, 13, 17, 19, 23, 29.

Rational number

A number that can be expressed as a fraction, with integers on the top and bottom. If written as a decimal, a rational number will either terminate that is, will have a finite number of decimal places or repeat (the digits after the decimal point will follow an obvious sequence). For example, 1 (1.0), ½ (0.5), ⅓ (0.$\overline{3}$ [the 3 continues repeating forever]), and ³⁵⁵⁄₃₈₉ (0.912596401028277788155...) are all rational numbers.

Square number (or perfect square)

A number equal to an integer squared (that is, multiplied by itself). 2 times itself is 4, so 4 is the second square. The square of a negative number is equal to the square of its positive counterpart: -3 × -3 = 3 × 3 = 9. The first ten square numbers are:

1, 4, 9, 16, 25, 36, 49, 64, 81, 100.

Square root

The inverse of squaring a number. The square root of a number *a* is the number which, when multiplied by itself, will produce *a*, and is denoted by the symbol $\sqrt{\ }$. So $\sqrt{25} = 5$ because $5^2 = 25$. In fact, though, any positive number has both a positive and a negative square root, as $(-5)^2$ is also 25. Negative numbers, however, have no real square roots, although they do have imaginary ones (see *i*, page 482).

Triangular number

One of a set of integers which correspond to the number of points required to produce a triangle, where each row of points has one more than the previous row. A triangular number will be the sum of a series of consecutive integers, starting from 1. Thus, the *n*th triangular number will equal n+(n-1)+(n-2)+(n-3)... until you get to 1.

The first ten triangular numbers are:

1	= 1
3	= 1+2
6	= 1+2+3
10	= 1+2+3+4
15	= 1+2+3+4+5
21	= 1+2+3+4+5+6
28	= 1+2+3+4+5+6+7
36	= 1+2+3+4+5+6+7+8
45	= 1+2+3+4+5+6+7+8+9
55	= 1+2+3+4+5+6+7+8+9+10

Or, more graphically:

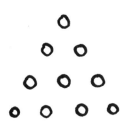

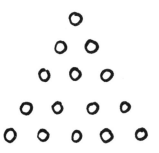

DIVISIBILITY TRICKS

In mental arithmetic, various tricks can be used to quickly check the divisibility of large numbers by smaller ones. Here are a few examples.

Divisibility by 3

To check whether or not a number is divisible by 3, simply add all the digits together and check whether the sum of these is divisible by 3. If the result is still too large to be conveniently divided mentally, the digits of the result can be added again until it's clear (if the number is divisible, you should be able to keep going until you end up with 3, 6, or 9):

Is 5,952 divisible by 3?

$5 + 9 + 5 + 2 = 21$, so 5,952 is divisible by 3.

Divisibility by 7

To be honest, it's usually quickest to work this out with long division, but there is a method to determine whether or not a number is divisible by 7.

Is 21,987 divisible by 7?

Begin by removing and doubling the final digit of the number.

$$7 \times 2 = 14$$

Subtract this from the remaining digits:

$$2198 - 14 = 2184.$$

Do the same again to this number:

$$4 \times 2 = 8$$

$$218 - 8 = 210.$$

And keep going until you get to a multiple of 7:

$$0 \times 2 = 0$$

$$21 - 0 = 21 = 3 \times 7, \text{ so } 21{,}987 \text{ is divisible by } 7.$$

Divisibility by 9

The same as the rule for divisibility by 3, but here the digits can always eventually be added up to make 9.

Is 64,152 divisible by 9?

$$6 + 4 + 1 + 5 + 2 = 18$$

$$1 + 8 = 9, \text{ so } 64{,}152 \text{ is a multiple of } 9.$$

Divisibility by 11

This is a bit more complicated. Begin by separating out the alternate digits of the original number (starting from the left-hand side), and add them together.

Is 95,428,399 divisible by 11?

9 5 4 2 8 3 9 9

$$9 + 4 + 8 + 9 \quad = \quad 30$$

$$5 + 2 + 3 + 9 \quad = \quad 19.$$

Now subtract the smaller of these results from the bigger one. If the result is 0 or a multiple of 11, the original number is divisible by 11.

$$\begin{array}{r} 30 \\ - 19 \\ \hline 11 \end{array}$$

so 95,428,399 is divisible by 11.

You could just use a calculator, of course.

π (3.14159265358979323 ...)

π (pi) is one of the better-known numbers in this collection, its importance having been drummed into us in school. It is, of course, the number that defines the relationship between the circumference and diameter of a circle (C = πD, a.k.a. C=2πr; see illustration below), and it is named after the first letter of the Greek words for periphery or perimeter.

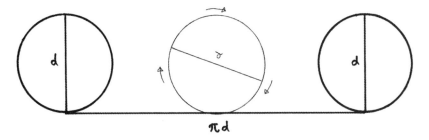

Strangely, though, π also appears in a vast number of other fields, particularly quantum physics and astronomy, which appear to have no relation to circles. It's even been the subject of legislation (see Indiana Pi Bill, page 389).

For all its scientific importance, π is perhaps more memorable for being a non-terminating, non-repeating decimal—an irrational (see page 461) and also a transcendental number. Technological advances in the late twentieth century allowed vast numbers of the digits of π to be calculated by computer, and the current record is about 1.2 trillion decimal places.

Despite the lack of any real point in doing so, memorizing the digits of π has become an almost obsessive pastime among some people. In October 2006, retired engineer Akira Haraguchi memorized 100,000 digits, beating his own previous record of 83,431 places. Pi devotees often use complex mnemonic devices in their efforts, such as *The Cadaeic Cadenza*, a short story by Mike Keith, the words of which correspond in length to the first 3834 digits of π.

For the less ambitious, this limerick should suffice:

The ratio C over D
When they're parts of a circle, is three
Point one four one five
Nine two six five three five
Eight nine seven nine three two three!

These π devotees often also celebrate Pi Day on March 14th, by eating π pie. Depressingly, this is one of the funnier running gags of the mathematical world.

THE EVOLUTION OF ZERO

To most of us, the idea of life without zero is inconceivable. From the most basic financial transactions to the circuitry of all electronic equipment (see The Binary System, page 490), the zero underpins every aspect of modern life. The value and meaning of zero are among the first things children learn.

But for many centuries, the idea of a number that represented nothing was counterintuitive and controversial, raising philosophical as well as mathematical questions. Europe's first mathematics, after all, was concerned mainly with counting and measuring solid objects, and you can't count to nothing. The story of zero is also largely the story of how the West adopted a positional decimal number system over the more primitive Roman one.

Around 3,000 B.C.—first evidence of a primordial decimal number system in the Indus valley, in what is now India. The civilization of this area was mathematically enormously advanced, and remained ahead of others for centuries in its understanding of number theory.

Mid-1,000s B.C.—The Babylonians developed a rather complex sexagesimal (base-60) positional notation system, which required some placeholder to represent an unoccupied space. It could be used to distinguish, say, 101 from 11 but could not be called analogous to modern 0, because it was never written at the end of a number and was not considered to have a value in itself (and, consisting only of an empty space, could not be written on its own). Between 700 and 300 B.C., the Babylonians developed symbols similar to the current one to represent zero, but still did not have a number resembling modern zero.

300 B.C. onward—Hindu cultures adopted something closer to the modern zero and gave a Sanskrit name to the null value—*sunya* (related to the word zero etymologically).

The Greeks—by contrast, had philosophical difficulty with the idea of naming zero—it seemed contradictory that "nothing" could be "something," especially as the Greek mathematical tradition, unlike the Hindu one, was concerned largely with counting and measuring physical objects. Geometry was the real strength of the Greek mathematicians. This philosophical doubt eventually extended to medieval religious arguments about the existence or nonexistence of a vacuum.

However, Greek mathematician Ptolemy, influenced by the Babylonians, developed the "Hellenistic zero" in A.D. 130. He gave it a symbol similar to the current one—a circle with a long overbar. It would take a long time to spread to the rest of Europe, though, and Ptolemy, like the Babylonians, did not view 0 as a number in its own right.

The Romans—did not use a numeric zero symbol, preferring the word *nullus* or *nihil* (nothing), alongside their other numerals. The word was occasionally used alongside other numbers in tables (the oldest surviving example dates from c. A.D. 525), but the Roman system, which was used in the West for centuries, was not positional and had little need for a zero.

A.D. 498—The now-ubiquitous decimal number system was by this time fully established in modern-day India. The mathematician Aryabhata described a decimal positional system where *"Sthanam sthanam dasa gunam"*—"place to place, ten times in value"—but viewed the zero as an indicator of an empty position rather than a number itself.

A.D. 628—Hindu mathematician Brahmagupta laid down a set of rules for zero, negative numbers, and some simple algebraic rules, in his book *Brahmasputha-siddhanta*. These mostly correspond to those used today, but modern mathematics disagrees with his assertion that $0 \div 0 = 0$. Dividing by zero remained a thorny issue for some time (see page 476).

Around A.D. 665—The use of zero as a placeholder was also popular in the Americas, in the vigesimal (base-20) system of the Long Count Calendar, which the Maya, among other civilizations, used to predict major celestial events so they could plan their sacrifices. It used a shell to represent 0, and was probably developed by the Olmecs and before, spreading to the Maya. However, this development appears not to have spread beyond Central America.

A.D. 820—Brahmagupta's writings were introduced to the wider world, centuries later, by Al-Khwarizmi (c. 790–840), a Persian mathematician who invented algebra (in his book *Al-Jabr wa-al-Muqabilah*) and gave his name to the algorithm. In doing so, he brought together Greek and Hindu knowledge of mathematics. Arabic numerals had developed over the previous two centuries from Hindu ones, and would eventually become the standard across Europe.

A.D. 976—the first appearance of Hindu-Arabic numerals in Europe in the *Codex Vigilanus*, a historical record of Spain. Zero, however, was not included by the monks who compiled the book.

11th century—The Indian decimal numeral system reached widespread use in Europe through the Iberian Peninsula, brought by the Moors along with Hindu-Arabic numerals. The Italian mathematician Fibonacci (see The Fibonacci Sequence, page 480) had traveled to numerous trading ports and favored the Arabic system, becoming instrumental in promoting it in his *Liber Abaci* of 1202. The new system had many conservative opponents in the Catholic Church—the word "cipher" is derived from the Arabic *sifr* (zero or empty), possibly because the idea of the zero was so hard for ordinary Europeans to grasp that the term came to be used for anything unclear, like a coded message. Even then, zero was viewed less as a number in its own right than as a modifier digit that could distinguish 3 from 300. Arabic numerals, including zero, didn't become truly widespread until the development of the printing press.

1440—Gutenberg developed the printing press, and with it came a new ability to disseminate information. The socioeconomic changes of the Renaissance led to enormous growth in trade, and a growing mercantile class used the new numbers. Use of Arabic numerals was no longer limited to mathematicians, but it took centuries for the zero to be fully accepted.

Up to the present day—Growing European control of most of the world, particularly economically, meant that Hindu-Arabic numerals were spread worldwide.

Dividing by Zero

One of the most perplexing problems with zero, even now, is how to divide a number by zero. Taking $a/0$ to equal 0, as Brahmagupta did in 628, seems to suggest that 0 times itself could equal anything other than 0. Taking it to equal ∞, as Bhaskara did 500 years later, makes a little more sense, but there is the problem that infinite nothing is still nothing.

As always, computers cause as many problems as they solve—a computer required to divide by zero may generate an incorrect result, or (worse) expend all its resources trying to solve the impossible problem, and not having the resources for anything else. Many programs are designed to spot a divide-by-zero error before it can cause problems, but this was small consolation to the crew of the *USS Yorktown,* a U.S. Navy cruiser whose computer network hit a divide-by-zero error. The network crashed, and with it went control of the ship's propulsion, leaving it paralyzed in port.

A convenient, if perhaps rather unfair, solution is simply to remove this calculation from the field of mathematics altogether. Recent computer math standards require a division by zero to produce the result NaN—Not a Number—much like zero itself was all those centuries ago ...

ROMAN NUMERALS

You probably at least half-know these already, but this does seem an appropriate place for a refresher on the system of ancient Roman numerals, although these days you're unlikely to have any pressing need to use or read them. Their modern use is largely confined to clock faces, statues, and formal documents.

The decimal number system now used worldwide uses positional notation, with the position of each digit indicating its significance (see Base, page 457, for a more detailed explanation). This system derived from a need for a number system that allowed complex theoretical mathematics to be performed.

Despite their prominence in engineering, architecture, and trade, the Romans, unlike the Greeks, produced little in the way of abstract mathematical theory. The Roman numeral system is based essentially on counting things, and although Roman numbers are also letters of the alphabet, this was not their original source. The system appears to have begun with Etruscan shepherds, who carved notches into tally sticks when counting their flocks. To make the process easier, they would carve a second stroke with each fifth notch, two crossed strokes for each tenth one, and so on. Gradually, the Romans adapted the shepherds' system into one that used the letters of their alphabet.

I—one
V—five
X—ten
L—50
C—100
D—500
M—1000

Putting a little bar over the digit multiplies its value by 1,000, and was common for numbers above 4,000 or so:

$\overline{\text{IV}}$—4,000
$\overline{\text{M}}$—1,000,000
$\overline{\text{MDCCVII}}$—1,700,007

Unlike in our decimal system, the placement of the symbol has little to do with its significance (that is, the M in MXI is not ten times bigger than the M in MI). The numerals, in most cases, simply add together, and are usually written largest first (for example, MLXVI). However, this is not always the case, and working out Roman numerals isn't always just a question of adding everything together. To make the writing process less cumbersome, the Romans would often express numbers that fell just short of one of the convenient quantities above as a larger number less a smaller number—because of their tally-based system, it was quicker to write "fifty less one" than "forty-nine." This is done simply by writing the smaller number to the left of the larger one:

IV = 4 (though IIII was also common)

IX = 9

LD = 450

MCMLXVIII = 1968

There was no real method of writing zero. Any Roman needing to express this concept would have to write out the word *nullus* (meaning nothing). After the decline of the Roman Empire, the numbers continued to be commonly used until the introduction of modern Arabic numerals around the fourteenth century (see The Evolution of Zero, page 470).

THE FIBONACCI SEQUENCE

The Fibonacci sequence is a sequence of numbers, defined by the fact that each term is the sum of the previous two terms. Therefore the first fifteen terms are:

0, 1, 1, 2, 3, 5, 8, 13, 21, 34, 55, 89, 144, 233, 377.

The sequence is named after Leonardo of Pisa, also known as Fibonacci (c.1170–1240), an Italian mathematician who was a major figure in spreading Arabic numerals to the rest of the world (see The Evolution of Zero, page 470) in his book *Liber Abaci* (the Book of Calculation, published in 1202). *Liber Abaci* also introduced the Fibonacci sequence as a solution to the following problem:

> A pair of rabbits is kept in an enclosure, supplied with food and water. After a month, this pair mates and produces a new pair of rabbits. Each new pair of rabbits begins producing offspring after one month, and produces exactly two every month after that. How many pairs of rabbits can be produced in each month over the course of a year, assuming each pair dies after producing two pairs of offspring?

The result is the Fibonacci sequence.

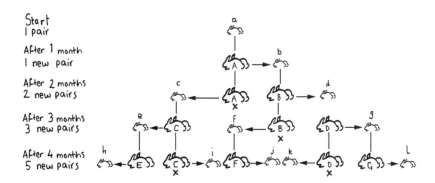

The Fibonacci sequence has attracted a great deal of interest because it crops up frequently in nature—even outside monogamous rabbits, which actually occur rather rarely. The Fibonacci sequence also appears in sunflowers, in the spiral pattern of the seeds in the center (which usually grow in formations of 55 clockwise and 89 counter-clockwise spirals of seeds—both Fibonacci numbers). A similar pattern exists in other flowers, pine cones and pineapples. It gives the most efficient even distribution of seeds in the space available.

The sequence is also strongly linked to the Golden Number (see page 46)—the aforementioned seeds emerge from each other at an angle of about 222.5°, or 360° divided by the Golden Number (the angle is also often given as 137.5°, which is 360°–222.5°—this is because the pattern of seeds forms two intertwining spirals, one with each of the Golden Angles). The angle allows the seeds to grow outward in a regular way— each seed in a spiral arm is turned by the same amount away from the previous one. Patterns of squares and spirals derived from the Fibonacci sequence closely relate to those derived from the Golden Number. As with the Golden Spiral, sightings of this phenomenon in nature can be rather spurious.

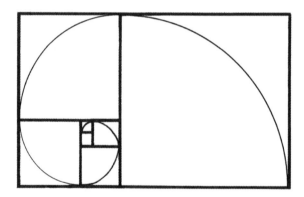

i(√-1) THE IMAGINARY UNIT

Finding the square root of a positive number, even one that humans would find difficult and lengthy, is now an extremely simple process for even the most basic calculators. The square root of a *negative* number, however, remains entirely impossible to find. Any positive number squared will produce a positive result, and so will the square of any negative number (in math, two negative numbers multiplied together will produce a positive result: $-3 \times -2 = +6$).

But i, the square root of -1, is not only mathematically existent but rather useful, too. For i is the basic unit of the imaginary numbers, an entire set of numbers centered around negative square roots, which can be manipulated according to many of the same rules as real numbers, and are often combined with real numbers to form complex numbers. $3 + 2i$, for instance, is a complex number. π (see page 469), however, is just a complicated one.

The seeming impossibility of the imaginary numbers meant that for years very few mathematicians would approach them. Even ordinary negative numbers seemed rather outlandish. Many figures of Renaissance mathematics dismissed the idea of a negative square root as absurd, but one, Girolamo Cardano (1501–76), acknowledged their existence and usefulness in solving cubic equations in his book *Ars Magna* (the Great Art). As well as being a mathematician, Cardano was a physicist, an inventor of many devices, including the combination lock, and an incorrigible (and not wholly honest) gambler—and hence, presumably, no stranger to negative numbers. Eventually, though, he was imprisoned in 1570 for heresy (he had published Jesus' horoscope), which left him looking rather like an ars magna.

After his death, Cardano's work was continued by his colleagues, but imaginary numbers were not fully accepted for many years. After all, one might well wonder what relevance imaginary numbers, being imaginary, could have to the real world. Well, you've probably seen sound waves represented like this:

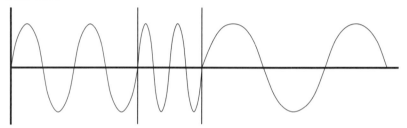

These are known as sine waves, because it's based on the sine—a trigonometric function you may well remember from school. In a right-angled triangle, the sine of any angle is equal to the length of the side opposite the angle divided by the hypotenuse (the side opposite the right angle is the hypotenuse, thus sin 90 = 1).

All sounds are made of one or more sine waves: A louder sound will have higher and deeper peaks and troughs, while sounds at higher frequencies will appear more horizontally "squashed" than lower ones. However, sound is by no means the only appearance of sine waves—they also appear in other oscillations, like the voltage of alternating current systems, in radio waves and light waves. Even the literal waves of the ocean are basically sine waves, though I wouldn't bother bringing graph paper to the beach with you.

Without going too deeply into the complicated math of this*, the relationship between i (which, confusingly, is often written j in engineering contexts) and π allows sine waves to

---

* For a more mathematically rigorous but still very accessible explanation, I'd recommend the final chapter of David Acheson's *1089 and All That.*

be expressed in relatively simple ways using complex numbers, really reducing the work involved in calculating the math of oscillations. Hence, a number that seems mathematically impossible is still enormously helpful to engineers and scientists everywhere.

MISLEADING STATISTICS

Numbers exert enormous control over our lives as statistics, where they are cited to support assertions and determine policy. All too often, though, the statistics are misleading, whether unintentionally or otherwise.

Any credible study should have a large enough sample size—that is, enough things or people being studied—to rule out anomalies. The smaller the sample, the higher the chance of results that don't reflect the population at large. Furthermore, a survey that overrepresents a particular group of people, whether by how it's run or by pure chance, might show a bias. For instance, a political survey conducted in the rural center of a large northern state will probably be biased toward the political right, while the same study conducted in the middle of a big city in that same state would get the opposite result.

It's all in the selection

Selection bias is also an issue, occurring when the sample selected is inherently skewed. There are many ways of doing this—one example might be surveying gym customers about their views on health, which would probably be unrepresentative, since gym users tend to be more health-conscious. The time period under scrutiny is also important: A short-term survey is not very useful for discussing long-term trends.

Self-selection bias is especially important in the media—surveys, especially political surveys, can be biased by the group of people who actually bother to do them. Website surveys are particularly problematic, because most websites have a specific audience and the cheapness of running them makes them useful to the press. Combine that with the political agendas of many newspapers, and you have an easy system for a newspaper to statistically support any claim it cares to make.

About a year and a half ago, a right-wing British tabloid newspaper ran a poll about reinstating capital punishment. Given the politics of its readership, the poll would probably have been skewed anyway. However, those who bothered to vote on the website and in telephone polls were even more likely to be in favor—as the process of voting requires action from the voter (rather than passively having someone phone them). Hence the poll is more likely to be accessed by those who want a change. Newspapers, particularly tabloids, often use emotional, one-sided coverage to sway those voting in these polls, just as they may in general elections. The capital punishment poll eventually found that 99 percent of readers favored its reinstatement, while more objective surveys suggest that only around 50–60 percent of Britons would agree.

It's the way you ask them

Loaded questions are an excellent way to get the data you want. In the United States, this has reached an incredible height with the "push poll"—an outwardly objective survey that hides unfounded accusations in its questions. In this political campaign technique, large numbers are polled, rumors are spread, and little or no effort is made to collect or analyze response data.

Averages (see page 456) can also be misleading. The mean, in particular, can be easily influenced by unusually high and low values. In a group of five people, where four earn $25,000 a year and one earns $250,000, the mean salary is $70,000, which is clearly unrepresentative. For this reason, median salaries are generally used for official purposes, though these data are far from perfect. Almost all official data, for instance, exclude people who are working illegally.

Lies, damned lies, and statistics

But all this is nothing compared to the way statistics are used to draw conclusions. One has to remember, when looking at any set of statistics, that correlation does not imply causality—just because two factors coincide doesn't mean one causes the other. For instance, we could consider that generally, people who wear glasses tend to be considered more intelligent. Does that mean glasses make you more intelligent or that intelligence somehow affects the eyes? Probably not. It seems far more likely that either more intelligent children are more likely to spend time reading at a young age, which may affect their eyes, or (as has recently been suggested) intelligence in small children is linked to visual exploration of the area closest to them.

This is a mistake even the most eminent scientists can make. In the study of malaria, for example (which gets its name from the Italian words *mala aria*—"bad air"), for centuries European scientists mostly assumed that because cases of the disease occurred mainly around swamps and marshes, the smelly air to be found in these places was what caused it. Although moderately effective treatments were developed, millions of people died because of an assumption that held back progress in treatment and prevention. It wasn't until the end of the nineteenth century that it was conclusively proved that mosquitoes transmitted malaria. This had been suggested long before—even the ancient Egyptians seem to have known it. Worldwide mosquito control efforts over the twentieth century—including mass pesticide use and supplying mosquito nets—massively reduced the incidence of malaria, although it remains a deadly disease in Africa.

This sort of misinterpretation isn't confined to science, or to numerology. It seems to me to be a fundamental problem with people's mental software. We evolved to recognize patterns in data of all kinds—whether it's the hunter recognizing the familiar shape of a deer in a dense forest, or a mathematician spotting a similarity between two complicated sequences of numbers—but with that comes the danger of seeing patterns that aren't there. In numerology, this means coincidentally encountering a particular number a few times in a day and assuming it's somehow auspicious. In statistics, the danger in identifying a nonexistent pattern can be much more serious.

THE BINARY SYSTEM

The binary number system contains just two digits—1 and 0—but is at the core of all electronic devices. It is the simplicity of the system that allows it to be used by machines—an electronic pulse is high or low voltage, one or zero—but by combining many electronic "bits," hugely complex data can be expressed.

Just as the decimal system works on powers (see page 458) of ten, the binary system works on ascending powers of two. Any positive integer can be expressed as a sum of ascending powers of two, with only one of each power at most being needed. Three, for instance, is written in binary as 11—the sum of 2^1 and 2^0, while 17,689 appears as:

$$100010100011001$$

Numbering the digit positions by powers of two:

1	0	0	0	1	0	1	0	0	0	1	1	0	0	1
14	13	12	11	10	9	8	7	6	5	4	3	2	1	0

$$2^{14} = 16,384 +$$
$$2^{10} = 1,024 +$$
$$2^{8} = 256 +$$
$$2^{4} = 16 +$$
$$2^{3} = 8 +$$
$$2^{0} = 1 +$$
$$= 17,689$$

Or, as the age-old nerdy joke goes: There are only 10 kinds of people in the world—those who understand binary, and those who don't.

In electronics, the binary impulses are usually interpreted by a system of logic gates—tiny components that receive one or two binary inputs, each either 1 or 0, and output a binary pulse according to the "logic" involved. Millions of logic gates can be fit onto a single computer chip, and this mind-bogglingly complex system of inputs and outputs is essentially what gives a computer its power. This was true even before electronics was invented—Charles Babbage's Analytical Engine, a mechanical calculating device designed from the 1830s onward and often considered the forerunner of modern computers, would have relied on a system of logic gates which were purely mechanical, had it ever been built.

The byter bit

The binary system is perhaps most obvious in computer memory storage. Each binary bit (a one or zero) is part of a byte*—a group of eight bits, traditionally enough to represent a single character of text—of which 1024 form a kilobyte (KB), though 1000 is sometimes used here.† A megabyte (MB) is formed by 1024 kilobytes, or 1,048,576 bytes, and 1024 megabytes make a gigabyte (GB). So, to put all this into context, this brief explanation of the binary system has made a 69-kilobyte file, which in turn is made up of about 561,152 binary bits; a 4-minute MP3 is made up of about 32 million bits, and an 80-gigabyte iPod hard disk can be reduced to about 687 billion ones and zeroes.

---

* The name byte has given rise to a number of hilarious nerd puns for other small units of memory, such as a nybble (4 bits) or the dynner (32 bits). The Jargon File at http://catb.org/jargon/ is a good source for many, many more examples of this kind of computer lore.

† There's some confusion about exactly how a kilobyte should be defined. The Greek prefixes "kilo," "mega," and "giga" properly mean thousand, million and billion respectively, and it's natural enough for people to see computer memory in these decimal terms. However, the physical binary storage is generally in multiples of 1024 bytes because that's a power of two. Although this may seem insignificant, it can cause fairly major differences as the storage units get bigger—a difference of 24 bytes (2.4 percent) at the kilobyte level increases to around 73MB (7.3 percent) at the gigabyte level. This difference can be exploited for sales purposes: A hard drive with around 250,000,000,000 bytes of memory can be advertised as being 250GB, whereas in fact it's about 233GB. In 2000, in an effort to correct this problem, a new system of prefixes that specifically referred to the relevant powers of two was introduced, working from the kilo-binary-byte (KiB, always 1024 bytes) upward.

ODDS AND ODDITIES

Probability is the branch of mathematics concerned with measuring the likelihood of a given outcome, which is usually expressed as a decimal, percentage or fraction. Where the outcome is random, like rolling a die, the probabilities are evenly distributed; that is, the probability of any given number is the same as any other (in this case, ⅙). Where there are more possibilities for one outcome than another (for instance, you're more likely to pick an E from a Scrabble bag than an X), the probability will be higher for that outcome.

Probabilities of multiple events in sequence can be figured out by multiplying the probabilities of the individual events—the probability of rolling a 6 on a die three times in succession is ⅙ × ⅙ × ⅙ = ¹⁄₂₁₆ or about 0.5%. The probabilities resulting from each individual event or sequence of events always add up to 1 in the end.

The easiest probabilities to figure out are those for random things where the chance of each outcome is equal—for instance, the probability of a coin toss landing on heads is 0.5, which is also the probability of it landing on tails. There is a tiny probability of its landing on the edge and staying on there—but we'll ignore that for the moment to look at a couple of interesting applications which show how counterintuitive probability can be.

The birthday problem

If there are 23 people in a room, what is the probability of two or more of them sharing the same birthday? One might think the probability is very low—after all, there are 365 days in the year, and only 23 people. In fact, though, it's more likely than not. Why is this?

First off, we'll assume for the sake of simplicity that all the birthdays are equally distributed throughout the year, and that no one was born on a February 29th. The probability of a person being born on a given day, therefore, is ⅟₃₆₅ , since there are 365 days in the year and a person is equally likely to be born on each one of them.

The trick here is to remember that it doesn't *matter* which people, or how many people, share a birthday, or which day it is. We could try and figure out the probabilities for every possible grouping and each day, but that would take forever, and there's an easier way. We know that the probability of two or more people sharing the same birthday (which we'll call P[s]) and the probability of no two people sharing the same birthday (P[ns]) must add up to 1, because the probabilities of all the outcomes of a given event always add up to 1.

Therefore, we can simply calculate the odds of no two people sharing the same birthday (that is, the probability of every single person being born on a different day) and then subtract that from 1 to get the probability that at least two people will.

Imagine now that you're going through the room carrying a clipboard and wearing a white coat, asking each person their birthdate, and assuring them that they'll be released once the study is complete. The first person in our big probability calculation could be born on any day, so the first term is $365/365$. The next person can't have the same birthday as the first, but still has 364 possible birthdays, so the second term is $364/365$. And so it goes on for all 23 of them, as each person has to have a birthday from a slowly narrowing range of them.

$$P(ns) = 365/365 \times 364/365 \times 363/365 \times \ldots \times 343/365 = 0.493$$

$$1 - 0.493 = 0.507, \text{ or } 50.7\%.$$

Hence, it's more likely than not (barely) that two or more people will share the same birthday. As the number of people increases, it quickly gets more likely, rising to a 99 percent chance for a group of 57 people. However, it's only absolutely certain when there are 366 people in the room, as it's still just possible for every person to have a different birthday until there are more people than days.

The Monty Hall problem

This next one's a bit trickier and has been around in some form for quite some time. It's named after Monty Hall, former host of the game show *Let's Make a Deal*. The show provides the template for this problem, which has apparently fooled even eminent scientists.

The rules of the game show are as follows. There are three doors. Behind one is a brand new sports car, but behind the other two are dud prizes (sometimes goats, for comical effect). The car is randomly placed. In the first round, you, the player, must choose one of the doors, with no knowledge of what's behind any of the doors.

Then begins the second round. Our host, who knows which door is the winning one, makes things a bit more complicated by opening one of the other two doors at random—never the winning one or your chosen door—even if you picked the winning door in the first round, that won't be revealed until the end. You are now allowed to stick with your original door or change your choice to the other unopened door. The door you choose now will be opened to reveal your prize.

Given that you're now presented with two doors, one of which conceals a car and the other a goat, it might seem that your chances of winning are equally likely, and it doesn't matter what you do. In fact, you should always switch.

The trick here is to remember that the first two rounds are connected, rather than being independent events, and that you don't know which door's correct until both rounds are over. With that in mind, we'll consider the probabilities.

You have a ⅓ chance of choosing the winning door in the first round. If you do so, switching doors in the next round would cause you to lose, no matter which of the other two doors the host opens. However, you have a ⅔ chance of picking a losing door in the first round. In that case, the host will have to open the other losing door. Now, switching doors will guarantee you the car.

You have no idea, of course, whether the first door you've chosen is correct, but there's a ⅔ chance it wasn't, and this probability is not altered by the door the host opens. It's twice as likely as not that you chose the wrong door the first time, and hence twice as likely that switching will win you the car. It's no guarantee of victory, but switching doors in the second round should win ⅔ of the time.

JOHN NASH AND GAME THEORY

The Cold War is chiefly remembered for the stockpiling by both sides of terrifying quantities of nuclear weapons. These weapons were never used against their targets, except as bargaining chips in a sinister and byzantine doctrine known as "Mutually Assured Destruction." American strategists devised complex predictions of possible Russian first strikes, and planned retaliatory strikes to ensure Western victory (insofar as anyone wins in a global nuclear war, anyway), no matter which strategy the U.S.S.R. pursued. These plans relied on a view of humans as coldly rational, scheming, self-interested beings with little interest in altruism or a greater good.

At the heart of this worldview was the American mathematician John Forbes Nash (b. 1928), who produced pioneering work in the field of game theory—a branch of mathematics dedicated to analyzing human behavior mathematically, originating in attempts to predict the outcomes of chess and card games. Nash, along with a number of colleagues, advanced game theory and began applying it to global politics while working at the RAND Corporation, then a military think tank, during the 1950s. For Nash in particular, all human interactions could be viewed in terms of Machiavellian self-interest.

The game theorists developed various game scenarios designed to mimic the behavior of these self-interested hypothetical people—a well-known example is the Prisoner's Dilemma (see page 500), invented by Nash's colleagues at RAND. They claimed that such behavior could be applied not simply to games, but to every aspect of human existence, including the Cold War. By viewing the U.S.S.R. as implacably hostile but also self-interested, they led RAND to promote the doctrine of mutually assured destruction. Like the Prisoner's Dilemma, each side had the opportunity to betray and annihilate the other, but there would be serious consequences in doing so.

But despite their influence on the policy of the Cold War, the worldview of game theory seems to have major flaws. Tests of a game called So Long Sucker (as the name implies, the game is won by forming and then breaking alliances) on secretaries at RAND were failures—loyalty ended up trumping their desire to win the game.* Nash, whose life inspired the 2002 film *A Beautiful Mind*, was diagnosed with paranoid schizophrenia in 1959, but his work remained influential. Game theory is not simply concerned with nuclear paranoia—it

---

* Interestingly, it was the same compassion and initiative that saved the world when it was closest to destruction. On September 26, 1983, a Russian army engineer named Stanislav Petrov was on duty at a surveillance station when an alarm went off, as though America had launched a strike. Petrov realized it could be a false alarm (as it turned out, a computer error) and that the future of the world rested with him. He disobeyed protocol by refusing to alert the Soviet command, preventing nuclear apocalypse but destroying his own career.

has important applications in economics, political science, and computer science. Nash, now fully recovered, received a Nobel Prize in Economics for his work in 1994, and some people have claimed that his work in game theory has created a world ruled by numbers.

The Prisoner's Dilemma

Two bank robbers, A and B, have been arrested by the police. The police have found illegal firearms in both their houses, and it seems clear that these are the weapons recently used in a major bank hold-up. Despite the discovery of the guns, however, the police have failed to find sufficient evidence to secure a conviction for the robbery. They intend, by separating the two prisoners, to force one to betray and testify against the other.

Each prisoner is thereby presented with a dilemma. If A betrays B, he will go free and B, as the only one to be convicted, will get a long ten-year sentence. A, however, realizes B is probably thinking the exact same thing about him. If neither betrays the other, they will both get a few months for possessing the illegal guns. If they both betray each other, they'll both be convicted for the robbery and end up with five-year sentences—not as long as if only one were betrayed, but far worse than if neither betrayed the other.

The maxims of game theory dictate that the best thing for each prisoner, in terms of personal gain, is to betray the other. At best, you get away with the crime. Given that the other prisoner is probably also intending to betray you, you gain a reduction in your sentence by betraying him.

BILLIONS

There is great confusion surrounding the usage of the word "billion." The problem is that the United States and most other English speaking countries use the term to mean 1,000,000,000—one thousand million, or 10^9, while most of Europe uses it to mean a million million—1,000,000,000,000 or 10^{12}. The European billion may make a little more sense given the "bi" prefix, which would suggest a billion is a million to the power of two, a trillion is a million to the power of three, etc. In most of these countries, the word "milliard" is used for a thousand million and sometimes "billiard" for a thousand million million, "trilliard" for a thousand million million million, and so on.

The difference between them stems from two different systems of working with very large numbers—the Long Scale used by mainland Europe, and the Short Scale used by America and most English-speaking countries. The Long Scale assigns a different word to numbers over a million that are a million times larger than the previous one, while the Short Scale does so using a factor of a thousand—a Long Scale trillion is 10^{18}, while a Short Scale one is only 10^{12}. As the numbers get bigger, so does the difference—by a factor of a thousand each time.

The United Kingdom used what we now call the Long Scale from around the sixteenth century, and its adoption by Germany spread it around to most of Europe. France, where the original Long-Scale billion and trillion were invented, then switched to the Short Scale in the early eighteenth century. This usage spread to French colonies in America, although France officially switched *back* to the Long Scale in 1961. The U.K. stayed with the Long Scale officially until 1974, when the government there announced a conversion to Short Scale numbers in official literature. However, even today people in Britain are likely to confuse the two.

THE WHEAT AND CHESSBOARD PROBLEM

This problem, often used to demonstrate the speed of exponential growth, has its origins in a story of India in about the sixth century A.D. Supposedly, an Indian mathematician called Sessa was the inventor of the game we now know as chess (an early version known as *Chaturanga*) and was called before his king to demonstrate his invention. The king was so pleased, he offered to give Sessa any reward he could think of.

Sessa asked the king only for wheat (rice, in some versions)—one grain on the first square of the chessboard, two on the second, four on the third, eight on the fourth and so on, doubling each time until he reached the last of the 64 squares. At first the king derided this seemingly paltry request, but as the numbers were added up he realized it was enough wheat to bankrupt him completely: $18,446,744,073,709,551,615$ (2^{64}-1) grains. Even with modern methods, producing that much wheat would require harvesting all the arable land on Earth eighty times over.

Sessa can't have received anything like his entire reward, and one variant of the story has the king getting an exacting revenge—out of feigned concern for Sessa, the king asked him to count every grain he received, to make sure he wasn't being short-changed. Although the Sessa story is probably the most common, there is also a version of the legend set in the Roman Empire. None of it—except the numbers—should be taken as true.

THINKING FOURTH-DIMENSIONALLY

As physics made strange and exciting new strides in the twentieth century, it became clear that there were problems with traditional scientific ideas, which viewed the universe as existing in three dimensions of space. Isaac Newton (1643–1727), whose theories formed the basis of physics until the twentieth century, saw time as flowing at a constant pace, regardless of anything else in the physical universe. For everyday life, where we rarely if ever travel at significant fractions of the speed of light, this works very nicely, and for a long time the idea was not challenged.

However, the experience of time was shown by Einstein's theories of relativity not to be independent of movement in the traditional physical world: Time appears to pass more slowly the faster the observer is traveling, and this process would be especially pronounced for someone moving close to the speed of light. (Albert Einstein lived 1879–1955.) The experience of space and time is relative, depending on the viewer's frame of reference. A well-known thought experiment involves a man traveling at nearly the speed of light for what seems to him to be a few minutes, only to return to Earth to find that decades have passed. Although travel at those speeds is obviously impossible at present (as well as presumably leaving the subject beyond severely jetlagged, into the realms of existential horror), the effect has been observed with atomic clocks on board the space shuttles. Even someone walking would experience time slightly differently than someone standing still, although the difference would be immeasurably tiny.

Anyway, all this suggests that time has to be related to the original three spatial dimensions in a much more complex way. With Einstein's Theory of Special Relativity as his starting point, the physicist Hermann Minkowski came up with a four-dimensional model of the universe in 1908, with time as the fourth dimension. Space and time can then be viewed as a "continuum" and, crucially, time can be distorted like space. Gravity can cause curvature in space-time, particularly where singularities (see Infinity, page 508) are involved. Light is known to bend around planets and stars because their gravity distorts space-time.

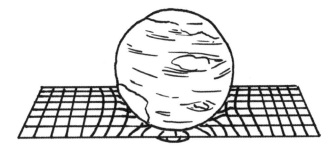

Another strand of mathematical theory, beginning some decades before, is concerned with a geometric fourth dimension of space, which is unrelated to time. The fourth dimension is perpendicular to the existing three, but as three-dimensional beings with basically two-dimensional vision, we couldn't actually see it. The concept is difficult to visualize (although some physicists and mathematicians have claimed to think in four dimensions), but we could view it in terms of regular shapes. If we consider a straight line with one dimension (length) to be representative of a one-dimensional universe, a square representative of a two-dimensional one (since a square has two dimensions—length and width), and a cube (which possesses length, width, and height) to represent a three-dimensional universe, the four-dimensional model is represented by a tesseract, or 4-dimensional hypercube. The tesseract is difficult to visualize and to draw, but could be considered like this: If a 3-dimensional cube is made of two 2-dimensional squares linked in a third dimension (with a total of 6 square faces), a 4-dimensional tesseract is made of two 3-dimensional cubes linked in a fourth dimension, creating a total of eight cubes.

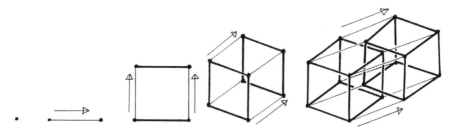

The 4-dimensional tesseract shown above does not look to us like a regular solid. But then, neither in fact does the cube look exactly like a regular cube—the edges that lead away from the viewpoint are slanted at a mathematically incorrect angle to conform to perspective, which is the method we have used to depict three-dimensional objects on a two-dimensional plane, ever since perspective painting was popularized during the Renaissance.

Similarly, we have to bend a few rules to display a 3D object as a 2D image, and the same goes for a 4D object. If we could see the tesseract in four dimensions, all eight cubes would look perfectly regular. As it is, they look slanted as below:

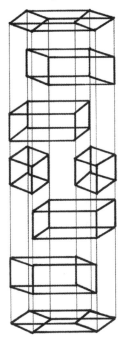

What use is a fourth spatial dimension anyway? One major application is in graphing functions that involve complex numbers (see page 483), but that sort of thing is really a very long way outside the scope of this book. From our perspective, it just seems rather an interesting idea—a four-dimensional being would in theory be able to see everything in 3D space, and would be able to see behind and inside objects that are obscured to us.

∞ (INFINITY)

Infinity is perhaps not a number in a true sense, but the mathematical representation of all that is inexhaustible and everlasting. Essentially, it is a number that can never be exceeded (children's claims of there being an "infinity plus 1" have not been subject to serious analysis—infinity plus anything is infinity), and which occupies a bizarre and fascinating place in our universe.

The universe is widely considered to be infinite in size and constantly expanding, although this is by no means certain. It may have some sort of defined edge, or the edges may somehow join up with each other—a person traversing one edge of the universe might simply end up on the opposite edge. As bizarre as that sounds, perhaps even stranger is the concept of the gravitational singularity—a point of infinite mass and zero size, where physical matter is compressed down almost to nothing.

There is a singularity at the heart of each black hole, thought to be the result of large stars collapsing in on themselves, whose gravity is so strong that not even light can escape it, which is why such a phenomenon would appear black. Anyone entering a black hole would be subjected to incredible gravitational stresses, described by Stephen Hawking and others as like "being turned into spaghetti," or sometimes referred to as "noodlizing." What happens after that is unknown, but unlikely to leave anyone alive. It is thought, however, that there is an enormous black hole at the heart of our galaxy and every other, and the gravitational pull of the black holes holds the galaxies together.

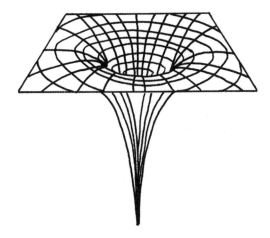

The entire universe is thought to have started off compressed into a singularity before the Big Bang. At this moment, around 14 billion years ago, the singularity exploded outward. Superheated matter and energy shot outward in all directions, and would gradually form everything there is in the universe today. It took hundreds of thousands of years even for the first atoms to form, and 100 million years for the first star to start shining. Our sun formed only after about 8 billion years. Even today, galaxies are still moving away from each other, suggesting that the universe is still expanding.

In temporal terms, the universe is probably not infinite. Current theory suggests that in about another 100 trillion years, the universe will simply expand too far and cool down too much. Stars will burn away and galaxies fall apart in a "Big Freeze," which will leave the universe dead, lacking the energy to support life. What will happen after that is another mystery, but the Big Freeze (also known as heat death) is not entirely certain. Other theories include a Big Crunch (the expansion process reverses and the universe collapses back into a singularity, which might then explode outward to form another universe in a Big Bounce) and a Big Rip (continued expansion tears the fabric of the universe apart).

In numbers, too, infinity is important. There is an infinite number of numbers, both positive and negative. Interestingly, there are different infinities of numbers—although there's an inexhaustible supply of whole numbers, there is an infinity of non-integers between each one.

This endless void seems to be a good place to end.

Shall I compare thee to a summer's ... er ... banana,

The Infinite Monkey Theorem

Back on Earth, infinity has found a place in the Infinite Monkey Theorem—the idea that, if you position an infinite number of monkeys or other non-human primates at typewriters, and leave them adequately fed and watered, one of them will eventually type out the complete works of Shakespeare, just by randomly pressing keys. The extreme improbability of any monkey doing that is counterbalanced by there being infinitely many monkeys (and, in some versions, infinite time), so one of them is bound to do it. The theorem was developed in 1913 by Émile Borel and Arthur Eddington, but wasn't tested until an experiment conducted in 2003 by researchers at Plymouth University in the United Kingdom. They aimed to investigate the Infinite Monkey Theorem by placing a computer with six crested macaques in a zoo enclosure. The results were, unsurprisingly, of little literary merit, with a stream of unconnected letters going on for several pages. The computer-illiterate primates also attempted to destroy the computer with a rock, as well as using it as a toilet. Some have claimed that this invalidates the Infinite Monkey Theorem, but surely without infinite monkeys you can't ever really know—basic probability tells us that even extremely unlikely things will still occasionally happen. Some commentators, however, have suggested that the Internet proves that no matter how many monkeys are bashing away at keyboards, they still won't produce anything worthwhile.